Anthropology in the New Guinea Highlands

An Annotated Bibliography

Garland Reference Library of Social Science (Vol. 17)

Anthropology
in the
New Guinea Highlands

An Annotated Bibliography

Terence E. Hays

Garland Publishing, Inc., New York & London

1976

Library of Congress Cataloging in Publication Data

Hays, Terence E
    Anthropology in the New Guinea highlands.

    (Garland reference library in social science ;
v. 17)
    Includes indexes.
    1. Ethnology—New Guinea—Bibliography.
2. New Guinea—Bibliography. I. Title.
Z5116.H38 [GN671.N5] 016.30129'95   75-24102
ISBN 0-8240-9972-9

Contents

CONTENTS

Preface

Anthropological research in the New Guinea Highlands has had a relatively short history, showing significant growth only in the past twenty-five years. Nevertheless the accumulated literature of interest to anthropologists is by now so extensive and widely-scattered even the specialist can scarcely attain a comprehensive awareness, much less a command, of it. The need for an ordered compilation of the relevant references is especially great for anthropologists with particular interests in Highlands peoples but is also felt by researchers whose concern is with Melanesia or Oceania in general.

The present volume is intended to largely fill this gap—not a void, surely, for it builds upon other, more broadly-focused works such as those listed in Part IB below. The efforts of previous bibliographers, which have been supplemented by systematic library research, are gratefully acknowledged.

The first and most important problem facing any bibliographer is the delimitation of the scope of inclusion. So far as subject matter is concerned the outline sketched below will indicate that I have tried to include references which would be of value to anthropologists from all of the subdisciplines as well as to geographers, historians and other social scientists. Some judgment is necessarily involved and what some will consider errors inevitable, but it is hoped that they are errors of commission rather than omission.

Determining the geographical boundaries of "the Highlands" is perhaps more difficult since these depend to some extent upon the nature of the problem a researcher is trying to solve. Many investigators have followed the geographer Brookfield, who suggests that "the essential distinguishing and unifying characteristic of the highland population concentrations is in cultivation methods" (Ref. 242, p. 438). For many purposes, however, this criterion seems too restrictive since it excludes the various "Ok" peoples of the

PREFACE

Papua New Guinea-Irian Jaya border area, the "Kukukuku" (Anga-speakers) and the populations of the Great Papuan Plateau. I have chosen to include these regions, excepting the extreme eastern and southern Anga who are unquestionably lowlanders, thus bounding the Highlands by the Kratke Ranges on the east, the southern slopes of the central cordillera, the Wissel Lakes of Irian Jaya on the west, and the northern slopes of the various ranges which form the cordillera. With the exceptions noted, the area concerned corresponds closely to that indicated on Brookfield's map in Ref. 242 (facing p. 436).

With this areal restriction several other limitations must be noted. While over two hundred journals and serial publications in four languages have been surveyed in the compilation of this bibliography, some relevant sources have doubtless been missed, especially those in languages other than English. With a few exceptions (e.g., *National Geographic, Natural History, Australian Museum Magazine* and *Walkabout)*, articles appearing in the popular press are excluded, as are unpublished papers delivered at meetings and conferences; unpublished masters and doctoral theses, however, are included. References are not cross-listed in the various sections but the two indexes should mitigate this deficiency to some extent. With only a few exceptions, those being major survey articles or monographs, a cutoff date of 1975 has been enforced with future editions planned to periodically update the coverage. In many cases the identification of ethnolinguistic groups has been difficult and sometimes impossible. This was variously due to authors' lack of specificity which could not be compensated for with the inadequate and incomplete maps presently available or to the use of variable names and spellings in designating the same or similar populations.

With these acknowledged deficiencies corrections, additions and deletions will be necessary in future editions and I thank my colleagues in advance for providing me with them. A more immediate debt is owed to my wife, Patricia, and Professor James B. Watson of the University of Washington. I hope that their continual assistance, patience and support over the past six years is partially compensated in this way.

PREFACE

Overview of Contents

The style of reference employed is that currently used by the American Anthropological Association with the exception of abbreviations used in Part III and explained there. Relevant ethnolinguistic groups are indicated in upper case letters in the body of the annotations, added parenthetically or set off beside the author's name as in Part II. In a few cases references were not available for examination and annotation but are included with a notation (usually asterisks beneath the citation) to that effect.

Part I, designated "General", includes reference works, collections and pertinent books and articles by authors who are not anthropologists but administrators, biologists, explorers, geographers, historians, journalists, missionaries or travellers. Some indication of the anthropologically-relevant content of these sources is provided in the annotations, which are fuller in this part than elsewhere in the bibliography.

Part II, "Social and Cultural Anthropology", includes works which are explicitly anthropological in content and authorship or, as in Section C, which deal in considerable detail with matters directly of concern to social and cultural anthropologists. Annotations are supplied except in Section B where titles are judged to be sufficiently descriptive.

Part III, "Linguistics", follows the same pattern, with only the more general works (Section A) requiring annotation.

Part IV, "Prehistory", involves perhaps the greatest degree of potential overlap within the bibliography. Many sources of importance to prehistorians are included in Part II, e.g., those dealing with technology and subsistence techniques. Included here are only those sources which deal directly with reconstructions of the possible origin of Highlands horti-culture (Section A) and excavation reports and artifact analyses (Section B). Annotations are provided in both sections.

Part V, "Physical Anthropology", includes a broader range of sources than the title immediately suggests, as in the many important contributions by medical professionals. In the majority of cases titles are sufficiently descriptive to obviate

PREFACE

annotation beyond ethnolinguistic group identifications.

Part VI, "Physical Environment", could be expanded almost indefinitely as the literature on flora and fauna, especially, is enormous. In the interests of economy I have restricted inclusion to only those works which are derived from research in specific Highlands locations or general surveys of important animal and plant groups which are found in the Highlands. Thus technical literature regarding particular species, genera or families is largely excluded as is the large and important body of material available for Australian flora and fauna. Annotations are supplied throughout.

The Author Index lists all authors included in the bibliography with appropriate reference numbers; in cases of multiple authorship only the senior author's name is incorporated in the index. The Ethnolinguistic Group Index is ordered alphabetically, as is the Author Index. Reference numbers are entered with the most commonly-used group name, following the spellings adopted by the foremost expert on New Guinea languages, S.A. Wurm (see Part IIIA); alternative names and spellings are also listed with directions to the main entries.

PART I   GENERAL

A.   General Surveys and Reference Works

1.   Essai, Brian
      1961   Papua and New Guinea: A Contemporary Survey.
              London: Oxford University Press.
              Journalist's survey intended for general
              audience; emphasis on administration and
              development.

2.   Evans-Pritchard, E.E.   (Supervisory Ed.)
      1972   Peoples of the Earth, Vol. 1.   Australia and
              Melanesia (Including New Guinea). London:
              The Danbury Press.
              Pictorial survey with brief text material,
              some written by anthropologists.

3.   Fisk, E.K.   (Ed.)
      1966   New Guinea on the Threshold: Aspects of
              Social, Political and Economic Development.
              Canberra: The Australian National University
              Press.
              Collection of papers on diverse topics by
              anthropologists, geographers and others.

4.   Hastings, Peter
      1969   New Guinea: Problems and Prospects.
              Melbourne: F.W. Cheshire.
              General survey of contemporary Papua New
              Guinea and Irian Jaya with emphasis on
              development and attendant problems.

5.   ----- (Ed.)
      1971   Papua New Guinea: Prospero's Other Island.
              Sydney: Angus and Robertson.
              Topical survey papers by anthropologists,
              biologists, geographers and others.

6.   New Guinea, Territory of
      1914-   Report(s) to the Council of the League of
      1940   Nations on the Administration of the
              Territory of New Guinea. Canberra:
              Government Printer.

7.   -----
      1946-   Report(s) to the General Assembly of the
              United Nations on the Administration of
              the Territory of New Guinea. Canberra:
              Government Printer.
              Both of above are annual reports now

published together with Reference 9;
mainly statistical compilations.

8. Oliver, Douglas
    1961   The Pacific Islands. (Revised Ed.) Garden
            City: Doubleday (Natural History Library).
            General survey of Pacific emphasizing
            European discovery and colonization;
            little material specifically on New
            Guinea Highlands.

9. Papua, Territory of
    1906-   Annual Report(s). Canberra: Government
            Printer.
            Mainly statistical reports but early
            issues often included patrol reports and
            brief articles on indigenous peoples;
            now incorporated in Reference 7.

10. Ryan, John
    1969   The Hot Land: Focus on New Guinea. New
            York: St. Martin's Press.
            Journalist's survey of post-World War II
            New Guinea, mainly concerning political
            developments and current events.

11. Ryan, Peter (General Ed.)
    1972   Encyclopaedia of Papua New Guinea. 3 Vols.
            Melbourne: Melbourne University Press.
            Basic reference work with hundreds of
            papers by specialists on many topics;
            lacks table of contents but Vol. 3
            includes index and gazetteer.

12. Tudor, Judy (Ed.)
    1969   The Handbook of Papua and New Guinea.
            (Sixth Ed.) Sydney: Pacific Publications.
            Statistical compendium with general
            descriptions by regions and topics;
            periodically updated and revised.

13. Wilkes, John (Ed.)
    1958   New Guinea and Australia. Sydney: Angus
            and Robertson.
            Collection of papers by specialists
            with emphasis on political development.

B. General Bibliographies

14. Bork-Feltkamp, A.J. van
    1941   Supplement to "Anthropologische Bibliographie

van den Indischen Archipel en van
Nederlandsch West-Indie" by J.P. Kleiweg
de Zwaan. Internationales Archiv fur
Ethnographie 39:1-130.
Includes early Dutch references to
exploration and research in Irian Jaya,
including Highlands.

15. Cammack, Floyd M. and Shiro Saito
    1962   Pacific Island Bibliography. New York:
           The Scarecrow Press.
           Based on materials in Pacific Collection,
           University of Hawaii Sinclair Library.
           Largely limited to sources published
           1948-1961; superseded by Taylor (Ref. 25).

16. Department of Anthropology and Sociology, The
    Australian National University
    1968   An Ethnographic Bibliography of New Guinea.
           3 Vols. Canberra: The Australian National
           University Press.
           Includes references through 1964 on wide
           variety of topics in addition to implied
           "ethnography"; volumes organized by
           Author, District and Proper Names (latter
           two are indexes).

17. Department of Anthropology and Sociology, University
    of Papua New Guinea
    1969- Man in New Guinea. (Beginning in 1975 to
           be renamed "Research in Melanesia") Boroko:
           University of Papua New Guinea.
           Occasional newsletter with short items of
           interest to researchers, listings of
           research in progress and current
           bibliography.

18. Dickson, Diane and Carol Dossor (Compilers)
    1971   World Catalogue of Theses on the Pacific
           Islands. Pacific Monograph Series, No. 1.
           Canberra: The Australian National University
           Press.
           Based on A.N.U. Department of Pacific
           History holdings and review of other
           catalogues. Includes B.A. (Honours),
           M.A. and doctoral theses through 1968;
           organized by region of Pacific and major
           subject headings.

19. Galis, K.W. (Ed.)
    1956   Bibliography of West New Guinea. Southeast
           Asia Studies, Bibliography Series. New
           Haven: Yale University.

3

Includes references (mostly Dutch) to
1955 including popular and scholarly
sources from anthropology, natural
history and current events.

20. Gill, Evan R.
1957   New Guinea: Catalogue of Books from the
Library of Evan R. Gill. Liverpool: Evan R.
Gill.
Based on collection amassed over period
of thirty-five years; organized under
headings of Annual Reports, Parliamentary
Papers, Government Publications and Other
Works.

21. Library, University of Papua New Guinea
1968- New Guinea Periodical Index: Guide to
Current Periodical Literature about New
Guinea. Boroko: University of Papua New
Guinea.
Quarterly listing of sources, both
popular and scholarly.

22. McGrath, W.A. (Compiler)
1965   New Guineana or Books of New Guinea 1942-
1964. Sydney: Margaret Woodhouse Bookshop.
Includes 900 items from various sources,
especially government documents; listed
alphabetically by author.

23. Reeves, Susan C. and May Dudley (Eds.)
1969   New Guinea Social Science Research and
Publications, 1962-67. New Guinea Research
Unit Bulletin No. 32. Port Moresby: New
Guinea Research Unit.
Bridges gap between A.N.U. bibliography
(Ref. 16) and "Man in New Guinea" (Ref.
17). Organized by administrative district
and subject with cross-indexing.

24. Richardson, Penelope and May Dudley (Eds.)
1967   Social Science Research in New Guinea 1965.
Current Anthropology 8:424-440.
Covers only 1965 with references
organized by administrative district;
followed by short essays by specialists
on research opportunities and priorities.

25. Taylor, Clyde R.H. (Ed.)
1965   A Pacific Bibliography: Printed Matter
Relating to the Native Peoples of Polynesia,
Melanesia and Micronesia. (Second Ed.)
London: Oxford University Press.

Standard reference work including sources
through 1962. Organized by regions which
are internally organized by subject;
includes author index.

C. Atlases and Geographical Surveys

26. Allied Forces, South West Pacific Area, Allied
    Geographical Section
    1942-   Area Study of Central Dutch New Guinea
    1945   (Sub-Division Wissel Lakes). Terrain
             Studies, No. 68. Washington: Government
             Printing Office.

27. -----
             Dutch New Guinea, Sub-Division Wissel Lakes.
             Terrain Studies, No. 21. Washington:
             Government Printing Office.
             Both are brief booklets giving some
             detail on terrain indicated; based
             principally on aerial photography.

28. Anas, Mohammad
    1958   Australian New Guinea: A Geographical
             Survey. Ph.D. Thesis, Canberra, The
             Australian National University.

29. -----
    1960   The Highlands of Australian New Guinea.
             Geographical Review 50:467-490.
             Both report results of field survey in
             mid-1950's. Major topics discussed
             include physical environment, population
             and economic development.

30. Blake, D.H.
    1972   Western District. In Peter Ryan, Gen. Ed.
             (Ref. 11), Vol. 2, pp. 1187-1193.
             General survey describing environment,
             population, administrative exploration
             and development. Includes map, but
             little detail shown.

31. Brookfield, Harold C. and Doreen Hart
    1971   Melanesia: A Geographical Interpretation of
             an Island World. London: Methuen.
             Comprehensive survey of environment,
             population distribution, cultural ecology
             and economic development. Comparison of
             forty-four agricultural systems includes
             eleven Highlands societies.

5

32. Brown, M.J.F.
    1970   Maps, Air Photographs and Land System
            Reports. In R. Gerard Ward and David A.M.
            Lea, Eds. (Ref. 49), pp. 98-99.
                Map of Papua New Guinea indicating areas
                for which maps, photo maps, air photos
                and land system reports are presently
                available.

33. Cumberland, Kenneth B.
    1954   Southwest Pacific: A Geography of Australia,
            New Zealand and Their Pacific Island
            Neighbourhoods. Wellington: Whitcombe and
            Tombs.
                General survey with little information on
                Highlands New Guinea; superseded by other
                works listed here.

34. Howlett, Diana R.
    1967   A Geography of Papua and New Guinea.
            Melbourne: Thomas Nelson.
                Brief survey of physical geography and
                related matters, especially subsistence
                and economic activities.

35. -----
    1971   Geography: In the Swamps, Rivers, High
            Valleys and Cordillera, a Land of Dramatic
            Contrasts. In Peter Hastings, Ed. (Ref. 5),
            pp. 4-22.
                General description of land, climate,
                vegetation, fauna, people, land use,
                towns and industries; includes some
                discussion of Highlands.

36. -----
    1973   Papua New Guinea: Geography and Change.
            Melbourne: Thomas Nelson.

                        * * * * *

37. Kennedy, T.F.
    1966   A Descriptive Atlas of the Pacific Islands.
            Sydney: A.H. and A.W. Reed.
                Includes only two maps of New Guinea
                with little detail shown; some statistics
                regarding area, population, climate and
                exports.

38. Lea, David A.M.
    1972   Sepik Districts, East and West. In Peter
            Ryan, Gen. Ed. (Ref. 11), Vol. 2, pp. 1030-
            1036.
                General survey describing geomorphology,

climate and vegetation, population and
economic development. Includes map, but
little detail shown.

39. Lea, David A.M. and G.R. Irwin
    1967   New Guinea: The Territory and Its People.
           London: Oxford University Press.
           Brief overview intended as high school
           textbook; includes chapter on "The Sweet
           Potato Growers" (i.e., Highlanders) and
           many excellent photographs.

40. Lennon, J.L.
    1972   Madang District. In Peter Ryan, Gen. Ed.
           (Ref. 11), Vol. 2, pp. 668-674.
           General survey describing geomorphology,
           climate, soil, vegetation, land use,
           population, settlement and development.
           Includes map, but little detail shown.

41. McAlpine, J.R.
    1972a Eastern Highlands District. In Peter Ryan,
           Gen. Ed. (Ref. 11), Vol. 1, pp. 284-289.
           General survey describing environment,
           history of contact and development.
           Includes map, but little detail shown.

42. -----
    1972b Southern Highlands District. In Peter Ryan,
           Gen. Ed. (Ref. 11), Vol. 2, pp. 1085-1091.
           General survey describing environment,
           population, land use, history of contact
           and development. Includes map, but
           little detail shown.

43. -----
    1972c Western Highlands District. In Peter Ryan,
           Gen. Ed. (Ref. 11), Vol. 2, pp. 1193-1199.
           General survey describing environment,
           population, development and prospects.
           Includes map, but little detail shown.

44. Niall, H.R.
    1972   Morobe District. In Peter Ryan, Gen. Ed.
           (Ref. 11), Vol. 2, pp. 793-799.
           General survey describing environment,
           population, agriculture and timber
           resources. Includes map, but little
           detail shown.

45. Ord, I.G.
    1967   Atlas of the South-west Pacific: With
           Special Emphasis on Papua and New Guinea.
           Brisbane: Jacaranda Press.

Includes sixteen maps of Papua and New
Guinea, most focusing in detail on
regions (including Highlands) and
topics, e.g., exploration, rainfall.

46. Readers Digest Association, Ltd.
    1968   The Readers Digest Complete Atlas of
            Australia Including Papua-New Guinea.
            Sydney: Readers Digest Association, Ltd.

                    * * * * *

47. Rumens, J.
    1972   Gulf District. In Peter Ryan, Gen. Ed.
            (Ref. 11), Vol. 1, pp. 507-515.
            General survey describing environment,
            population, settlement, subsistence and
            development. Includes map, but little
            detail shown.

48. Sinclair, James P.
    1972   Chimbu District. In Peter Ryan, Gen. Ed.
            (Ref. 11), Vol. 1, pp. 164-170.
            General survey describing geography,
            exploration, culture, agriculture and
            development. Includes map, but little
            detail shown.

49. Ward, R. Gerard and David A.M. Lea (Eds.)
    1970   An Atlas of Papua and New Guinea. Port
            Moresby: Department of Geography, University
            of Papua New Guinea and Glasgow: Collins-
            Longman.
            Topical coverage on standardized outline
            maps of Papua New Guinea (Irian Jaya
            excluded). Maps accompanied by short
            essays by specialists, most dealing with
            present development.

D. General Histories and Historical Surveys

50. Biskup, Peter, B. Jinks and H. Nelson
    1968   A Short History of New Guinea. Sydney:
            Angus and Robertson.
            Brief general introduction, intended as
            school textbook.

51. Gibbney, H.J.
    1972   Sources for History. In Peter Ryan, Gen.
            Ed. (Ref. 11), Vol. 2, pp. 1082-1085.
            Brief discussion of history of island,
            then subdivided by colonial regions.

Discusses, but does not systematically
list, newspaper, journal, archival and
library sources for historical research.

52. Healy, A.M.
1962   Native Administration and Local Government
in Papua, 1880-1960. Ph.D. Thesis, Canberra,
The Australian National University.
Historical survey and analysis of
administration and development, including
exploration, for time period indicated.

53. Hudson, W.J. (Ed.)
1971   Australia and Papua New Guinea. Sydney:
Sydney University Press.
Collection of papers on history of
Australian administration.

54. Hudson, W.J. and Jill Danen
1971   Papua and New Guinea Since 1945. In W.J.
Hudson, Ed. (Ref. 53), pp. 151-177.
General discussion of post-World War II
Australian administration.

55. Jack-Hinton, C.
1972   Discovery. In Peter Ryan, Gen. Ed. (Ref.
11), Vol. 1, pp. 246-257.
Discussion of European discovery from
early 1500's to 1830's; useful for
overview and important dates.

56. Jacobs, Marjorie
1972   German New Guinea. In Peter Ryan, Gen. Ed.
(Ref. 11), Vol. 1, pp. 485-498.
General discussion of area including
extreme Eastern Highlands only; emphasis
on administration and exploration 1884-
1914.

57. Joyce, Roger B.
1960   New Guinea. London: Oxford University
Press.
                * * * * *

58. -----
1971   Australian Interests in New Guinea Before
1906. In W.J. Hudson, Ed. (Ref. 53), pp.
8-31.
Discussion of period prior to penetration
of Highlands but includes important
background information.

59. -----
1972   Exploration. In Peter Ryan, Gen. Ed.

(Ref. 11), Vol. 1, pp. 385-389.
General survey of exploration of British
New Guinea, Mandated Territory, Papua
and Irian Jaya, including Highlands;
good for overview and important dates.

60. Joyce, Roger B., A.M. Healy and J.D. Legge
1972   British New Guinea. In Peter Ryan, Gen. Ed.
(Ref. 11), Vol. 1, pp. 115-121.
General discussion of area known as
Papua after 1906; emphasis on history of
administration and exploration.

61. Lagerberg, Cornelia S.I.J.
1962   Jaren van Reconstructie: Nieuw-Guinea van
1949 tot 1961. Ph.D. Thesis, Utrecht,
University of Utrecht.
* * * * *

62. Legge, J.D.
1946   Australian Colonial Policy: A Survey of
Native Administration and European
Development in Papua. M.A. Thesis,
Melbourne, University of Melbourne.
General survey as indicated, limited to
Papua.

63. -----
1956   Australian Colonial Policy: A Survey of
Native Administration and European
Development in Papua. Sydney: Angus and
Robertson.
Published version of Ref. 62.

64. -----
1971   The Murray Period: Papua 1906-1940. In
W.J. Hudson, Ed. (Ref. 53), pp. 32-56.
General discussion of administration
and exploration of Papua.

65. Mair, Lucy P.
1948   Australia in New Guinea. London: Christopher.
Brief history emphasizing administration
and development in Papua New Guinea.

66. Nelson, H.
1970   Contact and Administrative Control. In R.
Gerard Ward and David A.M. Lea, Eds. (Ref.
49), pp. 4-7.
Maps showing knowledge of Papua New
Guinea in 1880's, extent of administration
and control in 1923 and 1939, and areas
still restricted as of 1951-1965. Short
essay discussing general history 1920-69.

67. Price, A. Grenfell
1965 The Challenge of New Guinea: Australian Aid
to Papuan Progress. Sydney: Angus and
Robertson.
General history of Australian
administration and development in
Papua New Guinea.

68. -----
1972 Island Continent: Aspects of the Historical
Geography of Australia and Its Territories.
Sydney: Angus and Robertson.
General survey of Australian history
including chapter on Papua New Guinea.

69. Radford, Robin
1972 Missionaries, Miners and Administrators in
the Eastern Highlands. Journal of the
Papua and New Guinea Society 6:85-105.
Discussion of initial European entry into
Eastern Highlands 1919-1920's; includes
documentation through unpublished
archival materials.

70. Radi, Heather
1971 New Guinea Under Mandate 1921-1941. In
W.J. Hudson, Ed. (Ref. 53), pp. 74-137.
General discussion of administration of
Papua New Guinea between world wars.

71. Reed, Stephen W.
1939 Acculturation in New Guinea. Ph.D. Thesis,
New Haven, Yale University.
History of administration and contact
through late 1930's; includes little
directly related to Highlands.

72. -----
1943 The Making of Modern New Guinea: With
Special References to Culture Contact in
the Mandated Territory. American
Philosophical Society, Memoirs, No. 18.
Philadelphia: American Philosophical
Society.
Published version of Ref. 71.

73. Roe, Margriet
1971 Papua-New Guinea and War 1941-5. In W.J.
Hudson, Ed. (Ref. 53), pp. 138-150.
General discussion of World War II
and its effects in Papua New Guinea.

74. Rowley, C.D.
    1971   The Occupation of German New Guinea 1914-21.
           In W.J. Hudson, Ed. (Ref. 53), pp. 57-73.
           General discussion of Australian
           accession and control of Mandated Territory
           following World War I.

75. Souter, Gavin
    1963   New Guinea: The Last Unknown. Sydney:
           Angus and Robertson.
           Comprehensive and detailed history of
           discovery and exploration of Papua New
           Guinea and Irian Jaya, including special
           chapters on Highlands.

76. Veur, Paul W. van der
    1972   Dutch New Guinea. In Peter Ryan, Gen. Ed.
           (Ref. 11), Vol. 1, pp. 276-283.
           General survey of exploration and
           administration, European enterprises
           and missions in Irian Jaya, 1828-1962.

77. Willis, Ian
    1969   Who Was First? The First White Man into
           the New Guinea Highlands. Journal of the
           Papua and New Guinea Society 3:32-45.
           Critical examination of competing claims
           of "discovery" of Highlands of Papua New
           Guinea.

E. Observations and Reminiscences by Non-Anthropologists

78. Anderson, James L. and Donald M. Hogg
    1969   New Guinea. Sydney: A.H. and A.W. Reed.
           Picture book with photographs of various
           Highlanders and brief text by Hogg, a
           journalist.

79. Archbold, Richard A.
    1940   Flight to the Stone Age. New York Academy
           of Sciences, Transactions 2:95-98.
           Brief report by mammalogist on American
           Museum of Natural History 1938-1939
           expedition to Baliem Valley, Irian Jaya,
           including some notes on DANI people.

80. -----
    1941   Unknown New Guinea. National Geographic
           79:315-344.
           More detailed account of AMNH expedition
           describing discovery and exploration of

Baliem Valley; includes numerous
photographs and descriptions of DANI
gardens, settlements and customs.

81. Archbold, Richard A. and Austin L. Rand
    1941   Latchkey to a Savage Tribe. Natural History
    47:193-199.
    Brief description of initial contact
    with Pesegem DANI near Lake Habbema in
    1938; describes pig-killing and feast,
    including photographs.

82. Archbold, Richard A., Austin L. Rand and L.J. Brass
    1942   Results of the Archbold Expeditions, No. 41.
    Summary of the 1938-39 New Guinea Expedition.
    American Museum of Natural History, Bulletin
    79:197-288.
    Primarily a detailed report on flora and
    fauna of Baliem Valley region, but
    includes photographs and notes on DANI
    gardens and villages.

83. Attenborough, David
    1960   Quest in Paradise. London: Lutterworth.
    Ornithologist's account of collecting
    trips to Asai, Ganz, Jimmi and Wahgi
    Valleys; includes detailed notes and
    photographs on hunting, ornamentation
    and salt-making. (GANTS, KARAM, NARAK
    and WAHGI).

84. Barrett, Charles L.
    1954   Isles of the Sun. London: William Heineman.
    Journalist's account of travels and
    visits to Chimbu, Nondugl, Goroka and
    Wabag. (ASARO, CHIMBU, ENGA and WAHGI).

85. Bastian, Paul G.
    1969   Medical Aid for Bosavi Cannibals.
    Geographical Magazine 41:547-551.
    Journalistic description of medical
    services in Mt. Bosavi region of Southern
    Highlands. (BOSAVI).

86. Bearup, A.J.
    1936   The Ramu and Wahgi Valleys of New Guinea.
    Australian Geographer 3:3-14.
    Medical officer's report of 1934 survey
    in Kainantu and Mogei regions; brief
    notes on customs and 12 photographs.
    (AGARABE and HAGEN).

87. Beaver, Wilfred N.
     1912   Report by Mr. W.N. Beaver on the Search
            Party Led by Him in Connection with the
            Kikori Expedition. Territory of Papua,
            Annual Report for 1910-11. Canberra:
            Government Printer. pp. 178-187.
            Brief account by patrol officer of
            search for Smith party (see Ref's below)
            in Mount Murray and Samberigi Valley
            regions of Southern Highlands; includes
            passing notes on SAU people.

88. -----
     1920   Unexplored New Guinea. London: Seeley,
            Service.
            Reminiscences of patrol officer; includes
            chapter on 1910 patrol (see Ref. 87) to
            Mount Murray and Samberigi Valley. Some
            details on villages, houses, appearance,
            dress, weapons and crops of SAU people.

89. Bell, L.L.
     1911   Exploring in Papua. Victorian Geographical
            Journal 28:31-63.
            Summary description of 1910 Smith (see
            Ref's below) expedition to Mount Murray
            and Samberigi Valley regions; includes
            various notes on SAU people.

90. Bergman, Sten
     1957   Through Primitive New Guinea. (Transl. from
            Swedish) London: Robert Hale.
                        * * * * *

91. Bernarding, Georg
     1969   Aus der Diozese Mount Hagen. Steyler
            Missions-Chronik, pp. 55-59.
            History of Catholic missions in Western
            Highlands; includes map of Catholic
            dioceses and statistics on converts.
            (HAGEN)

92. Bernatzik, Hugo A.
     1935a A Flight into the Stone Age: Life in
            Unexplored New Guinea. Geographical
            Magazine 2(1):79-93.
            Popular account of travels in BENABENA
            area including notes on villages, houses,
            fortifications, gardens, appearance,
            dress, cane-swallowing and warfare, with
            five photographs.

93. -----
     1935b South Seas. (Transl. from German) New York:
             Henry Holt.
             More detailed account of travels in Ref.
             92, including additional photographs.
             (BENABENA).

94. Bjerre, Jens
     1956 The Last Cannibals. (Transl. from Danish)
             New York: Morrow.
             Popular account of travels including
             chapters on visits to Menyamya, Goroka,
             Nondugl, Minj, Banz and Mount Hagen;
             notes on various customs and some
             photographs. (ASARO, HAGEN, MENYA and
             WAHGI).

95. -----
     1964 Savage New Guinea. (Transl. from Danish)
             New York: Hill and Wang.
             Description of museum collecting trip to
             Southern and Western Highlands; color
             photographs and considerable detail on
             ceremonies, customs and myths of Mendi,
             Tari, Lake Kutubu, Laiagam and Simbai
             Valley. (ENGA, FOI, HULI, KARAM and
             MENDI).

96. Blood, Ned
     1949 Sheep Airlift in New Guinea. National
             Geographic 96:831-844.
             Photo-essay on introduction of sheep to
             experimental stations at Nondugl and
             Kerowagi in Wahgi Valley. (CHIMBU and
             WAHGI).

97. Brass, L.J.
     1972 Archbold Expeditions. In Peter Ryan, Gen.
             Ed. (Ref. 11), Vol. 1, pp. 25-28.
             Brief descriptions of routes of seven
             Archbold (AMNH) expeditions, two to
             Highlands regions: the 3rd (1938-39) to
             Baliem Valley, Irian Jaya, and the 6th
             (1959) to Eastern Highlands regions.

98. Brongersma, Leo D. and G.F. Venema
     1962 To the Mountains of the Stars. (Transl.
             from Dutch). London: Hodder and Stoughton.
             Popular account of 1959 expedition to
             Juliana Summit, Irian Jaya; includes
             many photographs and various notes on
             SIBIL and STAR MOUNTAINS people.

99. Brown, Edwin
    1969   The Kainantu Villager. Journal of the Papua
            and New Guinea Society 6(3):61-63.
            Brief description of customs and
            appearance of AGARABE people.

100. Campbell, Stuart
     1938   The Country between the Headwaters of the
             Fly and Sepik Rivers in New Guinea.
             Geographical Journal 92:232-258 and map
             ff. p. 288.
             Report of prospecting expeditiion in
             1936-37, including descriptions of dress,
             ornamentation, weapons, villages, house
             types, crops and some customs of Feramin,
             Kiarikmin, Telefomin and Ok Elip people;
             some photographs. (TELEFOL).

101. Cator, W.J.
     1938   Verslag van een tocht naar het Wisselmeer-
             district in Centraal Nieuw-Guinea.
             Nieuw-Guinea 2:329-340.
             Dutch patrol officer's account of brief
             visit in 1937 to Lake Paniai, Wissel Lakes
             region, Irian Jaya. (KAPAUKU).

102. Champion, Ivan F.
     1928   Report of Sub-Patrol -- Northwestern Patrol.
             Territory of Papua, Annual Report for 1926-27,
             App. B. Canberra: Government Printer. pp.
             102-117.
             Brief account of patrol to headwaters of
             Fly and Sepik Rivers (see Ref. 103).
             (FAIWOL and TELEFOL).

103. -----
     1932   Across New Guinea from the Fly to the Sepik.
             London: Constable.
             Popular account of administrative patrol
             in 1926-27 and 1927-28 to headwaters of
             Fly and Sepik Rivers. Includes passing
             descriptions of villages, gardens, houses,
             appearance, ornamentation and customs of
             Unkiamin, Sitamin, Feramin, Telefomin,
             Aptalmin and Karikmin peoples, with some
             photographs. (FAIWOL and TELEFOL).

104. -----
     1937   Lake Kutubu. Pacific Islands Monthly 7(11):
             33-34.
             Brief description of establishment of
             patrol post at Lake Kutubu in Southern
             Highlands. (FOI).

105. -----
      1938   The Bamu-Purari Expedition. Territory of
              Papua, Annual Report for 1936-37. Canberra:
              Government Printer. pp. 21-22.
              Brief summary of exploratory patrol to
              various regions of Southern Highlands
              (see Ref. 106). (AUA, AUGU, BOSAVI,
              FOI, GAWIGL, HULI, MENDI, MIKARU, POLOPA
              and TURAMA-KIKORI RIVERS FAMILY).

106. -----
      1940   The Bamu-Purari Patrol, 1936. Geographical
              Journal 96:190-206, 243-257 and map ff. p. 304.
              Detailed account of exploratory patrol to
              Mount Bosavi, Lake Kutubu, Wage River,
              Mendi River, Mt. Giluwe, Kaugel River,
              Mt. Ialibu, Tua River and Karimui Plateau.
              Includes passing comments on people and
              villages, with photographs. (AUA, AUGU,
              BOSAVI, FOI, GAWIGL, HULI, MENDI, MIKARU,
              POLOPA and TURAMA-KIKORI RIVERS FAMILY).

107. -----
      1941   Territory of Papua -- Lake Kutubu Police
              Camp. Territory of Papua, Annual Report for
              1939-40. Canberra: Government Printer.
              pp. 29-37.
              Detailed report on establishment of patrol
              post at Lake Kutubu. (FOI).

108. Chinnery, E.W.P.
      1934a   The Central Ranges of the Mandated Territory
              of New Guinea from Mt. Chapman to Mt. Hagen.
              Geographical Journal 84:398-412 and map ff.
              p. 464.
              Description of routes of Leahy brothers'
              prospecting expeditions and early patrols
              by author, J.K. McCarthy and J.L. Taylor
              to Eastern and Western Highlands, with
              detailed map. (BENABENA, CHIMBU, CHUAVE,
              GAHUKU, GANTS, HAGEN, KAMANO, MENYA,
              NARAK, SINASINA and WAHGI).

109. -----
      1934b   Mountain Tribes of the Mandated Territory of
              New Guinea from Mount Chapman to Mount Hagen.
              Man, Vol. 34, Art. 140, pp. 113-121.
              Description of peoples contacted by author
              and others in early 1930's (see Ref. 108).
              (BENABENA, CHIMBU, CHUAVE, GAHUKU, GANTS,
              HAGEN, KAMANO, MENYA, NARAK, SINASINA and
              WAHGI).

110. Clancy, D.J.
     1962   Through the Strickland Gorge. Australian
            Territories 2(1):12-19.
            Summary report of administrative patrol
            in 1954 to Tari, Lake Kutubu, Lagaip
            River and Lake Kopiago regions; includes
            four photographs and passing references
            to peoples encountered. (DUNA, FOI, HEWA
            and HULI).

111. Colijn, A.H.
     1937   Naar de eeuwige sneeuw van Nieuw Guinea.
            Amsterdam: Scheltens and Giltay.
            Popular account by leader of Dutch
            geographical expedition in 1936 to
            Carstensz Pyramid region, Irian Jaya;
            some references to UHUNDUNI people met.

112. Cotlow, Lewis
     1966   In Search of the Primitive. Boston: Little,
            Brown.
            Adventurer's reminiscences including
            chapters on visits to Menyamya, Okapa,
            Goroka, Chimbu, Minj, Mount Hagen,
            Laiagam, Wabag, Aiome and Baliem Valley.
            Includes descriptions of various customs.
            (ASARO, BENABENA, CHIMBU, DANI, ENGA,
            FORE, GAHUKU, KARAM, MENYA and WAHGI).

113. Courage, Michael and Dermot Wright
     1967   New Guinea Venture. London: Robert Hale.
            Popular account of experiences of
            Voluntary Service Overseas worker
            (Courage) with KARAM of Simbai Valley.

114. Cox, Paul and Ulli Beier
     1971   Home of Man: The People of New Guinea.
            Melbourne: Thomas Nelson.
            Photographs accompanied by traditional
            New Guinea poems and songs; people shown
            unidentified but include Highlanders.

115. Dean, Beth and Victor Carell
     1958   Softly, Wild Drums: In New Guinea Today.
            Sydney: Ure Smith.
            Popular account of brief visits in 1950's
            to Minj, Mount Hagen, Ogelbeng, Wapenamanda,
            Wabag, Bibia and Mendi; includes a few
            photographs and observations on customs.
            (ENGA, HAGEN, MENDI and WAHGI).

116. Derrick, Christopher
     1972   Asaro Valley People -- New Guinea. In E.E.
            Evans-Pritchard, Ed. (Ref. 2), pp. 88-91.

Very brief sketch of Gururumba people of
Goroka region; includes color photographs.
(ASARO).

17. Detzner, Hermann
1921   Vier jahre unter kannibalen, von 1914 bis
       zum waffenstillstand unter Deutscher flogge
       im unerforschten innern von Neuguinea.
       Berlin: A. Scherl.

18. -----
    1928- Stammesgemeinschaften im "Zentralgebirge"
    1929   von Deutsch-Neuguinea. Mitteilungen aus den
           Deutschen Schutzgebieten 36:112-130.

19. -----
    1935   Moeurs et coutumes des Papous: Quatre ans
           chez les cannibales de la Nouvelle-Guinee.
           (1914-1918). Paris: Payot.
           Three references above describe German
           officer's experiences in New Guinea
           including claimed (qualified in Ref. 119)
           "discovery" of Highlands areas of Wahgi
           Valley and southern slopes of Bismarck
           Range.

20. Eechoud, J.P.K.
    1953   Met kapmes en kompas door Nieuw-Guinea.
           Amsterdam: C. de Boer.

21. -----
    1957   Vergeten aarde: Nieuw Guinea. Amsterdam:
           C. de Boer.
           Two references constitute Dutch
           administrative officer's reminiscences
           of Irian Jaya including account of
           establishment of patrol post at Wissel
           Lakes in 1938; passing references to
           KAPAUKU people and neighbors.

22. Elsmore, Ray T.
    1945   New Guinea's Mountain and Swampland Dwellers.
           National Geographic 88:670-694.
           Allied Air Force officer's description of
           experiences in Baliem Valley of Irian
           Jaya and Telefomin area; includes
           photographs and passing comments on
           customs of DANI and TELEFOL.

23. Flierl, Johannes
    1927   Forty Years in New Guinea. (Transl. from
           German) Chicago: Wartburg Press.

19

124. -----
1931 Forty-Five Years in New Guinea: Memoirs of
      the Senior Missionary. (Transl. from
      German) Second and Revised Ed. (of Ref.
      123) Columbus, Ohio: Lutheran Book Concern.

125. -----
1932 Unter wilden: Missionarische anfangsarbeit
      im innern von Neu Guinea. Ansbach, Bayern:
      Neuendettelsau.
      Three references comprise reminiscences
      of pioneer Lutheran missionary including
      discussion of Neuendettelsau Mission
      penetration of Eastern Highlands in 1919
      and 1920's.

126. Flint, Leo A.
1923 Report on the Patrol through the Samberigi
      Valley, Mount Murray District, Delta
      Division. Territory of Papua, Annual Report
      for 1921-22. Canberra: Government Printer.
      pp. 141-152.
      Detailed report of 1922 patrol with H.M.
      Saunders (see below) with some comments
      on SAU people.

127. Frerichs, Albert C. and Sylvia Frerichs
1957 Anutu Conquers in New Guinea. Columbus,
      Ohio: Warburg Press.
      Survey of activities of Lutheran mission
      in New Guinea with passing descriptions
      of customs encountered including those
      of various Highlands groups.

128. Gaisseau, Pierre D.
1957 Visa to the Prehistoric World. (Transl.
      from French) London: F. Muller.
      Popular account by leader of French
      cinematographic expedition to Baliem
      Valley and Oranje Range of Irian Jaya
      (cf. Saulnier below). (DANI and GOLIATH
      FAMILY).

129. Gilliard, E. Thomas
1951 New Guinea's Paradise of Birds. National
      Geographic 100:661-688.
      Ornithologist's account of 1950 AMNH
      expedition to Wahgi Valley, Kubor Range,
      Mount Hagen and Mount Wilhelm areas;
      includes many photographs of birds and
      people. (CHIMBU, HAGEN and WAHGI).

130. -----
1953a Exploring New Guinea for Birds of Paradise.

20

Natural History 62:248-255, 287.
Brief account of same expedition as in
Ref. 130. (CHIMBU, HAGEN and WAHGI).

31. -----
      1953b New Guinea's Rare Birds and Stone Age Men.
             National Geographic 103:421-488.
             Description of 1952 AMNH expedition to
             sa e areas as in Ref's 129 and 130;
             many photographs (most in color) of
             animals, birds and people. (CHIMBU,
             HAGEN and WAHGI).

32. -----
      1954   In Quest of Birds of Paradise. Natural
             History 63:104-111, 140-142.
             Brief account of 1952 expedition as in
             Ref. 131, but including Baiyer Valley;
             some photographs of people and birds.
             (CHIMBU, HAGEN, KYAKA ENGA and WAHGI).

33. -----
      1955   To the Land of the Head-hunters. National
             Geographic 108:437-486.
             Description of 1953 AMNH expedition to
             Hindenburg Range and Telefomin area;
             includes many photographs (most in color)
             of birds and people. (TELEFOL).

34. -----
      1957   A Stone Age Naturalist. Natural History 66:
             344-351.
             Brief account of Telefomin man and his
             ornithological knowledge; includes some
             photographs of people and houses.
             (TELEFOL).

35. -----
      1961   Birds of the Victor Emanuel and Hindenburg
             Mountains, New Guinea. American Museum of
             Natural History, Bulletin 123:1-86.
             Primarily detailed ornithological report
             but includes photographs of landscapes,
             houses and people of Telefomin area.
             (TELEFOL).

136. Harrer, Heinrich
      1964   I Come from the Stone Age. (Transl. from
             German) London: Rupert Hart-Davis.
             Popular description of 1962 expedition
             to Carstensz Pyramid, Irian Jaya,
             including notes and photographs of DANI
             people of Baliem Valley and Mulia region.

137. Healy, M.J.
        1938   Patrol to Kukukuku Country Between the
                Tiveri and Upper Tauri Rivers. Territory
                of Papua, Annual Report for 1936-37.
                Canberra: Government Printer.   p. 24.
                Brief summary of patrol to Menyamya
                region. (MENYA).

138. Hides, Jack G.
        1935a   Approaching Mount Hagen Area.   Pacific
                Islands Monthly 5(10):44-46.
                Brief account of part of patrol with
                J.T. O'Malley in 1935 south of Mount
                Hagen area. (HULI and MENDI).

139. -----
        1935b   A Papuan Patrol. Australian Geographer 2(8):
                16-19.
                Brief summary of 1935 patrol up Fly River
                and across Southern Highlands to Kikori
                River. (HULI, MENDI, POLOPA and SAU).

140. -----
        1936   Papuan Wonderland. London: Blackie and Son.
                Popular account of 1935 patrol up Rentoul
                River, across Southern Highlands and down
                Kikori River.   (HULI, MENDI, POLOPA and SAU)

141. -----
        1938   Savages in Serge. Sydney: Angus and Robertson
                Popular account of various patrols and
                travels, mostly in Southern Highlands.
                (FOI, HULI, MENDI, POLOPA and SAU).

142. -----
        1939   Beyond the Kubea. Sydney: Angus and Robertson
                Popular account, similar to Ref. 141 in
                material covered, but emphasizing travels
                in Upper Strickland River region. (FOI,
                HULI, MENDI, POLOPA and SAU).

143. Hides, Jack G. and J.T. O'Malley
        1936   Expedition from the Strickland to the Purari
                River. Territory of Papua, Annual Report for
                1934-35. Canberra: Government Printer.
                pp. 23-25.
                Brief summary of 1935 patrol through
                Southern Highlands regions, especially
                Mendi, Wage and Erave Rivers and Samberigi
                Valley. (HULI, MENDI, POLOPA and SAU).

144. -----
        1936-   Aerial Reconnaissance of the Hides-O'Malley
        1937   Area in the Interior of Papua, Visited by

Them on Foot in the Early Half of 1936 and
to be Patrolled Later on by Mr. Champion.
Tijdschrift Nieuw-Guinea 1:62-68, 117-127.
Description of area patrolled and reported
in Ref's 138-143, but especially Lake
Kutubu region. (FOI).

145. Hitchcock, W.B.
1964   An Introduction to the Natural History of a
New Guinea Highland Community. Emu 63:351-372.
Biologist's description of 1963 bird and
mammal survey in Kubor Range near Minj;
includes lists of fauna collected and notes
on people's hunting techniques and uses of
plants. (WAHGI).

146. Hitt, Russell T.
1962   Cannibal Valley. New York: Harper and Row.
Missionary's description of Christian and
Missionary Alliance activities in 1950's,
mostly in Baliem Valley, Irian Jaya, but
some mention of work elsewhere. (DANI,
KAPAUKU, MONI and UHUNDUNI).

147. Holthuis, L.B.
1958   Freshwater Crayfish in Netherlands New Guinea
Mountains. South Pacific Commission, Quarterly
Bulletin 8(2):36-39.
Brief description by crustacean specialist
of crayfish in Wissel Lakes, Irian Jaya,
with details on KAPAUKU fishing techniques.

148. Holton, George and Kenneth E. Read
1971   The Human Aviary: A Pictorial Discovery of
New Guinea. New York: Charles Scribner's Sons.
Mainly book of photographs, many of
Highlanders though unidentified, with text
by anthropologist (Read).

149. Karius, C.H.
1928   Attempt to Cross New Guinea from the Fly to
the Sepik by Karius and Champion, Failed on
Account of Lack of Supplies. Territory of
Papua, Annual Report for 1926-27, App. A.
Canberra: Government Printer. p. 6.
Brief account of failed 1926-27 attempt
to find headwaters of Fly and Sepik Rivers.

150. -----
1929a   Expedition Across the Island of New Guinea
(and) Report on the Crossing of New Guinea.
Territory of Papua, Annual Report for 1927-28,
App. D. Canberra: Government Printer. pp. 87-
108.

Official report of 1927-28 patrol to
headwaters of Fly and Sepik Rivers with
Ivan F. Champion (see Ref's 102 and 103).
(FAIWOL and TELEFOL).

151. -----
    1929b Exploration in the Interior of Papua and
           North-East New Guinea: The Sources of the
           Fly, Palmer, Strickland and Sepik Rivers.
           Geographical Journal 74:305-322 and map ff.
           p. 416.
                Account of 1926 and 1927 expeditions to
                Hindenburg Range and Telefomin area; some
                notes on villages and houses but little
                on people; a few photographs (cf. Ref. 103).
                (FAIWOL and TELEFOL).

152. Karius, C.H. and Ivan F. Champion
    1928   Report of North-West Patrol, 3rd December
           1926, to 10th June 1927, and Sub-Patrol, 1st
           May to 14th July, 1927. Territory of Papua,
           Annual Report for 1926-27, App. A. Canberra:
           Government Printer. pp. 91-101.
                Official report of two patrols with
                brief notes on people of Fly and Sepik
                headwaters region (cf. Ref's 102, 103,
                149-151). (FAIWOL and TELEFOL).

153. Kerr, Martin D.
    1973   New Guinea Patrol. London: Robert Hale.
                Popular account of patrol officer's
                tours of duty, including five-month
                stay in Telefomin and five-week patrol
                in Mianmin area; passing notes on customs.
                (MIANMIN and TELEFOL).

154. Kienzle, Wallace and Stuart Campbell
    1938   Notes on the Natives of the Fly and Sepik
           River Headwaters, New Guinea. Oceania 8:
           463-481.
                Report of 1936-37 prospecting expedition
                describing villages, appearance and some
                customs of peoples of headwaters of Fly,
                Strickland, May and Sepik Rivers and Ok
                Om, Ok Fek and Ok Alip (cf. Ref. 100).
                (TELEFOL).

155. Kirk, Malcolm S.
    1969a Journey Into Stone Age New Guinea. National
           Geographic 135:568-592.
                Journalist's description of trip to Fly
                River headwaters; includes photographs
                and notes on FAIWOL, MIANMIN, OKSAPMIN
                and TELEFOL peoples.

24

082298

156. -----
           1969b New Guinea Festival of Faces. National
                  Geographic 136:148-156.
                    Color photographs taken at Mount Hagen
                    Show; include unidentified Highlanders,
                    probably ASARO, DUNA, ENGA, HAGEN and
                    WAHGI.

157. Leahy, Michael J.
           1935a Stone Age People of the Mount Hagen Area,
                  Mandated Territory of New Guinea. Man,
                  Vol. 35, Art. 202 , pp. 185-186.
                    Brief description of initial contact
                    with BENABENA, CHIMBU and WAHGI peoples
                    by prospecting expedition in 1930's.

158. -----
           1935b Tribal Wars in Unexplored New Guinea.
                  Walkabout 2(1):10-13.
                    Description of battle observed in early
                    1930's, with six photographs; people
                    unidentified but probably BENABENA.

159. -----
           1936   The Central Highlands of New Guinea.
                  Geographical Journal 87:229-262 and map
                  ff. p. 288.
                    Detailed diary of prospecting exploration,
                    ten expeditions in all, including Dunantina
                    and Kamamentina Rivers (1930), Marifutiga
                    River to Mount Hagen (1932), to west and
                    northwest of Mount Hagen (1934) and the
                    Wahgi Valley (1934); includes detailed
                    map and numerous photographs. (ASARO,
                    BENABENA, CHIMBU, CHUAVE, ENGA, GAWIGL,
                    HAGEN, KAMANO, KYAKA ENGA, SINASINA and
                    WAHGI).

160. Leahy, Michael J. and M. Crain
           1937   The Land That Time Forgot: Adventures and
                  Discoveries in New Guinea. London: Hurst
                  and Blackett.
                    Popular account of exploration 1930-34
                    (cf. Ref. 159); includes photographs
                    and passing comments on customs observed;
                    most information on ASARO, BENABENA,
                    CHIMBU, CHUAVE, SINASINA and WAHGI.

161. Maahs, Arnold
           1949   The Festival of the Pig. Walkabout 15(12):
                  17-20.
                    Brief description with five photographs
                    of pig feast; people unidentified but
                    probably WAHGI.

25

162.　-----
　　　1950a　Put Another Rock on the Fire. Walkabout
　　　　　　　16(3):44-45, 47-48.
　　　　　　　　　Brief description, with four photographs,
　　　　　　　　　of earth-oven feast; people unidentified
　　　　　　　　　but probably WAHGI.

163.　-----
　　　1950b　Salt-Makers of the Wahgi. Walkabout 16(1):
　　　　　　　15-18.
　　　　　　　　　Eleven photographs with brief description
　　　　　　　　　of vegetable salt-making process; people
　　　　　　　　　unidentified but probably WAHGI.

164.　-----
　　　1951　The Stone-Axe People. Geographical Magazine
　　　　　　　23:491-493.
　　　　　　　　　Four color photographs with detailed
　　　　　　　　　captions illustrating stone axe making at
　　　　　　　　　quarry of Make people, said to be near
　　　　　　　　　neighbors of Chimbu. (NARAK?)

165.　-----
　　　1953　New Guinea's Stone Age Men. Walkabout 19(2):
　　　　　　　29-35.
　　　　　　　　　Five photographs with brief description of
　　　　　　　　　axe-blade quarry on upper Jimmi River.
　　　　　　　　　(NARAK?)

166.　-----
　　　1955　Salt-Makers of New Guinea. Natural History
　　　　　　　64:352-354.
　　　　　　　　　Brief description, with photographs, of
　　　　　　　　　vegetable salt-making process in Wahgi
　　　　　　　　　Valley; people unidentified (cf. Ref. 163).
　　　　　　　　　(WAHGI?)

167.　-----
　　　1956　New Guinea Chiefs Give to Get Rich. Natural
　　　　　　　History 65:176-183, 223.
　　　　　　　　　Description, with photographs, of six-day
　　　　　　　　　moka ceremonial exchange at Ogelbeng.
　　　　　　　　　(HAGEN).

168.　McBride, Brian
　　　1963　A Patrol into the Porgera-Strickland Gorge
　　　　　　　Area. Australian Territories 3(2):32-41.
　　　　　　　　　Brief description of patrol with two
　　　　　　　　　photographs and passing comments on
　　　　　　　　　DUNA, ENGA, HEWA and IPILI peoples.

169.　McCarthy, John Keith
　　　1963　Patrol into Yesterday: My New Guinea Years.
　　　　　　　Melbourne: F.W. Cheshire.

Reminiscences of pioneer patrol officer
including two chapters on Menyamya area.
(MENYA).

70. McLeod, Helen
1961   Cannibals Are Human: A District Officer's
Wife in New Guinea. Sydney: Angus and
Robertson.
Memoirs and reminiscences including
residences in Lake Kutubu, Mendi and
Tari areas. (FOI, HULI and MENDI).

71. Manning, Helen
1969   To Perish for Their Saving. Eastbourne,
Sussex: Victory Press.
Reminiscences of missionary with long-
term residence in Seng Valley, Irian
Jaya. (JALÉ).

72. Mantovani, Ennio
1969   Baminwera-Yobai. Steyler Missions-Chronik,
pp. 65-69.
Brief discussion of Catholic Mission in
CHIMBU.

73. Mayr, Ernst and E. Thomas Gilliard
1954   Birds of Central New Guinea. American Museum
of Natural History, Bulletin 103:311-374.
Primarily ornithological report on 1950
and 1952 expeditions to Wahgi Valley but
includes discussion of deforestation,
local hunting and impact on bird fauna;
photographs of landscapes and birds.
(WAHGI).

74. Mjoberg, Eric
1917   A Proposed Aerial Expedition for the
Exploration of the Unknown Interior of
New Guinea. Geographical Review 3:89-106.
Outlines proposed route for hydroplane
expedition (never carried out) to include
Star Mountains and Telefomin area; includes
photographs and description of Tapiro
people of Nassau Range, Irian Jaya, from
works by Rawling and Wollaston (see Ref's
below).

75. Montgomery, D.E.
1960-   Patrol of Upper Chimbu Census Division,
1961   Eastern Highlands. Papua and New Guinea
Agricultural Journal 13(1):1-9.
Summary report of administrative patrol
with passing comments on CHIMBU people.

176. Putnam, Samuel
1963   Under the Mountain Wall. Harvard Medical
School, Alumni Bulletin, Winter, pp. 28-33.
Journalistic discussion of DANI people
as observed on Harvard Peabody Expedition
to Baliem Valley, Irian Jaya.

177. Rand, Austin L.
1943   Papuans I Have Known. Natural History 51:
84-94.
Popular account of 1938-39 Archbold (AMNH)
expedition to Baliem Valley, Irian Jaya;
includes notes on first contact with DANI
people with photographs of people and
gardens.

178. Reeson, Margaret
1972   Torn Between Two Worlds. Madang: Kristen
Press.
Missionary's description of MENDI people,
from time of first contact to present.

179. Ross, William A.
1937a   Mogei's Big Barbecue. Christian Family 32:
84-85, 98.
Missionary's brief description of pig
feast among HAGEN people.

180. -----
1937b   Ordinary Month -- Extraordinary Mission.
Christian Family 32:60-68, 75.
Descriptive account of village life in
HAGEN area.

181. -----
1937c   Unga Gets His Share. Christian Family 32:
132-133.
Brief description of wealth exchange among
HAGEN people.

182. -----
1938   Disarmament in Stone Age New Guinea.
Christian Family 33:53-54, 75.
Brief account of mission and administratio
pacification efforts in HAGEN area.

183. -----
1968   The Growth of Catholicism in the Western
Highlands. Journal of the Papua and New
Guinea Society 2:58-64.
General discussion emphasizing mission
progress among HAGEN people.

184. Ruhen, Olaf
1957   Land of Dahori: Tales of New Guinea.   London:
        Macdonald.
        Journalist's description of travels,
        mostly in Wahgi Valley; presented in
        form of stories said to be based on
        actual occurrences.

185. -----
1963   Mountains in the Clouds. Sydney: Angus and
        Robertson.
        Popularized history and survey of New
        Guinea, partly based on author's travels
        including Highlands regions.

186. -----
1968   New Guinea. In Isles of the South Pacific.
        Maurice Shadbolt and Olaf Ruhen, Eds.
        Washington, D.C.: National Geographic Society.
        pp. 190-207.
        Brief overview of Highlands peoples;
        includes color photographs of people and
        animals.

187. Sargent, Wyn
1974   People of the Valley. New York: Random House.
        Journalist's description of few months'
        stay in Baliem Valley, Irian Jaya; includes
        extensive discussion of customs and many
        photographs. (DANI).

188. Saulnier, Tony
1963   Headhunters of Papua. New York: Crown.
        Popular description of exploration of
        Oranje Range and other Highlands areas
        of Irian Jaya; passing descriptive notes
        and numerous photographs of DANI and
        GOLIATH FAMILY peoples (cf. Gaisseau,
        Ref. 128).

189. Saunders, H.M.
1923-   A Patrol in New Guinea. Queensland
1924   Geographical Journal 39:22-38.
        Summary of patrol to Mount Murray and
        Samberigi Valley regions of Southern
        Highlands; passing comments on customs
        observed and ten photographs. (SAU).

190. Scofield, John
1962a   Australian New Guinea: Civilization
        Challenges the Stone Age. National
        Geographic 121:604-637.
        Journalist's survey of Papua New Guinea;

29

many color photographs of unidentified
Highlanders, mostly taken at Mount Hagen
Show.

191. -----
     1962b Netherlands New Guinea: Bone of Contention
           in the South Pacific. National Geographic
           121:584-603.
           General survey of Irian Jaya including
           color photographs of DANI people of
           Baliem Valley.

192. Simpson, Colin
     1953 Adam with Arrows: Inside New Guinea. Sydney:
          Angus and Robertson.
          Journalist's description of travels
          including newly-opened areas of Highlands;
          descriptions of customs and numerous
          photographs of peoples encountered.
          (BARUA, ENGA, GANATI, MENYA, TAIRORA and
          TELEFOL).

193. -----
     1954 Adam in Plumes. Sydney: Angus and Robertson.
          Description of travels in 1953, including
          Goroka, Chimbu, Nondugl, Minj, Mount Hagen
          and Tari. (CHIMBU, GAHUKU, HAGEN, HULI
          and WAHGI).

194. -----
     1962 Plumes and Arrows. Sydney: Angus and
          Robertson.
          Collection of chapters from Ref's 192 and
          193, combined with material from additional
          book on non-Highlands New Guinea peoples.

195. Sinclair, James P.
     1954 Patrolling in the Restricted Areas of Papua
          and New Guinea. Australian Outlook 8:129-145.
          General discussion of logistics problems
          in administrative patrolling, especially
          regarding initial contacts.

196. -----
     1958 The Duna People of the Papuan Highlands:
          Their Way of Life. Walkabout 24(9):32-34,
          37-38; 24(10):30-32.
          General description of customs observed,
          with six photographs, and establishment
          of Koroba Patrol Post. (DUNA).

197. -----
     1961 Patrolling in the Territory of Papua and New
          Guinea. Australian Territories 1(4):26-33.

General discussion of reasons and
procedures in administrative patrolling.

198. -----
        1966   Behind the Ranges: Patrolling in New Guinea.
                Cambridge: Cambridge University Press.
                Detailed reminiscences of initial
                patrols in 1950's; interweaves history
                of exploration and administration with
                author's observations of peoples of
                Eastern and Southern Highlands; includes
                numerous photographs. (BARUA, DUNA, ENGA,
                HULI, IPILI, MENDI, MENYA and WAFFA).

199. -----
        1969   The Outside Man: Jack Hides of Papua.
                Melbourne: Lansdowne Press.
                Biography of administrative officer Hides
                (see Ref's above) and history of early
                exploration, especially Southern Highlands.

200. -----
        1971   The Highlanders. Milton, Queensland: Jacaranda
                Press.
                Primarily book of photographs (most in
                color) covering wide range of Highlanders;
                many taken on author's early patrols.

201. -----
        1973a   Faces of New Guinea. Milton, Queensland:
                Jacaranda Press.
                Book of photographs, similar to Ref. 200.

202. -----
        1973b   Wigmen of Papua. Milton, Queensland: Jacaranda
                Press.
                Book of photographs, mostly taken on
                early and initial contact patrols among
                DUNA, ENGA, HEWA, HULI and IPILI peoples.

203. Sippo, W.
        1962   Pushing Back the Frontier. Australian
                Territories 2(4):4-9.
                General discussion of patrolling in Tari
                area with five photographs of HULI people.

204. Smedts, Matthew
        1955   No Tobacco, No Hallelujah: Tale of a Visit to
                the Stone-Age Capaukoos. London: W. Kimber.
                Journalist's popular account of visit to
                Wissel Lakes region, Irian Jaya; includes
                photographs and some notes on KAPAUKU.

205. Smith, Robin and Keith Willey
      1969   New Guinea: A Journey Through 10,000 Years.
             Melbourne: Lansdowne Press.
             Book of photographs by Smith with text
             by journalist Willey; includes many
             Highlanders but unidentified.

206. Spinks, K.L.
      1934   Mapping the Purari Plateau, New Guinea.
             Geographical Journal 84:412-416 and map
             ff. p. 464.
             Brief description of 1930's exploration
             by Leahy brothers, with Spinks as surveyor
             (see Ref's 157-160 above); includes notes
             on countryside of Goroka, Wahgi Valley,
             Mount Hagen, Ganz River and Jimmi River
             areas.

207. -----
      1936   The Wahgi River Valley of Central New Guinea.
             Geographical Journal 87:222-225 and map ff.
             p. 288.
             Detailed description of landscape and
             local WAHGI names for mountain ranges;
             accompanies Ref. 159.

208. Staniforth-Smith, M.
      1912   The Kikori Expedition. Territory of Papua,
             Annual Report for 1910-11. Canberra:
             Government Printer. pp. 165-171.
             Official report of administrative patrol
             to Mount Murray and Samberigi Valley
             regions. (SAU).

209. Stonor, C.R.
      1951   The Chimbu Tribe: A Mountain People of New
             Guinea. Geographical Magazine 23:483-490.
             Traveller's notes and observations of
             customs of CHIMBU people; includes seven
             photographs.

210. Stutterheim, J.F.
      1939   Het een en ander omtrent de stam der
             kapnaoekoe's aan de Wisselmeren. Koloniaal
             Tijdschrift 28:183-188.
             Brief notes on KAPAUKU people by early
             Dutch administrator.

211. Sykes, S.V.
      1955   Into Upland Papua. Geographical Magazine
             28:155-168.
             Five color photographs and various notes
             on TELEFOL people of Sepik headwaters
             observed on petroleum exploration.

212.	Taylor, James L.
	1935	Resume -- Mount Hagen Patrol. Report to the
		Council of the League of Nations on the
		Administration of the Territory of New Guinea
		for 1933-34, App. B. Canberra: Government
		Printer. pp. 113-117.
		Brief summary of Ref. 215.

213.	-----
	1939	Exploring Central New Guinea. Pacific Islands
		Monthly 9(9):44-46.
		Brief synopsis of Ref. 215.

214.	-----
	1940a	Explorations of Unknown New Guinea: Taylor
		Patrol Report. Pacific Islands Monthly 10(8):
		37-42; 10(9):37-41; 10(10):32-37; 10(11):50-54.
		Published version of Ref. 215.

215.	-----
	1940b	Interim Report on the Hagen-Sepik Patrol
		1938-39. Report to the Council of the League
		of Nations on the Administration of the
		Territory of New Guinea for 1938-39, App. B.
		Canberra: Government Printer. pp. 137-149.
		Detailed account of exploratory patrol with
		numerous notes on peoples encountered.
		(DUNA, ENGA, HAGEN, HEWA, HULI, MIANMIN
		and TELEFOL).

216.	-----
	1961	From Wabag to Kelefomin. Australian
		Territories 1(2):28-35.
		Summary report of patrol described in
		Ref. 215.

217.	-----
	1971	Hagen-Sepik Patrol 1938-1939: Interim Report.
		New Guinea 6(3):24-45.
		Reprinting of Ref's 212 and 215.

218.	Temple, Philip
	1962	Nawok! The New Zealand Expedition to New
		Guinea's Highest Mountains. London: J.M.
		Dent and Sons.
		Popular account of 1961 attempt to ascend
		Carstensz Pyramid, Irian Jaya; includes
		photographs and notes on DANI of Baliem
		and Ilaga Valleys.

219.	Tillemans, H.
	1950	Gebruiken op Nieuw-Guinea: regenverdrijving
		bij de bergbewoners van Centraal Nieuw-Guinea

rond de Wisselmeren. Nieuw-Guinea 11: 88-96,
143-152, 183-192.
Missionary's account of numerous brief
visits to Wissel Lakes, Irian Jaya, in
late 1930's. (KAPAUKU).

220. Vial, Leigh G.
1939a The Kaman: Glimpses of Life amongst Some of
New Guinea's Native Peoples. Walkabout 5(7):
17-22.
Patrol officer's brief notes on CHIMBU
people, including notes on customs and
seven photographs.

221. -----
1939b Knights of the Stone Age. Asia 39:408-412.
Brief discussion of warfare among Kaman
(near Kubor Range), including seven
photographs. (CHIMBU).

222. -----
1939c Natives of Our Mandate. Walkabout 5(6):
21-24.
Five photographs and brief general comment
on CHIMBU people.

223. -----
1940 Stone Axes of Mount Hagen, New Guinea.
Oceania 11:158-163.
Description of axe-blade quarry on Ganz
River discovered on 1938-39 patrols.
(CHIMBU).

224. -----
1941 Down the Wahgi: A New Guinea Patrol.
Walkabout 7(9):16-20.
Brief description of salt-making among
CHIMBU; includes five photographs.

225. -----
1942a A New Guinea Journey. Geographical Magazine
14:234-241.
Description of stone-axe manufacture,
with various notes and five photographs
of CHIMBU people.

226. -----
1942b They Fight for Fun. Walkabout 9(1):5-9.
Brief description, with five photographs,
of warfare among CHIMBU.

227. White, Osmar
1965 Parliament of a Thousand Tribes: A Study of
New Guinea. Indianapolis: Bobbs-Merrill.

Journalist's discussion of contemporary
Papua New Guinea and social changes
occurring in early 1960's.

228. Williams, Maslyn
     1964   The Stone Age Islands: New Guinea Today.
            Garden City: Doubleday.
            Journalist and film-maker recounts brief
            visits in early 1960's to various parts
            of Eastern and Southern Highlands; passing
            observations on customs and some original
            photographs. (ASARO, HAGEN, HULI, MENDI,
            MENYA and WAHGI).

229. Zöllner, Ilse
     1972   Taufe in Angguruk. In die Welt fur die Welt:
            Berichte der Vereinigten Evangelischen Mission
            (Essen) 8(6):4-7.
            Missionary's report on progress since
            1961 in converting JALÉ people of Irian
            Jaya.

PART II   SOCIAL AND CULTURAL ANTHROPOLOGY

A. General Surveys and Comparative Studies

230. Abramson, J.A.
      1969   Style in New Guinea Highlands Shields.
              Mankind 7:59-66.
                  Comparison based on museum collections,
                  published descriptions and field research.
                  (HAGEN, KYAKA ENGA, MENDI, NARAK and
                  TELEFOL).

231. Allen, Michael R.
      1967   Male Cults and Secret Initiations in
              Melanesia. Melbourne: Melbourne University
              Press.
                  Comparative and theoretical analysis of
                  male initiation ceremonies, including
                  numerous Highlands societies.

232. -----
      1972   Initiation. In Peter Ryan, Gen. Ed. (Ref. 11),
              Vol. 1, pp. 552-558.
                  General description and discussion of
                  initiation rites, especially emphasizing
                  Highlands societies.

233. Anthropos Institut
      1968   Anthropica, Gedenkschrift zum 100, Geburtstag
              von P. Wilhelm Schmidt. Studia Instituti
              Anthropos, Vol. 21. St. Augustin bei Bonn:
              Verlag des Anthropos-Instituts.
                  Memorial volume to Pater Schmidt; includes
                  papers on Highlands societies.

234. Barnes, J.A.
      1962   African Models in the New Guinea Highlands.
              Man, Vol. 62, Art. 2, pp. 5-9.
                  General discussion of applicability of
                  unilineal descent models to Highlands
                  social organization.

235. Berndt, Catherine H.
      1972   Myths and Tales. In Peter Ryan, Gen. Ed.
              (Ref. 11), Vol. 2, pp. 822-829.
                  General survey with references to some
                  Highlands cultures.

236. Berndt, Ronald M.
      1964   Warfare in the New Guinea Highlands. In
              James B. Watson, Ed. (Ref. 373), pp. 183-203.

General survey of literature and original
field research among FORE, KAMANO, USURUFA
and YATE; comparison of warfare customs
and suggested correlates.

237. -----
     1972   Social Control. In Peter Ryan, Gen. Ed.
            (Ref. 11), Vol. 2, pp. 1050-1065.
            Survey of literature and original field
            research; includes section on Highlands.

238. Berndt, Ronald M. and Peter Lawrence (Eds.)
     1971   Politics in New Guinea: Traditional and in
            the Context of Change: Some Anthropological
            Perspectives. Perth: University of Western
            Australia Press.
            Collection of papers originally published
            in journal Anthropological Forum; seven
            Highlands societies included.

239. Bettison, David G., Colin A. Hughes and Paul van der
Veur (Eds.)
     1965   The Papua-New Guinea Elections 1964.
            Canberra: The Australian National University
            Press.
            Collection of papers by anthropologists
            reporting first national House of Assembly
            election; includes three Highlands
            electoral districts.

240. Brennan, Paul W. (Ed.)
     1970   Exploring Enga Culture: Studies in Missionary
            Anthropology. Wapenamanda: Kristen Press.
            Collection of papers on ENGA society and
            culture by Lutheran missionaries.

241. Brookfield, Harold C.
     1960   Population Distribution and Labour Migration
            in New Guinea (A Preliminary Survey).
            Australian Geographer 7:233-242.
            Survey based on field research in Eastern
            Highlands and statistics collected in
            Port Moresby in 1958.

242. -----
     1961a   The Highland Peoples of New Guinea: A Study
            of Distribution and Localization.
            Geographical Journal 127:436-448.
            General description and survey of
            defining characteristics of Highlands
            societies with resulting delimiting of
            "Highlands" boundaries.

243. -----
      1961b Native Employment within the New Guinea
             Highlands. Journal of the Polynesian
             Society 70:300-313.
             Survey, similar to Ref. 241.

244. -----
      1962   Local Study and Comparative Method: An
             Example from Central New Guinea. Annals,
             Association of American Geographers, 52:
             242-254.
             Comparison of agricultural systems of
             thirty-one societies (including some
             lowlanders) and delimitation of
             "highlands" based on agricultural
             methods.

245. -----
      1964   The Ecology of Highland Settlement: Some
             Suggestions. In James B. Watson, Ed.
             (Ref. 373), pp. 20-38.
             General discussion of settlement patterns
             in relation to climate, terrain and
             ecology of sweet potato cultivation.

246. ----- (Ed.)
      1973   The Pacific in Transition: Geographical
             Perspectives on Adaptations and Change.
             New York: St. Martin's Press.
             Collection of papers by anthropologists
             and geographers, including discussions
             of some Highlands societies.

247. Brown, Paula
      1966   Social Change and Social Movements. In
             E.K. Fisk, Ed. (Ref. 3), pp. 149-165.
             Discussion of general characteristics of
             Highlands societies, reactions to contact
             with Europeans and resulting cults and
             movements; includes some illustrative
             data from field research in CHIMBU.

248. Bruijn, J.V. de
      1958   Anthropological Research in Netherlands New
             Guinea since 1950. Oceania 29:132-163.
             General survey with extensive bibliography
             limited to Irian Jaya; includes little on
             Highlands societies.

249. Bulmer, Ralph N.H.
      1968   The Strategies of Hunting in New Guinea.
             Oceania 38:302-318.

Survey based on literature and field
research among KARAM and KYAKA ENGA;
general discussion of game available and
its uses, economic and social significance
of hunting, and strategies and weapons
commonly used in Highlands and lowlands.

250. -----
1969   Opportunities for Research in Papua-New
Guinea and Irian Barat: Anthropology and
Sociology. In Susan C. Reeves and May Dudley,
Eds. (Ref. 23), pp. 200-202.
Discussion of relatively unstudied topics
and regions, suggesting priorities; also
suggests procedures for selecting field
site.

251. -----
1970   Intensive Ethnographic Studies. In R. Gerard
Ward and David A.M. Lea, Eds. (Ref. 49),
pp. 93-96.
Map of Papua New Guinea indicating areas
of completed intensive field research;
lists ethnographers, study locations and
period(s) of field work.

252. -----
1972a   Hunting. In Peter Ryan, Gen. Ed. (Ref. 11),
Vol. 1, pp. 543-546.
General survey including mention of
Highlands societies.

253. -----
1972b   Victims of Progress: The Plight of Ethnic
Minorities in Undeveloped Areas. In Marion
W. Ward, Ed. (Ref. 368), pp. 119-129.
General discussion of recently opened
areas of Papua New Guinea Highlands and
lack of development opportunities.

254. Burton-Bradley, B.G.
1972a   Amuck. In Peter Ryan, Gen. Ed. (Ref. 11),
Vol. 1, pp. 19-21.
Brief discussion of occurrence, similar
to Highlands "wild man behavior"; suggests
possible relation to diseases and drugs.

255. -----
1972b   Betel Chewing. In Peter Ryan, Gen. Ed.
(Ref. 11), Vol. 1, pp. 66-67.
Brief discussion of distribution,
materials used, techniques, chemical
properties, effects and social attitudes;
found in numerous Highlands societies.

256. Chappell, J.A.
       1964   Stone Mortars in the New Guinea Highlands:
               A Note on Their Manufacture and Use. Man,
               Vol. 64, Art. 182, pp. 146-147.
               Survey of contemporary uses of stone
               mortars, especially by CHIMBU and WAHGI
               peoples.

257. ------
       1966   Stone Axe Factories in the Highlands of
               East New Guinea. Proceedings of the
               Prehistoric Society 32:96-121.
               Report of field survey disclosing
               thirteen quarries in use in territories
               of CHIMBU, HAGEN, KARAM, MARING and SIANE.

258. Chowning, Ann
       1972   Child Rearing and Socialization. In Peter
               Ryan, Gen. Ed. (Ref. 11), Vol. 1, pp. 156-164.
               General survey, including references to
               Highlands societies.

259. ------
       1973   Child Rearing and Socialization. In H. Ian
               Hogbin, Ed. (Ref. 291), pp. 61-79.
               Expanded version of Ref. 258.

260. Clarke, William C.
       1966   From Extensive to Intensive Shifting
               Cultivation: A Succession from New Guinea.
               Ethnology 5:347-359.
               Comparison of agricultural systems of
               KARAM, MARING and TAIRORA, suggesting
               continuum of intensity.

261. ------
       1973a   Temporary Madness as Theatre: Wildman
               Behaviour in New Guinea. Oceania 43:198-214.
               Discussion incorporating original field
               data on MARING and information from
               literature on numerous Highlands and
               other New Guinea societies.

262. ------
       1973b   The Dilemma of Development. In Harold C.
               Brookfield, Ed. (Ref. 246), pp. 275-298.
               Discussion of ecological problems related
               to economic development with special
               reference to Highlands societies.

263. Colebatch, H.K., Peta Colebatbh, Marie Reay and
     Andrew J. Strathern
       1971   Free Elections in a Guided Democracy. In
               A.L. Epstein et al., Eds. (Ref. 271),

pp. 218-274.
General discussion of 1968 House of
Assembly election in electoral districts
of ENGA, GAWIGL, HAGEN, KYAKA ENGA,
NARAK and WAHGI peoples.

264. Cook, Edwin A.
1969 Some Recent Anthropological Research Trends
in Melanesia. Anthropologica 11:117-150.
Overview of post-World War II research,
organized by topic with Highlands
references distributed accordingly.

265. Cranstone, B.A.L.
1961 Melanesia: A Short Ethnography. London:
British Museum.
General survey based on collections held
by British Museum; some Highlands items
included.

266. -----
1972 Material Culture. In Peter Ryan, Gen. Ed.
(Ref. 11), Vol. 2, pp. 715-740.
Survey of entire island with some material
from Highlands, especially author's own
field research in Telefomin area.

267. Elkin, A.P.
1953 Social Anthropology in Melanesia: A Review
of Research. New York: Oxford University
Press.
Comprehensive review and discussion of
research up to 1950, including original
material from author's own field survey;
organized by region with accompanying
bibliographies.

268. Epstein, A.L.
1972 Law, Indigenous. In Peter Ryan, Gen. Ed.
(Ref. 11), Vol. 2, pp. 631-634.
General survey with passing reserences
to Highlands societies.

269. -----
1973 Law. In H. Ian Hogbin, Ed. (Ref. 291),
pp. 174-181.
Expanded version of Ref. 268.

270. ----- (Ed.)
1974 Contention and Dispute: Aspects of Law and
Social Control in Melanesia. Canberra: The
Australian National University Press.
Collection of papers by anthropologists
and others; Highland New Guinea included.

271. Epstein, A.L., R.S. Parker and Marie Reay (Eds.)
     1971   The Politics of Dependence: Papua New
            Guinea 1968   Canberra: The Australian
            National University Press.
            Proceedings of Waigani Seminar on
            political development in Papua New
            Guinea; includes some papers dealing
            with Highlands societies.

272. Epstein, T.S.
     1972   Economy, Indigenous. In Peter Ryan, Gen.
            Ed. (Ref. 11), Vol. 1, pp. 306-314.
            General survey discussion including
            passing references to Highlands.

273. -----
     1973   Economy. In H. Ian Hogbin, Ed. (Ref. 291),
            pp. 80-99.
            Expanded version of Ref. 272.

274. Fetchko, Peter
     1972   Anga Material Culture. M.A. Thesis,
            Washington, D.C., George Washington
            University.
            Comprehensive survey and detailed
            description of dress, architecture,
            gardening, hunting, warfare, salt
            manufacture and economics of all
            Anga-speaking groups ("Kukukuku");
            based on D.C. Gajdusek collections.
            (BARUA, GANATI, MENYA, SIMBARI,
            WANTAKIA and YAGWOIA).

275. Finney, Ruth S.
     1970   Would-Be Entrepeneurs? Motivation in Six
            New Guinea Districts. Ph.D. Thesis,
            Cambridge, Mass., Harvard University.
            Comparative study of high-school
            students in Chimbu, East New Britain,
            Eastern Highlands, Madang, Manus and
            Western Highlands Districts.

276. -----
     1971   Would-Be Entrepeneurs? A Study of
            Motivation in New Guinea. New Guinea
            Research Unit, Bulletin 41. Port Moresby.
            Published version of Ref. 275.

277. Gajdusek, D. Carleton
     1970   Physiological and Psychological
            Characteristics of Stone Age Man.
            Engineering and Science 33(6):26-33, 56-62.
            General discussion of numerous topics
            including cannibalism, maturation,

deformation and mutilation, response to
pain, mock combat, penile display,
echopraxia and echolalia; passing
references to various Highlands groups.

278. Gajdusek, D. Carleton, Peter Fetchko, Nancy J. van Wyk
and Steven G. Ono
1972 Annotated Anga (Kukukuku) Bibliography.
Bethesda, Md.: National Institute of
Neurological Diseases and Stroke, National
Institutes of Health.
Includes introductory essay and sketch
of Anga-speakers' cultural variations;
organized by broad subdisciplines within
anthropology. (BARUA, GANATI, MENYA,
SIMBARI, WANTAKIA, YAGWOIA and lowland
Anga).

279. Glasse, Robert M.
1972 Wigs. In Peter Ryan, Gen. Ed. (Ref. 11),
Vol. 2, pp. 1203-1204.
Very brief discussion of human hair wigs
worn in various Southern and Western
Highlands societies.

280. Glasse, Robert M. and Mervyn J. Meggitt (Eds.)
1969 Pigs, Pearlshells and Women: Marriage in
the New Guinea Highlands. Englewood Cliffs:
Prentice-Hall.
Collection of papers by anthropologists
on marriage in ten Highlands societies,
with general introductory essay.

281. Glick, Leonard B.
1972a Divination. In Peter Ryan, Gen. Ed.
(Ref. 11), Vol. 1, pp. 269-270.
Brief survey with passing references to
Highlands societies.

282. -----
1972b Medicine, Indigenous. In Peter Ryan, Gen.
Ed. (Ref. 11), Vol. 2, pp. 756-757.
Brief survey with passing references to
Highlands societies.

283. -----
1972c Musical Instruments in Ritual. In Peter
Ryan, Gen. Ed. (Ref. 11), Vol. 2, pp. 821-822.
Brief survey with passing references to
Highlands societies.

284. -----
1972d Sangguma. In Peter Ryan, Gen. Ed. (Ref. 11),
Vol. 2, pp. 1029-1030.

Brief discussion of kind of sorcery found
in some Highlands societies.

285. ------
     1972e Sorcery and Witchcraft. $\underline{In}$ Peter Ryan,
            Gen. Ed. (Ref. 11), Vol. 2, pp. 1080-1082.
            Brief survey with passing references to
            Highlands societies.

286. ------
     1973   Sorcery and Witchcraft. $\underline{In}$ H. Ian Hogbin,
            Ed. (Ref. 291), pp. 182-186.
            Expanded version of Ref. 285.

287. Harding, Thomas G.
     1972   Land Tenure. $\underline{In}$ Peter Ryan, Gen. Ed.
            (Ref. 11), Vol. 2, pp. 604-610.
            Brief survey with passing references to
            Highlands societies.

288. ------
     1973   Land Tenure. $\underline{In}$ H. Ian Hogbin, Ed.,
            (Ref. 291), pp. 106-121.
            Expanded version of Ref. 287.

289. History of Melanesia, The
     1969   The History of Melanesia. Canberra: The
            Australian National University Press and
            Port Moresby: University of Papua New Guinea.
            Proceedings of Waigani Seminar on
            history of New Guinea, including some
            papers specifically on Highlands.

290. Hogbin, H. Ian
     1972   Settlement Patterns. $\underline{In}$ Peter Ryan, Gen. Ed.
            (Ref. 11), Vol. 2, pp. 1036-1038.
            Brief survey with passing references to
            Highlands societies.

291. ------ (Ed.)
     1973   Anthropology in Papua New Guinea: Readings
            from the Encyclopaedia of Papua and New
            Guinea. Melbourne: Melbourne University
            Press.
            Collection of selected articles from
            Ref. 11; most extensively revised and
            expanded (originals written in 1967).

292. Hughes, Ian
     1971   Recent Neolithic Trade in New Guinea: The
            Ecological Basis of Traffic in Goods among
            Stone-Age Subsistence Farmers. Ph.D. Thesis,
            Canberra, The Australian National
            University.

Extensive survey of pre-contact trade
routes, especially in Eastern Highlands.

293. -----
     1973   Stone-Age Trade in the New Guinea Inland:
            Historical Geography without History. In
            Harold C. Brookfield, Ed. (Ref. 246),
            pp. 97-126.
            Article-length discussion of main points
            in Ref. 292.

294. Kelly, Raymond C.
     1968   Demographic Pressure and Descent Group
            Structure in the New Guinea Highlands.
            Oceania 39:36-63.
            General discussion of social structure
            in relation to demographic imbalances,
            land availability and redistributive
            mechanisms; based on literature and
            focusing on CHIMBU, ENGA and SIANE.

295. Kerr, Harland B.
     1973   The Proto Kainantu Kinship System of the
            East New Guinea Highlands. In Howard P.
            McKaughan, Ed. (Ref. 1122), pp. 769-799.
            Reconstruction based on available
            material on AGARABE, AUYANA, AWA,
            BINUMARIEN, GADSUP, TAIRORA and USURUFA
            languages.

296. La Fontaine, Jean
     1973   Descent in New Guinea: An Africanist View.
            In The Character of Kinship. Jack Goody,
            Ed. Cambridge: Cambridge University Press.
            pp. 35-51.
            General discussion of Highlands social
            organization; based on literature.

297. Langness, Lewis L.
     1967a Hysterical Psychosis: The Cross-Cultural
            Evidence. American Journal of Psychiatry
            124(2):47-56.
            Comparison of syndromes in BENABENA
            with various Highlands and other
            societies.

298. -----
     1967b Rejoinder to R. Salisbury. Transcultural
            Psychiatric Research 4:125-130.
            Comparison of BENABENA "hysterical
            psychosis" with similar phenomena in
            ASARO and SIANE in debate with R.F.
            Salisbury (cf. Ref. 343).

299.   ------
       1968   Dr. Langness Replies. American Journal of
               Psychiatry 125(1):159-160.
                    Response to psychiatrist (W.M. Pfeiffer)
                    in continuing debate on BENABENA
                    syndrome (cf. Ref's. 297 and 298).

300.   ------
       1969   Possession in the New Guinea Highlands.
               Transcultural Psychiatric Research 6:95-100.
                    Continuation of debate on BENABENA and
                    others (cf. Ref's 297-299).

301.   ------
       1972a   Ethics. In Peter Ryan, Gen. Ed. (Ref. 11),
               Vol. 1, pp. 375-380.
                    Brief survey with passing references to
                    Highlands societies.

302.   ------
       1972b   Political Organization. In Peter Ryan,
               Gen. Ed. (Ref. 11), Vol. 2, pp. 922-935.
                    General survey with discussion of some
                    Highlands societies.

303.   ------
       1972c   Possession, Spirit. In Peter Ryan, Gen.
               Ed. (Ref. 11), Vol. 2, pp. 955-956.
                    Brief discussion emphasizing Highlands
                    material (cf. Ref's 297-300).

304.   ------
       1973a   Ethics. In H. Ian Hogbin, Ed. (Ref. 291),
               pp. 187-200.
                    Expanded version of Ref. 301.

305.   ------
       1973b   Traditional Political Organization. In
               H. Ian Hogbin, Ed. (Ref. 291), pp. 142-173.
                    Expanded version of Ref. 302.

306.   Lawrence, Peter
       1972   Religion and Magic. In Peter Ryan, Gen.
               Ed. (Ref. 11), Vol. 2, pp. 1001-1012.
                    General survey with passing references
                    to Highlands societies.

307.   ------
       1973   Religion and Magic. In H. Ian Hogbin, Ed.
               (Ref. 291), pp. 201-226.
                    Expanded version of Ref. 306.

308. Lawrence, Peter and Mervyn J. Meggitt (Eds.)
     1965   Gods, Ghosts and Men in Melanesia: Some
             Religions of Australian New Guinea and
             the New Hebrides. New York: Oxford
             University Press.
                 Collection of papers by anthropologists;
                 includes five Highlands societies and a
                 general introductory essay by editors.

309. Lepervance, Marie de
     1967-   Descent, Residence and Leadership in the
     1968   New Guinea Highlands. Oceania 38:134-158,
             163-189.
                 General analysis and comparison of
                 political and social organization in
                 numerous Highlands and Melanesian
                 societies.

310. -----
     1972   Social Structure. In Peter Ryan, Gen. Ed.
             (Ref. 11), Vol. 2, pp. 1065-1079.
                 General survey with discussion of
                 Highlands social organization.

311. -----
     1973   Social Structure. In H. Ian Hogbin, Ed.
             (Ref. 291), pp. 1-60.
                 Expanded version of Ref. 310.

312. McArthur, A. Margaret
     1972a   Food. In Peter Ryan, Gen. Ed. (Ref. 11),
             Vol. 1, pp. 433, 442-447.
                 General survey with passing references
                 to Highlands societies.

313. -----
     1972b   Salt. In Peter Ryan, Gen. Ed. (Ref. 11),
             Vol. 2, pp. 1026-1028.
                 General survey with discussion of some
                 Highlands examples.

314. McElhanon, Kenneth A. (Ed.)
     1974   Legends from Papua New Guinea. Ukarumpa:
             Summer Institute of Linguistics.
                 Collection of texts recorded by
                 missionaries; includes some Highlands
                 societies.

315. Maude, H.C.M. and H.E.M. Maude
     1972   String Figures. In Peter Ryan, Gen. Ed.
             (Ref. 11), Vol. 2, pp. 1102-1104.
                 Brief general discussion; found in most
                 if not all Highlands societies.

316. May, Ronald J. (Ed.)
     1973 Priorities in Melanesian Development.
           Canberra: The Australian National
           University Press.
             Proceedings of Waigani Seminar on
             development problems; includes some
             papers directly related to Highlands.

317. Meggitt, Mervyn J.
     1967 Uses of Literacy in New Guinea and
           Melanesia. Bijdragen tot de Taal-, Land-
           en Volkenkunde 123:71-82.
             General discussion of Melanesian
             attitudes and views regarding literacy;
             includes direct references to ENGA of
             Wabag region.

318. -----
     1969a Introduction. In Robert M. Glasse and
           Mervyn J. Meggitt, Eds. (Ref. 280),
           pp. 1-15.
             Survey of marriage in Highlands
             describing common features and points
             of variation.

319. -----
     1969b Uses of Literacy in New Guinea and
           Melanesia. In Literacy in Traditional
           Societies. Jack Goody, Ed. Cambridge:
           Cambridge University Press. pp. 298-310.
             Same as Ref. 317.

320. Moyle, Alice M.
     1972 Music (1). In Peter Ryan, Gen. Ed.
           (Ref. 11), Vol. 2, pp. 809-817.
             General survey with passing references
             to Highlands societies.

321. National Research Council
     1967 Behavioral Science Research in New Guinea.
           Publication 1493. Washington, D.C.:
           National Research Council.
             Collection of papers by anthropologists
             and others on diverse topics.

322. Newton, Douglas
     1972 Art. In Peter Ryan, Gen. Ed. (Ref. 11),
           Vol. 1, pp. 29-50.
             General survey with passing references
             to Highlands societies.

323. Panoff, Michel
     1972 Calendars. In Peter Ryan, Gen. Ed.
           (Ref. 11), Vol. 1, p. 130.

Very brief discussion of uses of
astronomical, climatic and natural
history observations on reckoning time;
includes reference to Meggitt's work
on Enga (see Section B below).

324. Pataki, Karen R.
1966 Missionary History and Influence within the
Eastern Highlands of the Territory of New
Guinea. M.A. Thesis, Seattle, University
of Washington.
Comparison of AUYANA, AWA, GADSUP and
TAIRORA recent history; based on field
and archival research.

325. Pataki, Kerry J.
1968 Time, Space, and the Human Community: An
Ecological Analysis of Settlement in the
Eastern Highlands of New Guinea. Ph.D.
Thesis, Seattle, University of Washington.
Comparison of settlement patterns of
AUYANA, AWA, GADSUP and TAIRORA; based
on field research.

326. Ploeg, Anton (Ed.)
1970 Land Tenure in West Irian. New Guinea
Research Unit, Bulletin 38. Port Moresby.
Collection of papers by anthropologists;
includes Highlands societies.

327. Potter, Michell (Compiler)
1973 Traditional Law in Papua New Guinea: An
Annotated and Select Bibliography.
Canberra: The Australian National University
Press.
Based on items in nine journals only;
includes 283 sources with indexes by
author, group and subject.

328. Pouwer, Jan
1966 Towards a Configurational Approach to
Society and Culture in New Guinea. Journal
of the Polynesian Society 75:267-286.
General theoretical discussion of
Highlands social structure and problems
in methodology; passing references to
DANI, KAPAUKU and STAR MOUNTAINS peoples
of Irian Jaya, as well as lowlands.

329. -----
1967 Toward a Configurational Approach to
Society and Culture in New Guinea. In
National Research Council (Ref. 321),
pp. 77-100.

Slightly different version of Ref. 328.

330. Prince, J.R.
1967   Science Concepts among New Guinea School
    Children: A Pilot Survey. Journal of the
    Papua and New Guinea Society 1:119-127.

331. -----
1969   Science Concepts in a Pacific Culture.
    Sydney: Angus and Robertson.

332. -----
1970   Views of Physical Causality in New Guinea
    Students. Journal of the Papua and New
    Guinea Society 4:99-107.

333. -----
1971   Sexual Attitudes of Some New Guinea Students.
    Journal of the Papua and New Guinea Society
    5:19-33.
        Four references report results of studies
        of New Guinea school children including
        some from Highlands regions.

334. Read, Kenneth E.
1954   Cultures of the Central Highlands, New
    Guinea. Southwestern Journal of Anthropology
    10:1-43.
        Earliest attempt to survey similarities
        and variations in Highlands societies;
        includes detailed description of GAHUKU
        social organization.

335. Reay, Marie
1965a   The Minj Open Electorate. In David G.
    Bettison et al., Eds. (Ref. 239), pp. 147-180.
        Discussion of first House of Assembly
        election (1964) in several electoral
        districts of Western Highlands. (HAGEN,
        KOBON and WAHGI).

336. -----
1965b   Women in Transitional Society. Australian
    Territories 5(3):2-24.
        General discussion of traditional and
        changing roles of women in New Guinea;
        passing references to Highlands peoples.

337. -----
1966   Women in Transitional Society. In E.K.
    Fisk, Ed. (Ref. 3), pp. 166-184.
        Slightly different version of Ref. 336.

38. Ryan, D'Arcy J.
    1972a Marriage. In Peter Ryan, Gen. Ed. (Ref. 11),
          Vol. 2, pp. 702-710.
          General survey with passing references
          to Highlands societies.

39. -----
    1972b Mok-Ink. In Peter Ryan, Gen. Ed. (Ref. 11),
          Vol. 2, pp. 788-789.
          Brief description of ceremonial exchange
          system found in various Southern
          Highlands societies; similar to moka
          and te of Western Highlands.

40. -----
    1972c Pearl-Shell. In Peter Ryan, Gen. Ed.
          (Ref. 11), Vol. 2, p. 895.
          Very brief description of one of major
          shells used as valuables throughout
          Highlands.

41. -----
    1972d Te. In Peter Ryan, Gen. Ed. (Ref. 11),
          Vol. 2, pp. 1114-1115.
          Brief description of ceremonial
          exchange system found in many Western
          Highlands societies.

42. -----
    1973 Marriage. In H. Ian Hogbin, Ed. (Ref. 291),
         pp. 122-141.
         Expanded version of Ref. 338.

43. Salisbury, Richard F.
    1966 Possession in the New Guinea Highlands:
         Review of Literature. Transcultural
         Psychiatric Research 3:103-108.
         Discussion of Highlands "wildman"
         behavior, conflicting with view of
         Langness (see Ref's. 297-300 above).

44. -----
    1967a Economic Research in New Guinea. In
          National Research Council (Ref. 321),
          pp. 106-120.
          General discussion of exchange, trade
          and economic development; passing
          references to Highlands societies.

45. -----
    1967b R. Salisbury Replies. Transcultural
          Psychiatric Research 4:130-134.
          Response to Langness (Ref. 298).

346. -----
      1968   Possession in the New Guinea Highlands.
              International Journal of Social Psychiatry
              14:85-94.
                  Continuation of Langness-Salisbury
                  debate (see Ref's. 297-300, 343, 345).

347. Sexton, Lorraine
      1974   Highlands New Guinea Warfare: An Ecological
              Analysis. M.A. Thesis, Philadelphia,
              Temple University.
                  Analysis and comparison of warfare of
                  CHIMBU and ENGA, based on literature.

348. Shaw, R. Daniel (Ed.)
      1974   Kinship in Papua New Guinea. Ukarumpa:
              Summer Institute of Linguistics.
                  Collection of descriptive papers by
                  missionaries.

349. Sheridan, R.J.
      1972   Music (2). In Peter Ryan, Gen. Ed.
              (Ref. 11), Vol. 2, pp. 817-821.
                  General survey with passing references
                  to Highlands societies.

350. Sillitoe, P.
      1972   Warfare in New Guinea: A Comparative Study.
              M.A. Thesis, Durham, North Carolina, Duke
              University.
                  Comparative study including numerous
                  Highlands societies; based on literature.

351. Sorenson, E. Richard
      1967   A Research Film Program in the Study of
              Changing Man. Current Anthropology 8:
              443-469 (incl. Comments and Reply).
                  General discussion of cinematography as
                  research tool; illustrated with numerous
                  photographs of Anga, FORE and GIMI.

352. Sorenson, E. Richard and D. Carleton Gajdusek
      1966   The Study of Child Behavior and Development
              in Primitive Cultures: A Research Archive
              for Ethnopediatric Film Investigations of
              Styles in the Patterning of the Nervous
              System. Pediatrics, Supplement, 37(1):
              Part 2, pp. 149-243.
                  Discussion of use of film in research;
                  includes references to and photographs
                  of numerous Highlands peoples; also
                  list and description of film holdings of
                  Child Growth and Development Project,
                  National Institutes of Health.

353. Stirling, Matthew W.
      1943 The Native Peoples of New Guinea. War
            Background Studies, No. 9. Washington,
            D.C.: Smithsonian Institution.
            General survey including photographs;
            Nogullo (?) people of Nassau Range,
            Irian Jaya, only Highlanders discussed.

354. Strathern, Andrew J.
      1969a Descent and Alliance in the New Guinea
            Highlands: Some Problems of Comparison.
            Royal Anthropological Institute, Proceedings
            for 1968, pp. 37-52. London.
            General discussion of Highlands social
            structure, especially with reference to
            BENABENA, CHIMBU, ENGA, GAHUKU, HAGEN,
            SIANE and WAHGI.

355. ------
      1969b Finance and Production: Two Strategies in
            New Guinea Highlands Exchange Systems.
            Oceania 40:42-67.
            Comparison of exchange systems in CHIMBU,
            ENGA, HAGEN, MARING, MENDI and SIANE.

356. ------
      1972 Moka. In Peter Ryan, Gen. Ed. (Ref. 11),
            Vol. 2, p. 788.
            Brief description of ceremonial exchange
            system found in various Western Highlands
            societies.

357. ------
      1973 Kinship, Descent and Locality: Some New
            Guinea Examples. In The Character of
            Kinship. Jack Goody, Ed. Cambridge:
            Cambridge University Press. pp. 21-33.
            General discussion of Highlands social
            structure.

358. ------
      1974 Anthropology and Problems of Social Change
            in Papua New Guinea. Man in New Guinea
            6(3):15-28.
            Inaugural lecture as Professor at
            University of Papua New Guinea; general
            discussion of research priorities and
            problems in contemporary New Guinea.

359. Strathern, A. Marilyn
      1966 Note on Linguistic Boundaries and the Axe
            Quarries. Proceedings of the Prehistoric
            Society 32:117-120.

Discussion of cultural and linguistic
relationships among peoples using stone
quarries described by Chappell (cf. Ref.
257). (CHIMBU, HAGEN, KARAM, MARING
and SIANE).

360. UNESCO (United Nations Educational, Scientific and
Cultural Organization)
1960   Symposium on the Impact of Man on Humid
Tropics Vegetation, Goroka. Sponsored by
the Administration of the Territory of
Papua and New Guinea and UNESCO Science
Co-operation Office for South East Asia.
Canberra: Government Printer.
Proceedings of symposium; includes
papers by administrators, anthropologists,
biologists and others, many relating to
Highlands ecosystems.

361. Valentine, Charles A.
1972   Social and Cultural Change. In Peter Ryan,
Gen. Ed. (Ref. 11), Vol. 2, pp. 1048-1050.
General survey with passing references
to Highlands societies.

362. -----
1973   Changing Indigenous Societies and Cultures.
In H. Ian Hogbin, Ed. (Ref. 291), pp. 227-234.
Expanded version of Ref. 361.

363. Vayda, Andrew P.
1966   Diversity and Uniformity in New Guinea.
Acta Ethnographica Academiae Scientarium
Hungariae 15:293-299.
Brief discussion of factors contributing
to diversity of cultures; passing
references to Highlands societies.

364. -----
1972   Pigs. In Peter Ryan, Gen. Ed. (Ref. 11),
Vol. 2, pp. 905-908.
General discussion with special emphasis
on Highlands societies.

365. Vayda, Andrew P., Anthony Leeds and D. Smith
1961   The Place of Pigs in Melanesian Subsistence.
In Symposium: Patterns of Land Utilization
and Other Papers. American Ethnological
Society, Proceedings. Viola E. Garfield, Ed.
Seattle: University of Washington Press.
pp. 69-77.
General discussion with passing references
to Highlands societies.

366. Ward, Marion W. (Ed.)
    1970   The Politics of Melanesia. Canberra: The
            Australian National University Press and
            Port Moresby: University of Papua New
            Guinea.
                Proceedings of Waigani Seminar; includes
                papers of direct relevance to Highlands
                societies.

367. ------ (Ed.)
    1971   Land Tenure and Economic Development:
            Problems and Policies in Papua New Guinea
            and Kenya. New Guinea Research Unit,
            Bulletin 40. Port Moresby.
                Collection of papers by anthropologists
                and others; includes Highlands cases.

368. ------ (Ed.)
    1972   Change and Development in Rural Melanesia.
            Canberra: The Australian National University
            Press and Port Moresby: University of Papua
            New Guinea.
                Proceedings of Waigani Seminar; includes
                papers on Highlands societies.

369. Ward, R. Gerard (Ed.)
    1972   Man in the Pacific Islands: Essays on
            Geographical Change in the Pacific Islands.
            New York: Oxford University Press.
                Collection of papers by geographers and
                others; includes references to Highlands
                societies.

370. Watson, James B.
    1963   A Micro-Evolution Study in New Guinea.
            Journal of the Polynesian Society 72:
            188-192.
                Description of extensive planned research
                project involving AUYANA, AWA, GADSUP and
                TAIRORA peoples. Published results
                include references under M. Leininger,
                R. Littlewood, H. McKaughan, K.J. Pataki,
                S. Robbins and J.B. Watson.

371. ------
    1964a   Anthropology in the New Guinea Highlands.
            In James B. Watson, Ed. (Ref. 373), pp. 1-19.
                General discussion of history of
                anthropological research in Highlands
                and major issues resulting therefrom.

372. ------
    1964b   A General Analysis of the Elections at
            Kainantu. Journal of the Polynesian

Society 73:199-204.
    Brief description of 1964 House of
    Assembly elections involving AGARABE,
    GADSUP, KAMANO and TAIRORA peoples.

373.   ------ (Ed.)
        1964c New Guinea: The Central Highlands. Special
               Publication. American Anthropologist, Vol.
               66, No. 4, Part 2.
               Collection of papers by anthropologists
               and others on diverse topics.

374.   ------
        1965   The Kainantu Open and South Markham Special
               Electorates. In David G. Bettison et al.,
               Eds. (Ref. 239), pp. 91-119.
               More extensive discussion than Ref. 372;
               covers AGARABE, AUYANA, AWA, BARUA,
               GADSUP, KAMANO and TAIRORA peoples.

375.   ------
        1967   Local Variation and Its Assessment in New
               Guinea. In National Research Council (Ref.
               321), pp. 53-71.
               General discussion of Highlands societies
               with passing references to various
               Eastern Highlands peoples.

376.   ------
        1968   Pueraria: Names and Traditions of a Lesser
               Crop of the Central Highlands, New Guinea.
               Ethnology 7:268-279.
               Discussion based on field survey of
               AGARABE, ASARO, BENABENA, CHIMBU, CHUAVE,
               GAHUKU, HAGEN, KAMANO, SIANE, TAIRORA
               and WAHGI peoples.

377.   White, J. Peter
        1967   Ethno-Archaeology in New Guinea: Two
               Examples. Mankind 6:409-414.
               Description of tools and rock paintings
               observed among ASARO, BOSAVI, FOI and
               TAIRORA peoples.

378.   Wolfers, Edward P.
        1972   Counting and Numbers. In Peter Ryan, Gen.
               Ed. (Ref. 11), Vol. 1, pp. 216-220.
               General survey including Highlands
               examples.

379.   Womersley, John S.
        1972   Plants, Indigenous Uses. In Peter Ryan,
               Gen. Ed. (Ref. 11), Vol. 2, pp. 908-912.
               General survey, excluding food plants.

56

8. Ethnographic and Topical Studies

380. Abramson, J.A. and Robert Holst: HEWA
1973 Hewa Sacred Bark Paintings and Styles in
New Guinea Art. Papua New Guinea Museum
Records 3:17-62.

381. Adam, Leonhard: FORE, KAMANO, USURUFA and YATE
1953 The Discovery of the Vierkantbeil or
Quadrangular Adze Head in the Eastern
Central Highlands of New Guinea. Mankind
4:411-423.
Adze collected by C.H. and R.M. Berndt.

382. Aitchison, T.G.: AGARABE (?)
1936 Peace Ceremony as Performed by the Natives
of the Ramu Headwaters, Central New Guinea.
Oceania 6:478-480.

383. Arndt, Gerald: ENGA
1970 Cultural Implications of the Enga Indigenous
Church. In Paul W. Brennan, Ed. (Ref. 240),
pp. 103-139.

384. Aufenanger, Heinrich: CHIMBU, CHUAVE and SINASINA
1946- Irdene gefäszflöte bei den Kuman im
1949 Wahgi-tal (Zentral-Neuguine). Anthropos
41-44:877-880.

385. -----
1957 The Niche Grave and the Farewell to the Soul
of the Deceased in Central New Guinea.
Anthropos 52:943-944. (also WAHGI).

386. -----
1958 How the Dirima People in Central New Guinea
Subdue a Ghost Who Harms the Living.
Anthropos 53:1024.

387. -----
1959a How Children's Faeces are Preserved in the
Central Highlands of New Guinea. Anthropos
54:236-237.

388. -----
1959b The Story-Telling Hut in the Highlands of
New Guinea. Anthropos 54:981-982. (also
GENDE).

389. -----
1959c The War-Magic Houses in the Wahgi Valley
and Adjacent Areas (New Guinea). Anthropos
54:1-26. (also GENDE, KANDAWO and WAHGI).

390.　------
　　　　1960a　The Kanggi Spirit in the Central Highlands
　　　　　　　　of New Guinea. Anthropos 55:671-688.
　　　　　　　　(also GENDE, KANDAWO and WAHGI).

391.　------
　　　　1960b　New Stone Implements from the Central
　　　　　　　　Highlands of New Guinea. Anthropos 55:
　　　　　　　　456-462. (also KANDAWO).

392.　------
　　　　1961a　A Children's Arrow-Thrower in the Central
　　　　　　　　Highlands of New Guinea. Anthropos 56:633.
　　　　　　　　(also WAHGI).

393.　------
　　　　1961b　The Cordyline Plant in the Central Highlands
　　　　　　　　of New Guinea. Anthropos 56:393-408.
　　　　　　　　(also WAHGI).

394.　------
　　　　1961c　The Use of Bones (Central Highlands, New
　　　　　　　　Guinea). Anthropos 56:869-882. (also
　　　　　　　　WAHGI).

395.　------
　　　　1962a　The Earthquake: Beliefs and Practices in the
　　　　　　　　Central Highlands, New Guinea. Anthropos
　　　　　　　　57:170-176. (also KANDAWO and WAHGI).

396.　------
　　　　1962b　Sayings with a Hidden Meaning (Central
　　　　　　　　Highlands, New Guinea). Anthropos 57:325-
　　　　　　　　335. (also WAHGI).

397.　------
　　　　1962c　The Sun in the Life of the Natives in the
　　　　　　　　New Guinea Highlands. Anthropos 57:1-44.
　　　　　　　　(also GENDE, KANDAWO and WAHGI).

398.　------
　　　　1963a　Customs, Beliefs, and Material Culture in
　　　　　　　　the Highlands of New Guinea. Anthropos 58:
　　　　　　　　187-208. (also WAHGI).

399.　------
　　　　1963b　Das enstehen einer handtrommel im Hochland
　　　　　　　　von Neuguinea. In Festschrift Paul Schebesta
　　　　　　　　zum 75. Studia Instituti Anthropos, Vol. 18.
　　　　　　　　Wien-Mödling: St. Gabriel Verlag. pp. 443-
　　　　　　　　445. (also WAHGI).

00. ------
    1964   Women's Lives in the Highlands of New
            Guinea. Anthropos 59:218-266. (also WAHGI).

01. ------
    1965a   Details of the Mengge People's Culture in
            the Highlands of New Guinea. Asian Folklore
            Studies 24:129-148.

02. ------
    1965b   The Gerua Cult in the Highlands of New
            Guinea. Anthropos 60:248-261. (also
            KANDAWO and WAHGI).

03. ------
    1965c   Notes on Animism and Magic Practices in the
            Eastern Highlands of New Guinea. Asian
            Folklore Studies 24:117-128. (also WAHGI).

04. ------
    1966a   Animals' Souls in the New Guinea Highlands.
            Anthropos 61:455-459. (also WAHGI).

05. ------
    1966b   Friendship in the Highlands of New Guinea.
            Anthropos 61:305-306.

06. ------
    1968   The Use of Plants in the New Guinea Highlands.
            In Anthropos Institut (Ref. 233), pp. 1-8.
            (also WAHGI).

07. ------
    1969   Die opferfreudigkeit der eingeborenen von
            Neuguinea. Steyler Missions-Chronik, pp. 78-80.

08. ------
    1970   Heilbringer und kulturheroen in Neuguinea.
            Verbum Roma 11:189-195.

09. ------
    1972   The Dinggan, Spirit of Disease in the Central
            Highlands of New Guinea. Ethnomedizin 1:
            373-396. (also GENDE).

10. Aufenanger, Heinrich: DUNA
    1967a   Aus dem leben der Duna am Kopiago See in
            Neu-Guinea. Zeitschrift für Ethnologie
            92:33-73.

11. ------
    1967b   Ergänzung zu dem beitrag 'Aus dem leben der
            Duna am Kopiago see in Neu-Guinea.'
            Zeitschrift für Ethnologie 92:277.

412. Aufenanger, Heinrich: ENGA
      1966   Ausschnitte aus der kultur einiger
             völkergruppen des Wabag-Distriktes im
             westlichen hochland von Neu-Guinea.
             Annali del Pontifico Museo Missionario
             Etnologico 30:257-287.

413. Aufenanger, Heinrich: GENDE and BIYOM
      1935-   Eine himmelsgeschichte aus dem Bismarck-
      1936a   gebirge. Steyler Missionsbote 63:204.

414. -----
      1935-   Wie die kanaken einen grossen begruben.
      1936b   Steyler Missionsbote 63:235-236.

415. -----
      1937-   Faustrecht. Steyler Missionsbote 64:
      1938   93-94.

416. -----
      1938   Etwas über zahl und zählen bei den Gende
             im Bismarckgebirge Neuguineas. Anthropos
             33:273-277.

417. -----
      1953   Drei mythen von den Gende in Zentral-
             Neuguinea. Anthropos 48:287-289.

418. -----
      1954   Wigs and Headrests in the Bundi and Nondugl
             Districts of the Middle Wahgi in the
             Central Highlands of Eastern New Guinea.
             Anthropos 49:313. (also WAHGI).

419. -----
      1955   Die stellung der ahnen im glauben und brauch
             des eingeborenen des Territoriums von
             Neu-Guinea. Ph.D. Thesis, Vienna, Universit
             of Vienna.

420. Aufenanger, Heinrich and Georg Höltker: GENDE and BIY
      1940   Die Gende in Zentral-Neuguinea: vom leben
             und denken eines Papua-stammes im Bismarck-
             Gebirge. Wien-Mödling: Missionsdruckerei
             St. Gabriel.

421. Aufenanger, Heinrich: KARAM
      1960   The Ayom Pygmies, Myth of Origin and Their
             Method of Counting. Anthropos 55:247-249.

422. -----
      1964   Aus der kultur der Simbai-pygmäen im
             Schradergebirge Neu-Guineas. Ethnos 29:
             141-174.

423. Aufenanger, Heinrich: KANDAWO
1957 The Parry Shield in the Western Highlands
of New Guinea. Anthropos 52:631-633.
(also WAHGI).

424. ------
1958 An Old Rock-Painting in the Kovun-Area
(Upper Jimmi River). Anthropos 53:623.

425. ------
1961 Descent Totemism and Magical Practices in
the Wahgi Valley (Central New Guinea).
Anthropos 56:281-283.

426. Aufenanger, Heinrich: SIANE (?)
1965 Mezauwe: 'Der grosse mann dort oben.'
Studie aus dem religiösen denken der
eingeborenen des Goroka-Gebietes in
hochland von Neuguinea. Zeitschrift für
Missionswissenschaft und Religionswissenschaft
49:191-197.

427. Aufenanger, Heinrich: WAHGI
1953 Kampfspeer mit knochenspitze und
holzschüssel mit schnabelförmigen ausgusz
vom Wahgi River in Zentral-Neuguinea.
Anthropos 48:977-981.

428. ------
1958a Children's Games and Entertainments among
the Kumngo Tribe in Central New Guinea.
Anthropos 53:575-584.

429. ------
1958b An Unusual Device for Hunting Birds in the
Wahgi Valley. Anthropos 53:1022.

430. ------
1965 Kumo, the Deadly Witchcraft in the Central
Highlands of New Guinea. Asian Folklore
Studies 24:103-115.

431. ------
1968 Notes of the Culture of the Kuli (New
Guinea). Asian Folklore Studies 27:147-156.

432. Bamler, Heinrich: FORE, KANITE, KEIGANA and YATE
1963- Magische und religiöse denkformen und
1964 praktiken der Keyagana, Kanite, Yate und
Fore im östlichen hochland von Neuguinea.
Baessler-Archiv 11:115-147.

433. Barnes, J.A.: ENGA (data from M.J. Meggitt)
     1967   Agnation among the Enga: A Review Article.
             Oceania 38:33-43.

434. ------
     1971   Agnatic Taxonomies and Stochastic Variation.
             Anthropological Forum 3:3-12.

435. Barrau, Jacques: (not available for examination)
     1957   Usage curieux d'une Aracee de la Nouvelle
             Guinée. Journal de la Botanique Appliquée
             et d'Agriculture Tropicale 4:348-349.

436. ------
     1958   Nouvelles observations au sujet des plantes
             hallucinogénes de la Nouvelle Guinée.
             Journal de la Botanique Appliquée et
             d'Agriculture Tropicale 5:377-379.

437. ------
     1962   Observations et travaux recents sur les
             vegeteaux hallucinogénes de la Nouvelle
             Guinée. Journal de la Botanique Appliquée
             et d'Agriculture Tropicale 9:245-250.

438. ------
     1965   Quelques notes à propos de plantes utiles
             des hautes terres de la Nouvelle-Guinée.
             Journal d'Agriculture Tropicale et de
             Botanique Appliquée 12:44-57.

439. Barth, Fredrik: FAIWOL
     1971   Tribes and Intertribal Relations in the
             Fly Headwaters. Oceania 41:171-191.

440. ------
     1975   Ritual and Knowledge among the Baktaman of
             New Guinea. New Haven: Yale University Press

441. Bergmann, H.F.W.: CHIMBU
     1971   The Kamanuku (The Culture of the Chimbu
             Tribes). 4 Vols. Harrisville, Pa.:
             H.F.W. Bergmann.

442. Berndt, Catherine H.: FORE, KAMANO, USURUFA and YATE
     1953   Socio-cultural Change in the Eastern Central
             Highlands of New Guinea. Southwestern
             Journal of Anthropology 9:112-138.

443. ------
     1954   Translation Problems in Three New Guinea
             Highlands Languages. Oceania 24:289-317.
             (YATE not included).

444.   ------
        1955   Mythology in the Eastern Central Highlands
                of New Guinea. Ph. D. Thesis, London,
                University of London, Landon School of
                Economics.

445.   ------
        1957   Social and Cultural Change in New Guinea:
                Communication and Views about 'Other
                People.' Sociologus 7:38-57,

446.   ------
        1959   Ascription of Meaning in a Ceremonial
                Context in the Eastern Central Highlands
                of New Guinea. In Anthropology in the
                South Seas: Essays Presented to H.D. Skinner.
                J.D. Freeman and W.R. Geddes, Eds. New
                Plymouth, N.Z.: T. Avery and Sons. pp. 161-
                183.

447.   ------
        1966   The Ghost Husband, Society and the Individual
                in New Guinea Myth. Journal of American
                Folklore 79(311):244-277. (KAMANO only).

448.   Berndt, Ronald M.: FORE, KAMANO, USURUFA and YATE
        1952-   A Cargo Movement in the Eastern Central
        1953   Central Highlands of New Guinea. Oceania
                23:40-65, 137-158, 202-234.

449.   ------
        1954   Contemporary Significance of Prehistoric
                Stone Objects in the Eastern Central
                Highlands of New Guinea. Anthropos 49:
                553-587.

450.   ------
        1954-   Kamano, Jate, Usurufa and Fore Kinship of
        1955a   the Eastern Highlands of New Guinea: A
                Preliminary Account. Oceania 25:23-53,
                156-187.

451.   ------
        1954-   Reaction to Contact in the Eastern Highlands
        1955b   of New Guinea. Oceania 24:190-228, 255-274;
                25:232-232.

452.   ------
        1955a   Interdependence and Conflict in the Eastern
                Central Highlands. Man, Vol. 55, Art. 116,
                pp. 105-107.

453.   ------
        1955b   Social Control among Central Highlanders of

New Guinea. Ph.D. Thesis, London, University of London, London School of Economics.

454. ─────
1958 A 'Devastating Disease Syndrome': Kuru Sorcery in the Eastern Central Highlands of New Guinea. Sociologus 8:4-28.

455. ─────
1962a Excess and Restraint: Social Control among a New Guinea Mountain People. Chicago: University of Chicago Press.

456. ─────
1962b The Other End of the Telescope. Australian Journal of Science 25(4):146-155.

457. ─────
1965 The Kamano, Usurufa, Jate and Fore of the Eastern Highlands. In Peter Lawrence and Mervyn J. Meggitt, Eds. (Ref. 308), pp. 78-104.

458. ─────
1970 Political Structure in the Eastern Central Highlands of New Guinea. Anthropological Forum 2:327-369. (also see Ronald M. Berndt and Peter Lawrence, Eds., Ref. 238, pp. 381-423).

459. Bijlmer, H.J.T.: DANI, DEM and UHUNDUNI
1923a Anthropological Results of the Dutch Scientific Central New Guinea Expedition of 1920, Followed by an Essay on the Anthropology of the Papuans. Nova Guinea 7(4

460. ─────
1923b Met de Centraal Nieuw-Guinea-Expeditie a 1920 naar een onbekenden volkstam in het hooggebergte. De Aarde en haar Volken, Nos. 5-9.

461. ─────
1938a De Mimika-Expeditie 1935-1936 naar Centraal Nieuw-Guinea. Tijdschrift van het Koninklijk Nederlandsch Aardrijkskundig Genootschap 55:240-259.

462. ─────
1938b Naar de achterhoek der aarde: de Mimika-Expeditie naar Nederlandsch Nieuw Guinea. Amsterdam: Scheltens and Giltay.

63. -----
1939 Tapiro Pygmies and Pania Mountain-Papuans.
Results of the Anthropological Mimika
Expedition in New Guinea 1935-1936.
Nova Guinea 3:113-184.

64. Blank, W.: ENGA
1963 Ein fruchtbarkeitsidol aus dem westlichen
hochland von Neuguinea. Anthropos 58:907.

65. Boelen, K.W.J.: KAPAUKU
1955 Begrippen stam an tuma bij de Ekagis.
Nieuw-Guinea 1:1-6.

66. Bouchard, J.F.: FORE
1972 The Impact of Roads on the Monetary
Activities of Subsistence Economics in the
Okapa Region of Papua New Guinea. University
of Papua New Guinea, Department of Geography,
Occasional Papers, No. 4. Port Moresby.

67. Bouchard, J.F.: SINASINA
1973 The Impact of Roads in the Gumine Region of
Papua New Guinea. University of Papua New
Guinea, Department of Geography, Occasional
Papers, No. 5. Port Moresby.

68. Bowers, Nancy: GAWIGL
1964 Further Note on a Recently Reported Root
Crop from the New Guinea Highlands. Journal
of the Polynesian Society 73:333-335.

69. -----
1965 Permanent Bachelorhood in the Upper Kaugel
Valley of Highland New Guinea. Oceania 36:
27-37.

70. -----
1968 The Ascending Grasslands: An Anthropological
Study of Ecological Succession in a High
Mountain Valley of New Guinea. Ph.D. Thesis,
New York, Columbia University.

71. -----
1971 Demographic Problems in Montane New Guinea.
In: Culture and Population: A Collection of
Current Studies. Carolina Population Center,
Monograph No. 9. Steven Polgar, Ed. Chapel
Hill. pp. 11-31.

72. Brandewie, Ernest B.: HAGEN
1964 Mount Hagen Open Electorate: The Campaign
among the Kumdi People. Journal of the
Polynesian Society 73:211-215.

65

473.   -----
       1966   An Internal Analysis of the Kinship System
               of the Mbowamb of the Central Highlands of
               New Guinea. Ph.D. Thesis, Chicago, Universit
               of Chicago.

474.   -----
       1967   Lucky: Additional Reflections on a Native
               Card Game in New Guinea. Oceania 38:44-50.

475.   -----
       1968a   New Guinea Sickness and Values: Their
               Discovery and Integration. In Dr. H. Otley
               Beyer: A Commemorative Issue. R. Rahmann
               and G. Ang, Eds. Cebu City: University of
               San Carlos. pp. 101-122.

476.   -----
       1968b   Reciprocity, Exchange and Social Structure
               in the Central Highlands of New Guinea. In
               Anthropos Institut (Ref. 233), pp. 25-36.

477.   -----
       1971   The Place of the Big Man in Traditional
               Hagen Society in the Central Highlands of
               New Guinea. Ethnology 10:194-210.

478.   -----
       1973   Serious Illness and Group Therapy among the
               Mbowamb, Central Highlands of New Guinea.
               Mankind 9:71-76.

479.   -----
       1974   A Note on Three Kinship Terms of the Mbowamb
               of the Central Highlands, New Guinea.
               Oceania 44:204-208.

480.   Brennan, Paul W.: ENGA
       1970   Enga Referential Symbolism: Verbal and
               Visual. In Paul W. Brennan, Ed. (Ref. 240),
               pp. 17-50.

481.   Broekhuijse, Jan Th.: DANI
       1967a   De Wiligiman-Dani: Een cultureel-
               anthropologische studie over religie en
               oorlogvoering in de Baliem-Vallie. Ph.D.
               Thesis, Utrecht, University of Utrecht.

482.   -----
       1967b   De Wiligiman-Dani: Een cultureel-
               anthropologische studie over religie en
               oorlogvoering in de Baliem-Vallie.
               Tilburg: H. Gianotten N.V.

483. Bromley, H. Myron: DANI
1960   A Preliminary Report on Law among the Grand
       Valley Dani of Netherlands New Guinea.
       Nieuw-Guinea Studien 4:235-259.

484. Bromley, H. Myron and Jacques Barrau: DANI
1965   Presence d'un Coix cultivé dans les
       montagnes de la Nouvelle-Guinée. Journal
       d'Agriculture Tropicale et de Botanique
       Appliquée 12:781-782.

485. Brookfield, Harold C.: CHIMBU
1959   Two Population Problem Areas of Papua-New
       Guinea. South Pacific 10(6):133-137.

486. -----
1962   Geography and Anthropology. Pacific
       Viewpoint 3(2):11-16.

487. -----
1966a But Where Do We Go From Here? In Eben H.
       Hipsley, Ed. (Ref. 1659), pp. 49-66.

488. -----
1966b The Chimbu: A Highland People in New Guinea.
       In Geography as Human Ecology: Methodology
       by Example. S.R. Eyre and G.R.J. Jones,
       Eds. London: Edward Arnold. pp. 174-198.

489. -----
1968   The Money That Grows on Trees: The
       Consequences of an Innovation with a Man-
       Environment System. Australian Geographic
       Studies 6:97-119.

490. -----
1973   Full Circle in Chimbu: A Study of Trends
       and Cycles. In Harold C. Brookfield, Ed.
       (Ref. 246), pp. 127-160.

491. Brookfield, Harold C. and Paula Brown: CHIMBU
1963   Struggle for Land: Agriculture and Group
       Territories among the Chimbu of the New
       Guinea Highlands. London: Oxford University
       Press.

492. Brown, David J.J.: POLOPA
1973   Doing Nothing is also Doing Something.
       LSE, The Magazine of the London School of
       Economics 46:12-14.

493. Brown, Paula: CHIMBU
1960   Chimbu Tribes: Political Organization in the
       Eastern Highlands of New Guinea.

Southwestern Journal of Anthropology 16:
22-35.

494. -----
    1961   Chimbu Death Payments. Journal of the
            Royal Anthropological Institute 91:77-96.

495. -----
    1962a   Anthropology and Geography. Pacific
            Viewpoint 3:7-11.

496. -----
    1962b   Non-Agnates among the Patrilineal Chimbu.
            Journal of the Polynesian Society 71:
            57-69.

497. -----
    1963   From Anarchy to Satrapy. American
            Anthropologist 65:1-15.

498. -----
    1964   Enemies and Affines. Ethnology 3:335-356.

499. -----
    1966   Goodbye to All That? In Eben H. Hipsley,
            Ed. (Ref. 1659), pp. 31-48.

500. -----
    1967a   The Chimbu Political System. Anthropological
            Forum 2:36-52. (also see Ronald M. Berndt
            and Peter Lawrence, Eds., Ref. 238, pp. 207-
            223).

501. -----
    1967b   Kondom. Journal of the Papua and New Guinea
            Society 1(2):26-34.

502. -----
    1969   Marriage in Chimbu. In Robert M. Glasse and
            Mervyn J. Meggitt, Eds. (Ref. 280), pp. 77-95.

503. -----
    1970a   Chimbu Transactions. Man, N.S., 5:99-117.

504. -----
    1970b   Mingge-money: Economic Change in the New
            Guinea Highlands. Southwestern Journal of
            Anthropology 26:242-260.

505. -----
    1972   The Chimbu: A Study of Change in the New
            Guinea Highlands. New York: Schenkman.

506. ------
       1974   Mediators in Social Change: New Roles for
               Big-Men. Mankind 9:224-230.

507. Brown, Paula and Harold C. Brookfield: CHIMBU
       1959   Chimbu Land and Society. Oceania 30:1-75.

508. ------
       1967   Chimbu Settlement and Residence: A Study
               of Patterns, Trends and Idiosyncracy.
               Pacific Viewpoint 8:119-151.

509. Brown, Paula and Gillian Winefield: CHIMBU
       1965   Some Demographic Measures Applied to
               Chimbu Census and Field Data. Oceania 35:
               175-190.

510. Bruijn, J.V. de: KAPAUKU
       1939a   Gegevens omtrent de bevolking in het
               Wisselmerengebied. Nieuw-Guinea 4:259-271.

511. ------
       1939b   Verslag van een tocht maar het brongebied
               van de Edere of Elegeboe-rivier in Centraal
               Nieuw-Guinea. Nieuw-Guinea 4:301-315.

512. ------
       1939c   Verslag von een tocht van Enarotali via
               Itodah, Jamopa, Obaja, Kamero naar Orawja.
               Nieuw-Guinea 4:259-271.

513. ------
       1970   Ekagi Land Tenure. In Anton Ploeg, Ed.
               (Ref. 326), pp. 13-23.

514. Bulmer, Ralph N.H.: CHIMBU
       1962   Chimbu Plume Traders. Australian Natural
               History 14:15-19.

515. Bulmer, Ralph N.H.: KARAM
       1964   Edible Seeds and Prehistoric Stone Mortars
               in the Highlands of East New Guinea. Man,
               Vol. 64, Art. 183, pp. 147-150.

516. ------
       1965   Beliefs Concerning the Propagation of New
               Varieties of Sweet Potato in Two New Guinea
               Highlands Societies. Journal of the
               Polynesian Society 74:237-239. (also KYAKA).

517. ------
       1966   Birds as Possible Agents in the Propagation
               of the Sweet Potato. The Emu 65:165-182.
               (also KYAKA).

518.   -----
        1967   Why is the Cassowary Not a Bird? A Problem
                of Zoological Taxonomy among the Karam of
                the New Guinea Highlands. Man, N.S., 2:5-25.

519.   -----
        1968a   Karam Colour Categories. Kivung 1:120-133.

520.   -----
        1968b   Worms that Croak and Other Mysteries of
                Karam Natural History. Mankind 6:621-639.

521.   -----
        1970a   Which Came First, the Chicken or the
                Egg-head? In Échanges et Communications:
                Melanges offerts à Claude Lévi-Strauss,
                Vol. 2, Jean Pouillon and Pierre Maranda,
                Eds. The Hague: Mouton. pp. 1069-1091.

522.   -----
        1970b   Why is the Cassowary Not a Bird? Australian
                External Territories 10(1):7-9.

523.   -----
        1971   Science, Ethnoscience and Education. Papua
                New Guinea Journal of Education 7:22-33.

524.   Bulmer, Ralph N.H. and J.I. Menzies: KARAM
        1972-   Karam Classification of Marsupials and
        1973   Rodents. Journal of the Polynesian
                Society 81:472-499; 82:86-107.

525.   Bulmer, Ralph N.H. and Michael J. Tyler: KARAM
        1968   Karam Classification of Frogs. Journal of
                the Polynesian Society 77:333-385.

526.   Bulmer, Ralph N.H.: KYAKA ENGA
        1957   A Primitive Ornithology. Australian Museum
                Magazine 12:224-229.

527.   -----
        1960a   Leadership and Social Structure among the
                Kyaka People of the Western Highlands
                District of New Guinea. Ph.D. Thesis,
                Canberra, The Australian National University.

528.   -----
        1960b   Political Aspects of the Moka Ceremonial
                Exchange System among the Kyaka People of
                the Western Highlands of New Guinea.
                Oceania 31:1-13.

529.   -----
        1964   Hagen and Wapenamanda Open Electorates: The

Election among the Kyaka Enga. Journal of the Polynesian Society 73:216-223.

530. -----
1965 The Kyaka of the Western Highlands. In Peter Lawrence and Mervyn J. Meggitt, Eds. (Ref. 308), pp. 132-161.

531. Bulmer, Ralph N.H. and Susan Bulmer: KYAKA ENGA
1962 Figurines and Other Stones of Power among the Kyaka. Journal of the Polynesian Society 71:192-208.

532. Burnett, R.M.: MARING (?)
1963 Some Cultural Practices Observed in the Simbai Administrative Area, Madang District. Papua New Guinea Agricultural Journal 16: 79-84.

533. Bus, G.A.M.: ENGA
1951 The Te Festival or Gift Exchange in Enga (Central Highlands of New Guinea). Anthropos 46:813-824.

534. Catley, A.: (not available for examination)
1963 Notes on Insects as Food for Native People in Papua and New Guinea. Papua and New Guinea Scientific Society, Transactions, 4(1):10-12.

535. Chenoweth, Vida: DUNA
1969 An Investigation of the Singing Styles of the Dunas. Oceania 39:218-230.

536. Chenoweth, Vida: GADSUP
1966 Song Structure of a New Guinea Highlands Tribe. Ethnomusicology 10:285-297.

537. Chenoweth, Vida and Darlene Bee: AWA
1971 Comparative-Generative Models of a New Guinea Melodic Structure. American Anthropologist 73:773-782.

538. Clarke, William C.: MARING
1968 The Ndwimba Basin, Mismarck Mountains, New Guinea: Place and People. Ph.D. Thesis, Berkeley, University of California.

539. -----
1971 Place and People: An Ecology of a New Guinean Community. Berkeley: University of California Press.

71

540. Clarke, William C. and James M. Street: MARING
     1967   Soil Fertility and Cultivation Practices
             in New Guinea. Journal of Tropical
             Geography 24:7-11.

541. Clarke, William C. and Ian Hughes: BARUA
     1974   Salt-Making among the Baruya People of
             Papua New Guinea. Australian Natural
             History 18(1):22-24.

542. Cook, Edwin A.: NARAK
     1966   Cultural Flexibility: Myth and Reality.
             Anthropos 61:831-838.

543. -----
     1967   Manga Social Organization. Ph.D. Thesis,
             New Haven, Yale University.

544. -----
     1969   Marriage among the Manga. In Robert M.
             Glasse and Mervyn J. Meggitt, Eds. (Ref.
             280), pp. 96-116.

545. -----
     1970   On the Conversion of Non-Agnates into
             Agnates among the Manga, Jimi River,
             Western Highlands District, New Guinea.
             Southwestern Journal of Anthropology 26:
             190-196.

546. Craig, Barry: TELEFOL
     1966   Art of the Telefomin Area, New Guinea.
             Australian Natural History 15:218-224.

547. -----
     1967   The Houseboards of the Telefomin Sub-
             District, New Guinea. Man, N.S., 2:260-
             273 and 1 Plate.

548. -----
     1968a   Bark Paintings and Rock Art of the Mountain
             Ok. Mankind 6:595-597. (also KAWOL and
             TIFAL).

549. -----
     1968b   Making Fire by Percussion in the Telefomin
             Area, New Guinea. Mankind 6:434-435.
             (also FAIWOL, KAWOL, MIANMIN and TIFAL).

550. -----
     1970   Art Styles of New Guinea. The Franciscan
             12(2):88-95.

551. Craig, Ruth: TELEFOL
          1969   Marriage among the Telefolmin. In Robert M.
                  Glasse and Mervyn J. Meggitt, Eds. (Ref.
                  280), pp. 176-197.

552. Cranstone, B.A.L.: TELEFOL and TIFAL
          1965a   The British Museum Ethnographic Expedition
                  to New Guinea, 1963-4: A Preliminary
                  Report. British Museum Quarterly 29(3-4):
                  109-118 and Plates XXVIII-XXXI.

553. ------
          1965b   A House Board from Telefomin, Territory of
                  New Guinea. British Museum Quarterly
                  30(1-2):56-59 and Plate XII.

554. ------
          1967   Some Boards from a New Guinea haus tamberan.
                  Man, N.S., 2:274-277 and 3 Plates.

555. ------
          1968   War Shields of the Telefomin Sub-District,
                  New Guinea. Man, N.S., 3:609-624 and 8
                  Plates.

556. ------
          1971   The Tifalmin: A 'Neolithic' People in New
                  Guinea. World Archaeology 3:132-142.

557. Criper, Clive: CHIMBU
          1965   The Chimbu Open Electorate. In David G.
                  Bettison et al., Eds. (Ref. 239),
                  pp. 120-146.

558. ------
          1967   The Politics of Exchange: A Study of
                  Ceremonial Exchange among the Chimbu.
                  Ph.D. Thesis, Canberra, The Australian
                  National University.

559. Diamond, Jared M.: FORE
          1966   Zoological Classification System of a
                  Primitive People. Science, 4 March,
                  151:1102-1104.

560. ------
          1968   Search for Birds of Northern New Guinea.
                  Explorers Journal 46(3):210-223. (also
                  MIKARU).

561. ------
          1971   Birds of the Karimui Basin, New Guinea.
                  National Geographic Society, Research
                  Reports, 1965 Projects, pp. 69-74.

Washington, D.C.   (also GIMI and PAWAIA).

562.   -----
         1972   Avifauna of the Eastern Highlands of New
                Guinea. Nuttall Ornithological Club,
                Publication No. 12. Cambridge, Mass.
                (also MIKARU).

563.   Dornstreich, Mark D.:   ENGA
         1973a An Ecological Study of Gadio Enga (New
                Guinea) Subsistence. Ph.D. Thesis, New
                York, Columbia University.

564.   -----
         1973b Food Habits of Early Man: Balance between
                Hunting and Gathering. Science, 19 January,
                179:306-307.

565.   Dornstreich, Mark D. and George E.B. Morren: ENGA
       and MIANMIN
         1974   Does New Guinea Cannibalism Have Nutritional
                Value? Human Ecology 2:1-12.

566.   Downs, I.F.G.:   CHIMBU, CHUAVE and SINASINA
         1941   Fighting Customs of the Yonggamugl, China
                Sina, Masul and Chuave Native Districts,
                Chimbu, Madang District. Report to the
                League of Nations on the Administration of
                the Territory of New Guinea for 1939-1940.
                Canberra: Government Printer.   p. 22.

567.   Dubbeldam, L.F.B.:   KAPAUKU
         1964   The Devaluation of the Kapauku-Cowrie as
                a Factor of Social Disintegration. In
                James B. Watson, Ed. (Ref. 373), pp. 293-
                303.

568.   Du Toit, Brian M.:   GADSUP
         1962   Structural Looseness in New Guinea.
                Journal of the Polynesian Society 71:
                397-399.

569.   -----
         1963   Organization and Structure in Gadsup Society.
                Ph.D. Thesis, Eugene, University of Oregon.

570.   -----
         1964a Filiation and Affiliation among the Gadsup.
                Oceania 35:85-95.

571.   -----
         1964b Gadsup Culture Hero Tales. Journal of
                American Folklore 77:315-330.

74

572. ------
      1969   Misconstruction and Problems in
              Communication. American Anthropologist
              71:46-53.

573. ------
      1972   Comment on E. Richard Sorenson, "Socio-
              Ecological Change among the Fore of New
              Guinea" (Ref. 935). Current Anthropology
              13:373.

574. ------
      1974   Akuna: A New Guinea Village Community.
              Rotterdam: A.A. Balkema. (1975).

575. Dwyer, Peter D.: SIANE
      1974   The Price of Protein: Five Hundred Hours
              of Hunting in the New Guinea Highlands.
              Oceania 44:278-293.

576. Eechoud, J.P.K.: KAPAUKU
      1939   Ethnographische gegevens omtrent de
              bevolking om an bij de Wisselmeren.
              Nieuw-Guinea 4:121-137, 181-192.

577. Eckert, Leroy and David Thomas: ENGA
      1970   The Nature of Christian Giving in Enga
              Society. In Paul W. Brennan, Ed. (Ref.
              240), pp. 190-211.

578. Ekman, Paul, E. Richard Sorenson and Wallace V.
      Friesen: FORE
      1969   Pan-Cultural Elements in Facial Displays
              of Emotion. Science, 4 April, 164:86-88.

579. Elkin, A.P.: ENGA
      1953   Delayed Exchange in Wabag Sub-District,
              Central Highlands of New Guinea, with
              Notes on the Social Organization. Oceania
              23:161-201.

580. Eyma, P.J.: KAPAUKU
      1940   Verslag van den tocht ten noorden van het
              Paniaimeer. Tijdschrift van het Koninklijk
              Nederlandsch Aardrijkskundig Genootschap
              57:423-441.

581. Feachem, Richard: ENGA
      1972   The Enga. Hemisphere 16(10):16-18.

582. ------
      1973a   The Christians and the Enga: "Misin i
              Foulim Mi!" New Guinea 8(1):36-44.

75

583. ------
        1973b   Domestic Water Use in the New Guinea
                Highlands: The Case of the Raiapu Enga.
                Water Research Laboratory, Report No. 132.
                University of New South Wales.

584. ------
        1973c   The Pattern of Domestic Water Use in the
                New Guinea Highlands. South Pacific
                Commission, Bulletin 23(3):10-14, 24.

585. ------
        1973d   The Raiapu Enga Pig Herd. Mankind 9:
                25-31.

586. ------
        1973e   The Religious Belief and Ritual of the
                Raiapu Enga. Oceania 43:259-285.

587. Finney, Ben R.: ASARO, BENABENA, GAHUKU, SIANE and
     YAVIYUFA
        1968   Bigfellow Man Belong Business in New
                Guinea. Ethnology 7:394-410.

588. ------
        1969   New Guinea Entrepeneurs: Indigenous Cash
                Cropping, Capital Formation and Investment
                in the New Guinea Highlands. New Guinea
                Research Unit, Bulletin 27. Port Moresby.

589. ------
        1970   "Partnership" in Developing the New Guinea
                Highlands, 1948-1968. Journal of Pacific
                History 5:117-134.

590. ------
        1973   Big Men and Business: Entrepeneurship and
                Economic Growth in the New Guinea Highlands.
                Honolulu: University of Hawaii Press.

591. Fischer, H.W.: DANI
        1915   Ethnographica van den Pesechem und aus
                südwest-Neu-Guinea. Nova Guinea 7:145-160.

592. Fischer, Hans: YAGWOIA
        1968   Negwa: Eine Papua-gruppe im wandel.
                Munich: Klaus Renner.

593. Fortune, Reo F.: KAMANO
        1947a   Law and Force in Papuan Societies.
                American Anthropologist 49:244-259.

594.   -----
         1947b   The Rules of Relationship Behaviour in
                 One Variety of Primitive Warfare. Man,
                 Vol. 47, Art. 115, pp. 108-110.

595.   -----
         1960   New Guinea Warfare: Correction of a Mistake
                 Previously Published. Man, Vol. 60, Art.
                 146, p. 108.

596. Franklin, Karl J.: KEWA
         1963   Kewa Ethnolinguistic Concepts of Body Parts.
                 Southwestern Journal of Anthropology 19:
                 54-63.

597.   -----
         1965   Kewa Social Organization. Ethnology 4:
                 408-420.

598.   -----
         1967   Names and Aliases in Kewa. Journal of the
                 Polynesian Society 76:76-81.

599.   -----
         1970   Metaphorical Songs in Kewa. In Stephen A.
                 Wurm and Donald C. Laycock, Eds. (Ref. 1148),
                 pp. 985-995.

600.   -----
         1971a   Practical Considerations of Folk Taxonomies.
                 Kivung 4:133-140.

601.   -----
         1971b   Some Comments on Eliciting Cultural Data.
                 Anthropological Linguistics 13:339-348.

602.   -----
         1972   A Ritual Pandanus Language in New Guinea.
                 Oceania 43:66-76.

603.   -----
         1974.   Kewa. In Kenneth A. McElhanon, Ed. (Ref.
                 314), pp. 124-138.

604. Franklin, Karl J. and Joice Franklin: KEWA
         1962   The Kewa Counting Systems. Journal of the
                 Polynesian Society 71:188-191.

605. Freund, A.P.H.: (not available for examination)
         1965   Salt-making in Inland New Guinea. Papua
                 and New Guinea Scientific Society,
                 Transactions 6:16-19.

606. Freund, Roland P.: ENGA
     1971   Those Enga! The More Things Change...
            New Guinea 6(3):52-56.

607. ------
     1972   An Approach to the Commercialization of
            Enga Agriculture. In Marion W. Ward, Ed.
            (Ref. 368), pp. 189-202.

608. Freund, Roland P., R. Hett and K. Reko: ENGA
     1970   The Enga Concept of God. In Paul W.
            Brennan, Ed. (Ref. 240), pp. 141-166.

609. Gajdusek, D. Carleton and Michael Alpers: FORE
     1972   Genetic Studies in Relation to Kuru. I.
            Cultural, Historical, and Demographic
            Background. American Journal of Human
            Genetics 24(6), Suppl., pp. S1-S38.

610. Gajdusek, D. Carleton and Vincent Zigas: FORE
     1961   Studies on Kuru. I. The Ethnologic
            Setting of Kuru. American Journal of
            Tropical Medicine and Hygiene 10:80-91.

611. Gardner, Robert and Karl G. Heider: DANI
     1969   Gardens of War: Life and Death in the
            New Guinea Stone Age. New York: Random
            House.

612. Gitlow, Abraham L.: HAGEN
     1947a Economics of the Mt. Hagen Tribes, New
            Guinea. Ph.D. Thesis, New York, Columbia
            University.

613. ------
     1947b Economics of the Mt. Hagen Tribes, New
            Guinea. American Ethnological Society,
            Monograph No. 12. New York: J.J. Augustin.

614. Glasse, Robert M.: FORE
     1967   Cannibalism in the Kuru Region of New
            Guinea. New York Academy of Sciences,
            Transactions 29:748-754.

615. ------
     1968   Cannibalisme et kuru chez les Fore de
            Nouvelle Guinée. L'Homme 8(3):22-36.

616. ------
     1969   Marriage in South Fore. In Robert M.
            Glasse and Mervyn J. Meggitt, Eds.
            (Ref. 280), pp. 16-37.

617. -----
      1970   Some Recent Observations on Kuru.
              Oceania 40:210-213.

618. Glasse, Robert M. and Shirley Lindenbaum: FORE
      1967   How New Guinea Natives Reacted to a Total
              Eclipse. Trans-action 5(2):46-52.

619. -----
      1969   South Fore Politics. Anthropological
              Forum 2:308-326. (also see Ronald M. Berndt
              and Peter Lawrence, Eds., Ref. 238, pp. 362-
              380).

620. Glasse, Robert M.: HULI
      1959a   The Huli Descent System: A Preliminary
              Account. Oceania 29:171-184.

621. -----
      1959b   Revenge and Redress among the Huli: A
              Preliminary Account. Mankind 5:273-289.

622. -----
      1962   The Cognatic Descent System of the Huli of
              Papua. Ph.D. Thesis, Canberra, The
              Australian National University.

623. -----
      1963   Bingi at Tari. Journal of the Polynesian
              Society 72:270-271.

624. -----
      1965   The Huli of the Southern Highlands. In
              Peter Lawrence and Mervyn J. Meggitt, Eds.
              (Ref. 308), pp. 27-49.

625. -----
      1968   Huli of Papua: A Cognatic Descent System.
              Cahiers de l'Homme, VIII. Paris: Mouton.

626. -----
      1968-   The Quadrangular Stone Axe of the Huli,
      1969   Southern Highlands of Papua. Anthropos
              63-64:571-574.

627. -----
      1974   Le masque de la volupté: Symbolisme et
              antagonisme sexuels sur les hauts plateaux
              de Nouvelle-Guinée. L'Homme 14(2):79-86.

628. Glasse, Robert M.: MIKARU
      1965   Leprosy at Karimui. Papua and New Guinea
              Medical Journal 8:95-98.

629. -----
          1966   La lepre à Karimui. L'Homme 6(2):82-87.

630. Glasse, Shirley: FORE   (also see Lindenbaum, S.)
          1964   The Social Effects of Kuru. Papua and
                  New Guinea Medical Journal 7:36-47.

631. Glick, Leonard B.: GIMI
          1963   Foundations of a Primitive Medical System:
                  The Gimi of the New Guinea Highlands.
                  Ph.D. Thesis, Philadelphia, University of
                  Pennsylvania.

632. -----
          1964   Categories and Relations in Gimi Natural
                  Science. In James B. Watson, Ed. (Ref.
                  373), pp. 273-280.

633. -----
          1967a   Medicine as an Ethnographic Category: The
                  Gimi of the New Guinea Highlands. Ethnology
                  6:31-56.

634. -----
          1967b   The Role of Choice in Gimi Kinship.
                  Southwestern Journal of Anthropology 23:
                  371-382.

635. -----
          1968   Gimi Farces. Oceania 39:64-69.

636. Godelier, Maurice: BARUA
          1969a   Land Tenure among the Baruya of New Guinea.
                  Journal of the Papua and New Guinea Society
                  3:17-23.

637. -----
          1969b   La "monnaie de sel" des Baruya de Nouvelle
                  Guinée. L'Homme 9:5-37.

638. -----
          1970   "Monnaie de sel" et circulation des
                  merchandises chez les Baruya de Nouvelle
                  Guinée. Cahiers Vilfredo Pareto 21:121-147.

639. -----
          1971   "Salt Currency" and the Circulation of
                  Commodities among the Baruya of New Guinea.
                  In Studies in Economic Anthropology.
                  American Anthropological Association,
                  Anthropological Studies No. 7. George
                  Dalton, Ed. pp. 52-73.

640. -----
1972   Le visible et l'invisible chez les Baruya
        de Nouvelle-Guinée. In Langues et
        techniques nature et société, Tome II,
        Approche ethnologique et naturaliste.
        Jacqueline M.C. Thomas and Lucien Bernot,
        Eds. Paris: Editions Klincksieck.
        pp. 263-269.

641. Godelier, Maurice and Jose Garanger: BARUYA
        1973   Outils de pierre, outils d'acier chez les
                Baruya de Nouvelle-Guinée. L'Homme 13:
                187-220.

642. Godelier, Maurice: SIANE (Data from R.F. Salisbury)
        1964   Economic politique et anthropologie
                economique: à propos des Siane de Nouvelle-
                Guinée. L'Homme 4:118-132.

643. Goldberg, Harvey: KAPAUKU (data from L. Pospisil)
        1966   A Note on Pospisil's "Correlates."
                American Anthropologist 68:1488-1491.

644. Goodenough, Ward H.: ENGA
        1952   Ethnological Reconnaissance in New Guinea.
                University of Pennsylvania, University
                Museum, Bulletin 17(1):5-37. (also MENYA).

645. -----
        1953   Ethnographic Notes on the Mae People of
                New Guinea's Western Highlands.
                Southwestern Journal of Anthropology 9:
                29-44.

646. Grandowski, Edwin: HAGEN
        1956   Lebensläufe bei den Aranda (Zentralaustralien)
                und den Hagenbergleuten (Neuguinea).
                Ethnosoziologischer Versuch einer
                Gegenüberstellung. Ph.D. Thesis, Berlin,
                University of Berlin.

647. Grove, D.S.: AGARABE (?)
        1948   Garden Ceremonies - Central Highlands
                District. Report to the General Assembly of
                the United Nations on the Administration of
                the Territory of New Guinea from 1st July,
                1947, to 30th June, 1948. Sydney: Government
                Printer. App. XVI, p. xlvii.

648. Gusinde, Martin: KARAM
        1957   A Pygmy Group Newly Discovered in New
                Guinea: A Preliminary Report. Anthropological
                Quarterly 30:18-26.

649. ―――――
      1958   Die Ayom-pygmäen auf New-Guinea: Ein
              forschungsbericht. Anthropos 53:497-
              574, 817-863.

650. Hage, Per: GAHUKU (data from K.E. Read)
      1973-   A Graph Theoretic Approach to the Analysis
      1974   of Alliance Structure and Local Grouping
              in Highland New Guinea. Anthropological
              Forum 3:280-294.

651. Harris, G.T.: DUNA
      1972   Labour Supply and Economic Development in
              the Southern Highlands of Papua New Guinea.
              Oceania 43:123-139.

652. Hatanaka, Sachiko: SINASINA
      1970a   Elections and Political Consciousness in
              the Chimbu District. Journal of the Papua
              and New Guinea Society 4(2):37-51.

653. ―――――
      1970b   Leadership and Its Background in the
              Highlands of New Guinea. University of
              Kyoto, Anthropology, Vol. 2. (Text in
              Japanese). (also UMAIROF).

654. ―――――
      1972   Leadership and Socio-Economic Change in
              Sinasina, New Guinea Highlands. New Guinea
              Research Unit, Bulletin 45. Port Moresby.

655. ―――――
      1973   Conflict of Laws in a New Guinea Society.
              Man, N.S., 8:59-73.

656. Hatanaka, Sachiko: UMAIROF
      1969a   Human Relationships among the Highlands
              People of New Guinea. Society of Japanese
              Social Psychologists, Social Psychology
              Annual Report No. 10. Tokyo. (Text in
              Japanese).

657. ―――――
      1969b   A Number of the Sisimin in New Guinea.
              University of Tokyo, Mathematics Seminar,
              Vol. 83. (Text in Japanese).

658. Hatanaka, Sachiko and Laurence W. Bragge: UMAIROF
      1973   Habitat, Isolation and Subsistence Economy
              in the Central Range of New Guinea. Oceania
              44:38-57.

659. Hayano, David M.: AWA
         1972   Marriage, Alliance and Warfare: The Tauna
                 Awa of New Guinea. Ph.D. Thesis, Los
                 Angeles, University of California.

660. -----
         1973a   Individual Correlates of Coffee Adoption
                 in the New Guinea Highlands. Human
                 Organization 32:305-314.

661. -----
         1973b   Sorcery Death, Proximity, and the Perception
                 of Out-Groups: The Tauna Awa of New Guinea.
                 Ethnology 12:179-191.

662. -----
         1974a   Marriage, Alliance, and Warfare: A View
                 from the New Guinea Highlands. American
                 Ethnologist 1:281-293.

663. -----
         1974b   Misfortune and Traditional Political
                 Leadership among the Tauna Awa of New
                 Guinea. Oceania 45:18-26.

664. Hays, Terence E.: TAIRORA
         1974   Mauna: Explorations in Ndumba Ethnobotany.
                 Ph.D. Thesis, Seattle, University of
                 Washington.

665. Head, Robert: GAWIGL
         1974   Gawigl. In Kenneth A. McElhanon, Ed.
                 (Ref. 314), pp. 91-102.

666. Healey, Alan: TELEFOL
         1962   Linguistic Aspects of Telefomin Kinship
                 Terminology. Anthropological Linguistics
                 4(7):14-28.

667. Healey, Christopher J.: KANDAWO, MARING and NARAK
         1973   Hunting of Birds of Paradise and Trade in
                 Plumes in the Jimi Valley, Western
                 Highlands District. M.A. Qualifying Essay,
                 Port Moresby, University of Papua New Guinea.

668. Heider, Eleanor Rosch: DANI (also see Rosch, E.)
         1972a   Probabilities, Sampling, and Ethnographic
                 Method: The Case of Dani Colour Names.
                 Man, N.S., 7:448-466.

669. -----
         1972b   Universals in Color Naming and Memory.
                 Journal of Experimental Psychology 93:10-20.

670. Heider, Eleanor Rosch and Donald C. Olivier: DANI
      1972   The Structure of the Color Space in Naming
             and Memory for Two Languages. Cognitive
             Psychology 3:337-354.

671. Heider, Karl G.:   DANI
      1966   The Dugum Dani: A Papuan Culture in West
             New Guinea. Ph.D. Thesis, Cambridge, Mass.,
             Harvard University.

672. -----
      1967a Archaeological Assumptions and
             Ethnographical Facts: A Cautionary Tale
             from New Guinea. Southwestern Journal of
             Anthropology 23:52-64.

673. -----
      1967b Speculative Functionalism: Archaic Elements
             in New Guinea Dani Culture. Anthropos 62:
             833-840.

674. -----
      1969a Attributes and Categories in the Study of
             Material Culture: New Guinea Dani Attire.
             Man, N.S., 4:379-391.

675. -----
      1969b The Dongson and the Dani: A Skeuomorph
             from the West Irian Highlands. Mankind 7:
             147-148.

676. -----
      1969c Sweet Potato Notes and Lexical Queries,
             or "The Problem of All Those Names for
             Sweet Potatoes in the New Guinea Highlands."
             Kroeber Anthropological Society, Papers 41:
             78-86.

677. -----
      1970a The Dugum Dani: A Papuan Culture in the
             Highlands of West New Guinea. Viking Fund
             Publications in Anthropology, No. 49. New
             York: Wenner-Gren Foundation and Chicago:
             Aldine.

678. -----
      1970b Hanging Stone Disks in the New Guinea
             Highlands. Mankind 7:292-294. (also JALE).

679. -----
      1972a Dani Kurelu - New Guinea. In E.E. Evans-
             Pritchard, Supervisory Ed. (Ref. 2),
             pp. 92-99.

680.   ------
        1972b   Dani of New Guinea. HRAFlex Books,
                Ethnocentrism Series, OJ1-004. New Haven:
                Human Relations Area Files.

681.   ------
        1972c   The Dani of West Irian. Warner Modular
                Publications, Module 2 (1972), pp. 1-75.

682.   ------
        1972d   The Grand Valley Dani Pig Feast: A Ritual
                of Passage and Intensification. Oceania
                42:169-197.

683.   Heim, Roger: GADSUP
        1964   Note succinte sur les champignons
                alimentaires des Gadsup (Nouvelle-Guinée).
                Cahiers du Pacifique 6:121-132.

684.   Heim, Roger: WAHGI
        1963   Diagnoses Latines des espéces de champignons
                ou nonda, associés à la folie du komugel
                tai du ndaal. Revue de Mycologie 28:277-283.

685.   ------
        1965a   Les champignons associés à la folie des
                Kuma, etude descriptive et iconographie.
                Cahiers du Pacifique 7:7-64.

686.   ------
        1965b   Sur un nouveau bolet utilisé par les Kuma,
                en Nouvelle-Guinée. Beiträge zur Biochemie
                und Physiologie von Naturstoffen: Festschrift
                Kurt Mothes zum 65 Geburtstag. Iena.
                pp. 247-249.

687.   ------
        1966a   Le boletus flammeus. Cahiers du Pacifique
                9:67-68.

688.   ------
        1966b   Les bolets sataniques. Essai sur les espèces
                du groupe Satanas. Revue de Mycologie 30:
                262-291.

689.   Heim, Roger and R.G. Wasson: WAHGI
        1964a   La folie des Kuma. Cahiers du Pacifique
                6:2-27.

690.   ------
        1964b   Note preliminaire sur la folie fongique des
                Kuma. Comptes Rendus des Sceances de
                l'Academie des Sceances 258:1593-1598.

691. -----
1965   The "Mushroom Madness" of the Kuma. Harvard
        University, Botanical Museum, Leaflet 21(1):
        1-36.

692. Heinicke, Victor: ENGA
1970   The Meaning of Identification: What the
        Engas Want from the Missionaries. In Paul
        W. Brennan, Ed. (Ref. 240), pp. 235-244.

693. Henty, E.E.: (not available for examination)
1960   Two Drug-Plants in Native Culture. Papua
        and New Guinea Scientific Society,
        Transactions 1:19-20.

694. Hide, Robin L.: SINASINA
1969   Worms and Sickness: A Note on Noise-
        Producing Worms and Mystical Belief among
        the Nimai of the New Guinea Highlands.
        Mankind 7:149-151.

695. -----
1971   Land Demarcation and Disputes in the Chimbu
        District of the New Guinea Highlands. In
        Marion W. Ward, Ed. (Ref. 367), pp. 37-61.

696. -----
1973   The Land Titles Commission in Chimbu: An
        Analysis of Colonial Land Law and Practice.
        New Guinea Research Unit, Bulletin 50.
        Port Moresby.

697. Höltker, Georg: CHIMBU
1942   Zeremonial-steinbeil von den Korugu im
        Wagi-tal im ostlichen Zentral Neuguinea.
        Ethnos 7:79-83.

698. Höltker, Georg: GENDE
1940-   Zur hamburger ethnographischen sammlung
1941   aus dem östlichen Zentral-Neuguinea.
        Anthropos 35-36:357-363.

699. Howlett, Diana R.: ASARO
1960   The Pre-Contact Society in the Goroka
        Valley. In UNESCO (Ref. 360), pp. 375-379.

700. -----
1962   A Decade of Change in the Goroka Valley,
        New Guinea: Land Use and Development in
        the 1950s. Ph.D. Thesis, Canberra, The
        Australian National University.

701. -----
1973   Terminal Development: From Tribalism to

Peasantry. In Harold C. Brookfield, Ed.
(Ref. 246), pp. 249-273.

702. Hughes, Ian: FORABA and MIKARU
1970 Pigs, Sago and Limestone: The Adaptive Use
of Natural Enclosures and Planted Sago in
Pig Management. Mankind 7:272-278.

703. Irwin, Barry: SINASINA
1972 The Liability Complex among the Chimbu
Peoples of New Guinea. Practical
Anthropology 19:280-285.

704. Jablonko, Alison: MARING
1968 Dance and Daily Activities among the Maring
People of New Guinea: A Cinematographic
Analysis of Body Movement Style. Ph.D.
Thesis, New York, Columbia University.

705. -----
1972 Comment on E. Richard Sorenson, "Socio-
Ecological Change among the Fore of New
Guinea" (Ref. 935). Current Anthropology
13:374-375.

706. Jablonko, Alison and Marek Jablonko: MARING
1963 Kerepe's House: A Housebuilding in New
Guinea. Psychological Cinema Register,
Pennsylvania State University, University
Park, Pa. (Film).

707. Jackson, Graham: HULI (data from R.M. Glasse)
1971 Glasse, the Huli and Descent. Journal of
the Polynesian Society 80:119-132.

708. Keil, Dana: BENABENA
1974 The Inter-Group Economy of the Nekematigi,
Eastern Highlands District, New Guinea.
Ph.D. Thesis, Evanston, Ill., Northwestern
University.

709. Kernan, Keith T.: KAPAUKU (data from L. Pospisil)
1965 A Transformational Analysis of the
Kapauku Kinship System. Kroeber
Anthropological Society, Papers 33:71-90.

710. Kirschbaum, F.: GENDE
1927 Ein neuentdeckter zwergstamm auf Neu-Guinea.
Anthropos 22:202-215.

711. Knight, J.: HAGEN
1972 A Local Christian Community -- Koge Parish.
Point 1:130-148. Goroka.

87

712. Koch, Klaus-Friedrich: JALÉ
          1967   Conflict and Its Management among the Jalé
                  People of West New Guinea. Ph.D. Thesis,
                  Berkeley, University of California.

713. ------
          1968a   Marriage in Jalémó. Oceania 39:85-109.

714. ------
          1968b   On "Possession" Behaviour in New Guinea.
                  Journal of the Polynesian Society 77:
                  135-146.

715. ------
          1970a   Cannibalistic Revenge in Jalé Warfare.
                  Natural History 79(2):41-43, 47, 49-50.

716. ------
          1970b   Structure and Variability in the Jalé
                  Kinship Terminology: A Formal Analysis.
                  Ethnology 9:263-301.

717. ------
          1970c   Warfare and Anthropophagy in Jalé Society.
                  Bijdragen tot de Taal-, Land- en
                  Volkenkunde 126:37-58.

718. ------
          1972a   Jalé - New Guinea Highlands. In E.E.
                  Evans-Pritchard, Supervisory Ed. (Ref. 2),
                  pp. 80-87.

719. ------
          1972b   Semantics of Kinship Terms: The Jalé Case.
                  Bijdragen tot de Taal-, Land- en
                  Volkenkunde 128:81-98.

720. ------
          1974a   The Anthropology of Warfare. An Addison-
                  Wesley Module in Anthropology, Module No.
                  52, pp. 1-23. Reading, Mass.: Addison-
                  Wesley.

721. ------
          1974b   Incest and Its Punishment in Jalé Society.
                  Journal of the Polynesian Society 83:84-91.

722. ------
          1974c   Sociogenic and Psychogenic Models in
                  Anthropology: The Functions of Jalé
                  Initiation. Man, N.S., 9:397-422.

723. ------
          1974d   War and Peace in Jalemó: The Management of

Conflict in Highland New Guinea. Cambridge,
Mass.: Harvard University Press.

724. Kock, A.C. de: GOLIATH FAMILY
1912   Eenige ethnologische en anthropologische
gegevens omtrent een devergstam in het
bergland van zuid Nieuw Guinea. Tijdschrift
Koninklijk Nederlandische Aardrijks
Genootschap 29:154-170.

725. Kooijman, S.: STAR MOUNTAINS
1962   Material Aspects of the Star Mountains
Culture. Nova Guinea (Anthropology) 2:
15-44.

726. Lacey, Roderic: ENGA
1973a   The Enga World View: Some Thoughts from a
Wandering Historian. Catalyst 3(2):37-47.

727. -----
1973b   Local Consciousness and National Identity:
Aspects of the Enga Case. In Ronald J.
May, Ed. (Ref. 316), pp. 89-102.

728. -----
1974   Oral Traditions as History: An Exploration
of Oral Sources among the Enga of the New
Guinea Highlands. Ph.D. Thesis, Ann Arbor,
University of Michigan.

729. Langlas, Charles M.: FOI
1974   Foi Land Use, Prestige Economics and
Residence: A Processual Analysis. Ph.D.
Thesis, Honolulu, University of Hawaii.

730. Langness, Lewis L.: BENABENA
1963   Notes on the Bena Council, Eastern Highlands.
Oceania 33:151-170.

731. -----
1964a   Bena Bena Social Structure. Ph.D. Thesis,
Seattle, University of Washington.

732. -----
1964b   Some Problems in the Conceptualization of
Highlands Social Structures. In James B.
Watson, Ed. (Ref. 373), pp. 162-182.

733. -----
1965   Hysterical Psychosis in the New Guinea
Highlands: A Bena Bena Example. Psychiatry
28:258-277.

734. -----
      1967   Sexual Antagonism in the New Guinea
             Highlands: A Bena Bena Example. Oceania
             37:161-177.

735. -----
      1968   Bena Bena Political Organization.
             Anthropological Forum 2:180-198. (also
             see Ronald M. Berndt and Peter Lawrence,
             Eds., Ref. 238, pp. 298-316).

736. -----
      1969   Marriage in Bena Bena. In Robert M. Glasse
             and Mervyn J. Meggitt, Eds. (Ref. 280),
             pp. 38-55.

737. -----
      1970   Entree into the Field: Highlands New Guinea.
             In Handbook of Method in Cultural
             Anthropology. Raoul Naroll and Ronald Cohen,
             Eds. Garden City: Natural History Press.
             pp. 220-225.

738. -----
      1972   Violence in the New Guinea Highlands. In
             Collective Violence. James F. Short, Jr.
             and Marvin E. Wolfgang, Eds. Chicago:
             Aldine-Atherton. pp. 171-185.

739. -----
      1974   Ritual, Power, and Male Dominance in the
             New Guinea Highlands. Ethos 2:189-212.

740. Leach, Edmund R.: KAPAUKU (data from L. Pospisil)
      1959   Social Change and Primitive Law. American
             Anthropologist 61:1096-1097.

741. Leach, Edmund R.: SIANE (data from R.F. Salisbury)
      1957   On Asymmetrical Marriage Systems.
             American Anthropologist 59:343-344.

742. Leininger, Madeleine M.: GADSUP
      1964   A Gadsup Village Experiences Its First
             Election. Journal of the Polynesian
             Society 73:205-209.

743. -----
      1966   Convergence and Divergence of Human Behavior:
             An Ethnopsychological Comparative Study of
             Two Gadsup Villages in the Eastern Highlands
             of New Guinea. Ph.D. Thesis, Seattle,
             University of Washington.

44. Lerche, G.: GAWIGL
     1969   Kogegruber: New Guineas hojland. Kuml,
             pp. 195-209.

45. LeRoux, C.C.F.M.: DANI, DEM, MONI and KAPAUKU
     1948   De bergpapoea's van Nieuw-Guinea en hun
             woongebied. 3 Vols. Leiden: E.J. Brill.

46. Lindenbaum, Shirley: FORE (also see Glasse, S.)
     1971   Sorcery and Structure in Fore Society.
             Oceania 41:277-287.

47. -----
     1972   Sorcerers, Ghosts, and Polluting Women:
             An Analysis of Religious Belief and
             Population Control. Ethnology 11:241-253.

48. Lindenbaum, Shirley and Robert M. Glasse: FORE
     1969   Fore Age Mates. Oceania 39:165-173.

49. Lloyd, Richard and Joy Lloyd: BARUA
     1974   Baruya. In Kenneth A. McElhanon, Ed.
             (Ref. 314), pp. 54-68.

50. Lorentz, H.A.: DANI
     1911   An Expedition to the Snow Mountains of
             New Guinea. Geographical Journal 37:477-
             500 and map ff. p. 588.

51. -----
     1913   Zwarte menschen -- witte bergen: Verhaal
             van den tocht naar het Sneeuwgebergte van
             Nieuw Guinea. Leiden: E.J. Brill.

52. Loving, Richard E.: AWA
     1973   Awa Kinship Terminology and Its Use.
             Ethnology 12:429-436.

53. Lowman, Cherry: MARING
     1968   Maring Big Men. Anthropological Forum 2:
             199-243. (also see Ronald M. Berndt and
             Peter Lawrence, Eds., Ref. 238, pp. 317-
             361).

54. -----
     1973   Displays of Power: Art and War among the
             Marings of New Guinea. New York: Museum
             of Primitive Art.

55. Luzbetak, Louis J.: WAHGI
     1954   The Socio-Religious Significance of a New
             Guinea Pig Festival. Anthropological
             Quarterly 27:59-80, 102-128.

91

756.   -----
        1956   Worship of the Dead in the Middle Wahgi
                (New Guinea). Anthropos 51:81-96.

757.   -----
        1958a   The Middle Wahgi Culture: A Study of First
                Contacts and Initial Selectivity.
                Anthropos 53:51-87.

758.   -----
        1958b   Treatment of Disease in the New Guinea
                Highlands. Anthropological Quarterly 31:
                42-55.

759.   McArthur, A. Margaret: ENGA (data from M.J. Meggitt)
        1967   Analysis of the Genealogy of a Mae-Enga
                Clan. Oceania 37:281-285.

760.   McArthur, A. Margaret: MARING (data from R. Rappapor
        1974   Pigs for the Ancestors: A Review Article.
                Oceania 45:87-123.

761.   McKaughan, Howard P.: GADSUP
        1974   Gadsup. In Kenneth A. McElhanon, Ed.
                (Ref. 314), pp. 85-90.

762.   McKaughan, Howard P. and Richard E. Loving: AWA
        1974   Awa. In Kenneth A. McElhanon, Ed. (Ref.
                314), pp. 45-53.

763.   McKaughan, Howard P. and Alex Vincent: TAIRORA
        1974   Tairora. In Kenneth A. McElhanon, Ed.
                (Ref. 314), pp. 189-197.

764.   Malone, Dennis and Steve Steffens: ENGA
        1970   The Christian Concept of Forgiveness and
                Enga Morality. In Paul W. Brennan, Ed.
                (Ref. 240), pp. 167-189.

765.   Matthiessen, Peter: DANI
        1962   Under the Mountain Wall: A Chronicle of
                Two Seasons in the Stone Age. New York:
                Viking Press.

766.   Mbaginta'o, Ivan: SIMBARI
        1971   The Anga Initiations. Journal de la
                Société des Océanistes 27(32):285-294.

767.   -----
        1972   Les esprit gierisseurs chez les Dunkwi
                Anga. Journal de la Société des Océanistes
                28(37):337-343.

768. Meggitt, Mervyn J.: ENGA
        1956   The Valleys of the Upper Wage and Lai
                Rivers, Western Highlands, New Guinea.
                Oceania 27:90-135. (also HULI and MENDI).

769.   -----
        1957a   Enga Political Organisation: A Preliminary
                Description. Mankind 5:133-137.

770.   -----
        1957b   House Building among the Mae Enga, Western
                Highlands. Oceania 27:161-176.

771.   -----
        1958a   The Enga of the New Guinea Highlands: Some
                Preliminary Observations. Oceania 28:253-
                330.

772.   -----
        1958b   Mae Enga Time-Reckoning and Calendar, New
                Guinea. Man, Vol. 58, Art. 87, pp. 74-77.

773.   -----
        1959   The Lineage System of the Mae Enga of New
                Guinea. Ph.D. Thesis, Sydney, University
                of Sydney.

774.   -----
        1960a   Comments in General Discussion. In UNESCO
                (Ref. 360), pp. 102-110, 133-147, 236-247
                and 394-400 (passim).

775.   -----
        1960b   Notes on the Horticulture of the Enga People
                of New Guinea. In UNESCO (Ref. 360),
                pp. 86-89.

776.   -----
        1962a   Dream Interpretation among the Mae Enga of
                New Guinea. Southwestern Journal of
                Anthropology 18:216-229.

777.   -----
        1962b   Growth and Decline of Agnatic Descent
                Groups among the Mae Enga of the New Guinea
                Highlands. Ethnology 1:158-165.

778.   -----
        1964a   The Kinship Terminology of the Mae Enga of
                New Guinea. Oceania 34:191-200.

779.   -----
        1964b   Male-Female Relationships in the Highlands
                of Australian New Guinea. In James B.

Watson, Ed. (Ref. 373), pp. 204-224.

780. -----
1965a   The Lineage System of the Mae-Enga of New
         Guinea. Edinburgh: Oliver and Boyd.

781. -----
1965b   The Mae Enga of the Western Highlands.
         In Peter Lawrence and Mervyn J. Meggitt,
         Eds. (Ref. 308), pp. 105-131.

782. -----
1967   The Pattern of Leadership among the Mae-
         Enga of New Guinea. Anthropological Forum
         2:20-35. (also see Ronald M. Berndt and
         Pater Lawrence, Eds., Ref. 238, pp. 191-206).

783. -----
1971   From Tribesmen to Peasants: The Case of
         the Mae Enga of New Guinea. In Anthropology
         in Oceania: Essays Presented to Ian Hogbin.
         L.R. Hiatt and C. Jayawardena, Eds. Sydney:
         Angus and Robertson. pp. 191-209.

784. -----
1972   System and Subsystem: The Te Exchange Cycle
         among the Mae Enga. Human Ecology 1:111-
         123. (also GAWIGL, HAGEN and KYAKA ENGA).

785. -----
1973   The Sun and the Shakers: A Millenarian
         Cult and Its Transformations in the New
         Guinea Highlands. Oceania 44:1-37, 109-
         126. (also IPILI).

786. -----
1974   "Pigs Are Our Hearts!" The Te Exchange
         Cycle among the Mae Enga of New Guinea.
         Oceania 44:165-203.

787. Meggitt, Mervyn J.: IPILI
1957   The Ipili of the Porgera Valley, Western
         Highlands District. Oceania 28:31-55.

788. -----
1958   Salt Manufacture and Trading in the Western
         Highlands of New Guinea. Australian Museum
         Magazine 12:309-313.

789. Meyer-Rochow, V.B.: BOSAVI and CHUAVE
1973   Edible Insects in Three Different Ethnic
         Groups of Papua and New Guinea. American
         Journal of Clinical Nutrition 26:673-677.

'90. Modjeska, Charles N.: DUNA
      1969   Among the Duna: An Anthropologist's
              Initiation. Journal of the Papua and New
              Guinea Society 3(1):5-12.

'91. Morren, George E.B.: MIANMIN
      1974   Settlement Strategies and Hunting in a New
              Guinea Society. Ph.D. Thesis, New York,
              Columbia University.

'92. Moylan, Thomas: KAPAUKU (data from L. Pospisil)
      1973   Disequilibrium in a New Guinea Local
              Ecosystem. Mankind 9:61-70.

'93. Moyne, Walter E.G. and Kathleen Haddon: KARAM
      1936   The Pygmies of the Aiome Mountains,
              Mandated Territory of New Guinea. Journal
              of the Royal Anthropological Institute 66:
              269-290.

'94. Murphy, John J.: CHIMBU
      1938   Stone Workers of New Guinea, Past and
              Present. Oceania 9:37-40.

'95. Naylor, Larry L.: DANI
      1972   Cultural Change and Development in the
              Balim Valley. Irian 1:101-103.

'96. Nelson, Harold E.: HAGEN
      1971a   Disease, Demography, and the Evolution of
              Social Structure in Highlands New Guinea.
              Journal of the Polynesian Society 80:
              204-216.

'97. -----
      1971b   The Ecological, Epistemological and
              Ethnographic Context of Medicine in a New
              Guinea Highlands Culture. Ph.D. Thesis,
              Seattle, University of Washington.

'98. Nelson, Harold E. and Gary L. Chisum: HAGEN
      1974   A Computer-Assisted Method for Age-
              Determination in Non-Literate Populations.
              Bijdragen tot de Taal-, Land- en
              Volkenkunde 130:132-137.

'99. Newman, Philip L.: ASARO
      1962a   Sorcery, Religion and the Man. Natural
              History 71(2):21-28.

300. -----
      1962b   Supernaturalism and Ritual among the
              Gururumba (New Guinea). Ph.D. Thesis.
              Seattle, University of Washington.

801. -----
        1964a   Religious Belief and Ritual in a New Guinea
                Society. In James B. Watson, Ed. (Ref.
                373), pp. 257-272.

802. -----
        1964b   "Wild Man" Behavior in a New Guinea Highlands
                Community. American Anthropologist 66:1-19.

803. -----
        1965   Knowing the Gururumba. Case Studies in
                Cultural Anthropology Series. New York:
                Holt, Rinehart and Winston.

804. Newman, Philip L.: AWA
        1972   Irahqkiah of New Guinea. 2 Vols. HRAFlex
                Books, Ethnocentrism Series, OJ1-001 and
                OJ1-002. New Haven: Human Relations Area
                Files.

805. Nilles, Johann (John): CHIMBU
        1938a   Häuserbau und häuserformen bei den östlichen
                Waugla und Kurugu im Wahgital Neuguineas.
                Anthropos 33:963-968.

806. -----
        1938b   Die siedlungsform bei den oestlichen Waugla
                und Kurugu im Wagital, Neuguinea. Anthropos
                33:664-670.

807. -----
        1939   Mädchen-reifefeier bei den östlichen Waugla
                im Bismarckgebirge Neuguineas. Anthropos
                34:402-406.

808. -----
        1940   Eine knaben-jugendweihe bei den östlichen
                Waugla im Bismarckgebirge Neuguineas.
                Internationales Archiv für Ethnographie
                38:93-98.

809. -----
        1942-   Digging Sticks, Spades, Hoes, Axes and
        1945   Adzes of the Kuman People in the Bismarck
                Mountains of East-Central New Guinea.
                Anthropos 37-40:205-212.

810. -----
        1943-   Natives of the Bismarck Mountains, New
        1944   Guinea. Oceania 14:104-123; 15:1-18.

811. -----
        1950a   The Kuman of the Chimbu Region, Central
                Highlands, New Guinea. Oceania 21:25-65.

12.   -----
      1950b   Some Essential Features of the Social
              Culture of the Kuman People of the
              Interior of New Guinea. Ph.D. Thesis,
              Sydney, University of Sydney.

13.   -----
      1953   The Kuman People: A Study of Cultural
              Change in a Primitive Society in the
              Central Highlands of New Guinea. Oceania
              24:1-27, 119-131..

14.   -----
      1968-   Eine mythe in der Kuman-Sprache.
      1969   Anthropos 63-64:561-565.

15.   Nouhuys, J.W. van: DANI
      1912   Eerste bijdrage tot de kennis van de taal
              der "Pesegem" van Centraal Nieuw-Guinea.
              Bijdragen tot de Taal-, Land- en Volkenkunde
              66:266-273.

16.   -----
      1913   Der bergstamm Pesegem im innern von
              Niederlandisch-Neu-Guinea. Nova Guinea
              7(1):1-33..

17.   Numazawa, Kiichi: KARAM and KOBON
      1968   Die riten der aufnahme in die altersklassen
              bei den Kobon und Karam im Schradergebirge
              (Neuguinea). In Anthropos Institut (Ref.
              233), pp. 272-292.

18.   -----
      1969   New Guinea Pygmies Expedition. Tokyo:
              Tairiku Shobo. (In Japanese).

19.   Numazawa, Kiichi: KOBON
      1971   Stories of Kobon People in the Schrader
              Mountains, New Guinea. Collectanea
              Universitatis Catholicae Nanzan 4:21-42.
              (Text in Japanese).

20.   Nunen, Bernard Otto van: MONI
      1966   The Community of Kugapa: A Report on
              Research Conducted in 1957-1958 among a
              Group of Moni in the Central Highlands of
              West New Guinea. M.A. Thesis, Sydney,
              University of Sydney.

21.   -----
      1973   The Community of Kugapa: A Report on
              Research Conducted in 1957-1958 among a
              Group of Moni in the Central Highlands of

Irian Jaya. Irian 2(2):1-100.

822. O'Brien, Denise: DANI
      1966   A Twentieth-Century Stone-Age Culture.
              Discovery 1(2):31-37. New Haven, Conn.

823. -----
      1967   The Economics of Dani Marriage: An Analysis
              of Marriage Payments in a Highland New
              Guinea Society. Ph.D. Thesis, New Haven,
              Yale University.

824. -----
      1969   Marriage among the Konda Valley Dani. In
              Robert M. Glasse and Mervyn J. Meggitt,
              Eds. (Ref. 280), pp. 198-234.

825. O'Brien, Denise and Anton Ploeg: DANI
      1964   Acculturation Movements among the Western
              Dani. In James B. Watson, Ed. (Ref. 373),
              pp. 281-292.

826. Ollier, C.D., D.P. Drover and Maurice Godelier: BARUA
      1971   Soil Knowledge amongst the Baruya of
              Wonenara, New Guinea. Oceania 42:33-41.

827. Osborne, Kenneth B.: KYAKA ENGA
      1970   A Christian Graveyard Cult in the New
              Guinea Highlands. Practical Anthropology
              17:10-15.

828. Pataki, Kerry J.: AUYANA
      1965   Shifting Population and Environment among
              the Auyana: Some Considerations on
              Phenomena and Schema. M.A. Thesis, Seattle,
              University of Washington.

829. -----
      1972   Comment on E. Richard Sorenson, "Socio-
              Ecological Change among the Fore of New
              Guinea." (Ref. 935). Current Anthropology
              13:376. (also AWA, GADSUP and TAIRORA).

830. Pedersen, Lise Rishoj: ENGA
      1963   A Woman's Carrying Net from New Guinea.
              Folk 5:259-264.

831. Perey, Arnold: OKSAPMIN
      1973   Oksapmin Society and World View. Ph.D.
              Thesis, New York, Columbia University.

832. Peters, Hermanus Lambertus: DANI
      1965a   Enkele hoofdstukken wit het sociaal-
              religieuze leven van een Dani-groep.

98

Ph.D. Thesis, Utrecht, University of
Utrecht.

833. -----
      1965b Enkele hoofdstukken wit het sociaal-
             religieuze leven van een Dani-groep.
             Venlo: Dagblad voor Noord-Limburg.

834. Ploeg, Anton: DANI
      1965   Government in Wanggulam. Ph.D. Thesis,
             Canberra, The Australian National
             University.

835. -----
      1966   Some Comparative Remarks about the Dani
             of the Baliem Valley and the Dani at
             Bokondini. Bijdragen tot de Taal-, Land-
             en Volkenkunde 122:255-273.

836. -----
      1969   Government in Wanggulam. Verhandelingen
             van het Koninklijk Instituut voor Taal-,
             Land- en Volkenkunde, Deel 57. The Hague:
             Martinus Nijhoff.

837. Posala, Haynes F.: AGARABE and KAMANO
      1969   Customs and Belief in Relation to Health
             and Disease in the Kainantu Subdistrict.
             Papua and New Guinea Medical Journal 12(3):
             91-95.

838. Pospisil, Leopold: KAPAUKU
      1956   Law among the Kapauku of Netherlands New
             Guinea. Ph.D. Thesis, New Haven, Yale
             University.

839. -----
      1958a Kapauku Papuans and Their Law. Yale
             University, Publications in Anthropology
             No. 54. New Haven.

840. -----
      1958b Kapauku Political Structure. In Systems
             of Political Control and Bureaucracy in
             Human Society. American Ethnological
             Society, Proceedings. Verne Ray, Ed.
             Seattle: University of Washington Press.
             pp. 9-22.

841. -----
      1958c Social Change and Primitive Law:
             Consequences of a Papuan Legal Case.
             American Anthropologist 60:832-837.

842.   -----
         1960a   The Kapauku Papuans and Their Kinship
                 Organization. Oceania 30:188-205. (see
                 Erratum, 1961, 32:71).

843.   -----
         1960b   Papuan Social Structure: A Rejoinder to
                 Leach. American Anthropologist 62:690-691.

844.   -----
         1963a   Kapauku Papuan Economy. Yale University,
                 Publications in Anthropology No. 67.
                 New Haven.

845.   -----
         1963b   The Kapauku Papuans of West New Guinea.
                 Case Studies in Cultural Anthropology Series.
                 New York: Holt, Rinehart and Winston.

846.   -----
         1965a   A Formal Analysis of Substantive Law:
                 Kapauku Papuan Laws of Inheritance. In
                 The Ethnography of Law. Special Publication.
                 American Anthropologist, Vol. 67, No. 6,
                 Part 2. Laura Nader, Ed. pp. 166-185.

847.   -----
         1965b   A Formal Analysis of Substantive Law:
                 Kapauku Papuan Laws of Land Tenure. In
                 Formal Semantic Analysis. Special
                 Publication. American Anthropologist,
                 Vol. 67, No. 5, Part 2. E.A. Hammel, Ed.
                 pp. 186-214.

848.   -----
         1966   A Note on Goldberg's Note. American
                 Anthropologist 68:1491-1494.

849.   -----
         1969   Structural Change and Primitive Law:
                 Consequences of a Papuan Legal Case. In
                 Law in Culture and Society. Laura Nader,
                 Ed. Chicago: Aldine. pp. 208-229.

850.   -----
         1971   Anthropology of Law: A Comparative
                 Theory. New York: Harper and Row.

851.   Pospisil, Leopold and D.J. de Solla Price: KAPAUKU
         1966   A Survival of Babylonian Arithmetic in New
                 Guinea? Indian Journal of History of
                 Science 1:30-33.

852. Pouwer, Jan: STAR MOUNTAINS
    1964 A Social System in the Star Mountains:
          Toward a Reorientation of the Study of
          Social Systems. In James B. Watson, Ed.
          (Ref. 373), pp. 133-161.

853. Quinlivan, Paul J.: TELEFOL
    1954 Afek of Telefolmin: A Fabulous Story
          from New Guinea Which Lead to a Strange
          Tragedy. Oceania 25:17-22.

854. Raich, Hermann: ENGA
    1967 Ein weiteres fruchtbarkeitsidol aus dem
          westlichen hochland von Neuguinea.
          Anthropos 62:938-939.

855. Rappaport, Roy A.: MARING
    1966 Ritual in the Ecology of a New Guinea
          People: An Anthropological Study of the
          Tsembaga Maring. Ph.D. Thesis, New York,
          Columbia University.

856. -----
    1967a Pigs for the Ancestors: Ritual in the
          Ecology of a New Guinea People. New Haven:
          Yale University Press.

857. -----
    1967b Ritual Regulation of Environmental Relations
          among a New Guinea People. Ethnology 6:
          17-30.

858. -----
    1969a Marriage among the Maring. In Robert M.
          Glasse and Mervyn J. Meggitt, Eds. (Ref.
          280), pp. 117-137.

859. -----
    1969b Population Dispersal and Land Redistribution
          among the Maring of New Guinea. In
          Contributions to Anthropology: Ecological
          Essays. National Museums of Canada,
          Bulletin No. 230, Anthropological Series,
          No. 86. David Damas, Ed. Ottawa: Queen's
          Printer for Canada. pp. 113-126.

860. -----
    1971a The Flow of Energy in an Agricultural
          Society. Scientific American 224(3):116-
          132.

861. -----
    1971b Nature, Culture, and Ecological Anthropology.
          In Man, Culture, and Society (Rev. Ed.).

Harry L. Shapiro, Ed. New York: Oxford
University Press. pp. 237-267.

862. -----
       1971c Ritual, Sanctity and Cybernetics. American
              Anthropologist 73:59-76.

863. -----
       1971d The Sacred in Human Evolution. Annual
              Review of Ecology and Systematics, Vol. 2,
              pp. 23-44. Palo Alto, Calif.

864. Rawling, Cecil G.: UHUNDUNI
       1911   Explorations in Dutch New Guinea.
              Geographical Journal 38:233-255 and map
              ff. p. 344.

865. -----
       1913   The Land of the New Guinea Pygmies: An
              Account of the Story of a Pioneer Journey
              of Exploration into the Heart of New
              Guinea. London: Seeley, Service.

866. Read, Kenneth E.: GAHUKU
       1951a Developmental Projects in the Central
              Highlands of New Guinea. South Pacific
              5:202-207.

867. -----
       1951b The Gahuku-Gama of the Central Highlands.
              South Pacific 5:154-164.

868. -----
       1952a Land in the Central Highlands. South
              Pacific 6:440-449, 465.

869. -----
       1952b Nama Cult of the Central Highlands, New
              Guinea. Oceania 23:1-25.

870. -----
       1952c Missionary Activities and Social Change in
              the Central Highlands. South Pacific 5:
              229-238.

871. -----
       1954   Marriage among the Gahuku-Gama of the
              Eastern Central Highlands, New Guinea.
              South Pacific 7:864-870.

872. -----
       1955   Morality and the Concept of Person among
              the Gahuku-Gama, Eastern Highlands, New
              Guinea. Oceania 25:233-282.

873. ------
    1959   Leadership and Consensus in a New Guinea
             Society. American Anthropologist 61:425-
             436.

874. ------
    1965   The High Valley. New York: Charles
             Scribner's Sons.

875. Reay, Marie: WAHGI
    1957   The Kuma: A Study of Tradition, Freedom and
             Conformity among a New Guinea People. Ph.D.
             Thesis, Canberra, The Australian National
             University.

876. ------
    1959a   Individual Ownership and Transfer of Land
             among the Kuma. Man, Vol. 59, Art. 109,
             pp. 78-82.

877. ------
    1959b   The Kuma: Freedom and Conformity in the
             New Guinea Highlands. Melbourne: Melbourne
             University Press.

878. ------
    1959c   Two Kinds of Ritual Conflict. Oceania 29:
             290-296.

879. ------
    1960   "Mushroom Madness" in the New Guinea
             Highlands. Oceania 31:137-139.

880. ------
    1962   The Sweet Witchcraft of Kuma Dream
             Experience. Mankind 5:459-463.

881. ------
    1964   Present-day Politics in the New Guinea
             Highlands. In James B. Watson, Ed. (Ref.
             373), pp. 240-256.

882. ------
    1965   Mushrooms and Collective Hysteria.
             Australian Territories 5(1):18-28.

883. ------
    1967   Structural Co-Variants of Land Shortage
             among Patrilineal Peoples. Anthropological
             Forum 2:4-19. (also see Ronald M. Berndt
             and Peter Lawrence, Eds., Ref. 238, pp. 175-
             190).

884. -----
         1969a   But Whose Estates? The Wahgi Smallholders.
                 New Guinea 4(3):64-68.

885. -----
         1969b   Myth and Tradition as Historical Evidence.
                 In The History of Melanesia (Ref. 289),
                 pp. 463-475.

886. -----
         1970   Roads and Bridges between Three Levels of
                 Politics. In Marion W. Ward, Ed. (Ref.
                 366), pp. 531-548.

887. -----
         1973-   Generating Political Conflict: Some
         1974   Consequences of Economic Exploitation of
                 the New Guinea Highlands. Anthropological
                 Forum 3:295-305.

888. -----
         1974   Changing Conventions of Dispute Settlement
                 in the Minj Area. In A.L. Epstein, Ed.
                 (Ref. 270), pp. 198-239.

889. Riebe, I.: KARAM
         1974   "...And Then We Killed.": An Attempt to
                 Understand the Fighting History of Upper
                 Kaironk Valley Kalam from 1900-1962.
                 M.A. Thesis, Sydney, University of Sydney.

890. Riesenfeld, Alphonse: CHIMBU
         1956   On the Relationship between the "Mt. Hagen"
                 and "Massim" Axes of New Guinea. In Die
                 Wiener Schule der Volkerkunde. J. Haekel
                 et al., Eds. Vienna: Verlag Ferdinand
                 Berger. pp. 473-475.

891. Robbins, Sterling G.: AUYANA
         1970   Warfare, Marriage and the Distribution of
                 Goods in Auyana. Ph.D. Thesis, Seattle,
                 University of Washington.

892. Rodrigue, Roger B.: HULI
         1963   A Report on a Widespread Psychological
                 Disorder Called "Lulu" Seen among the
                 Huli Linguistic Group in Papua. Oceania
                 33:274-279.

893. Rosch, Eleanor H.: DANI (also see Heider, E.R.)
         1973   Natural Categories. Cognitive Psychology
                 4:328-350.

94. Ross, John A.: CHIMBU
    1965 The Puberty Ceremony of the Chimbu Girl in
         the Eastern Highlands of New Guinea.
         Anthropos 60:423-432.

95. Ross, William A.: HAGEN
    1936 Ethnological Notes on Mt. Hagen Tribes.
         with Special Reference to the Tribe Called
         Mogei. Anthropos 31:341-363.

96. Rothenbush, Don: ENGA
    1970 Tension between the Individual and the
         Corporate in Enga Society. In Paul W.
         Brennan, Ed. (Ref. 240), pp. 319-333.

97. Ryan, D'Arcy J.: MENDI
    1955 Clan Organisation in the Mendi Valley.
         Oceania 26:79-90.

98. ------
    1958a Names and Naming in Mendi. Oceania 29:
          109-116.

99. ------
    1958b Some Decorated Fighting-Shields from the
          Mendi Valley, Southern Highlands District
          of Papua. Mankind 5:243-249.

00. ------
    1959 Clan Formation in the Mendi Valley.
         Oceania 29:257-289.

01. ------
    1962 Gift Exchange in the Mendi Valley: An
         Examination of the Socio-Political
         Implications of the Ceremonial Exchange
         of Wealth among the People of the Mendi
         Valley, Southern Highlands District, Papua.
         Ph.D. Thesis, Sydney, University of Sydney.

02. ------
    1969 Marriage in Mendi. In Robert M. Glasse
         and Mervyn J. Meggitt, Eds. (Ref. 280),
         pp. 159-175.

03. Sackschewsky, Marvin: ENGA
    1970 The Clan Meeting in Enga Society. In
         Paul W. Brennan, Ed. (Ref. 240), pp. 51-101.

04. Salisbury, Richard F.: SIANE
    1956a Asymmetrical Marriage Systems. American
          Anthropologist 58:639-655.

905.   -----
       1956b   Unilineal Descent Groups in the New
               Guinea Highlands. Man, Vol. 56, Art. 2,
               pp. 2-7.

906.   -----
       1957   Reply to Leach. American Anthropologist
               59:344-346.

907.   -----
       1958a   Economic Change among the Siane Tribes of
               New Guinea. Ph.D. Thesis, Canberra, The
               Australian National University.

908.   -----
       1958b   An "Indigenous" New Guinea Cult. Kroeber
               Anthropological Society, Papers 18:67-78.

909.   -----
       1960   Ceremonial Economics and Political
               Equilibrium. Sixth International Congress
               of Anthropological and Ethnological
               Sciences, Proceedings, Vol. 2, pp. 255-259.

910.   -----
       1962a   Early Stages of Economic Development in
               New Guinea. Journal of the Polynesian
               Society 71:328-339.

911.   -----
       1962b   From Stone to Steel: Economic Consequences
               of a Technological Change in New Guinea.
               Melbourne: Melbourne University Press.

912.   -----
       1964a   Changes in Land Use and Tenure among the
               Siane of the New Guinea Highlands, 1952-61.
               Pacific Viewpoint 5:1-10.

913.   -----
       1964b   Despotism and Australian Administration in
               the New Guinea Highlands. In James B.
               Watson, Ed. (Ref. 373), pp. 225-239.

914.   -----
       1964c   New Guinea Highland Models and Descent
               Theory. Man, Vol. 64, Art. 213, pp. 168-171.

915.   -----
       1965   The Siane of the Eastern Highlands. In
               Peter Lawrence and Mervyn J. Meggitt, Eds.
               (Ref. 308), pp. 50-77.

916. -----
1966a   Possession among the Siane (New Guinea).
          Transcultural Psychiatric Research 3:
          108-116.

917. -----
1966b   Structuring Ignorance: The Genesis of a
          Myth in New Guinea. Anthropologica 8:
          315-328.

918. Salisbury, Richard F. and Mary E. Salisbury: SIANE
1972   The Rural-Oriented Strategy of Urban
          Adaptation: Siane Migrants in Port
          Moresby. In The Anthropology of Urban
          Environments. Society for Applied
          Anthropology, Monograph No. 11. Thomas
          Weaver and Douglas White, Eds. pp. 59-68.

919. Schäfer, Alfons: CHIMBU
1938a   Im Wagital, dem paradies von Neuguinea.
          Steyler Missionsbote 66(2):29-33, 75-79.

920. -----
1938b   Kavagl -- der mann mit der zaunfahlkeule:
          Ein beitrag zur individuenforschung.
          Anthropos 33:107-113.

921. -----
1938c   Zur initiation im Wagi-tal. Anthropos
          33:401-423.

922. -----
1942   Ein frauenbegräbnis bei den Korugu im
          Wagi-tal, Zentral-Neuguinea. Ethnos 7:
          25-43.

923. -----
1945   Haus und siedlung in Zentral-Neuguinea.
          Ethnos 10:97-114.

924. Scheimann, Max: ENGA
1970   Motivations for Christianity: Satisfaction
          of Enga Needs. In Paul W. Brennan, Ed.
          (Ref. 240), pp. 334-371.

925. Schiefenhoevel, Wulf: BOSAVI
1971   Aspects of the Medical System of the
          Kaluli and Woragu Language-Group, Southern
          Highlands District. Mankind 8:141-145.

926. Schieffelin, Edward L.: BOSAVI
1968   The Sorrow of the Lonely and the Burning
          of the Dancers. Eighth International
          Congress of Anthropological and Ethnological

Sciences, Tokyo, Proceedings, Vol. 2,
pp. 342-345.

927. -----
1972   The Gisaro: Ceremonialism and Reciprocity
in a New Guinea Tribe. Ph.D. Thesis,
Chicago, University of Chicago.

928. Schuster, Meinhard: TELEFOL
1969   In the Heart of New Guinea: The Eriptaman.
Sandoz Bulletin 14:19-27.

929. Shand, R.T. and W. Straatmans: SINASINA
1974   Transition from Subsistence: Cash Crop
Development in Papua New Guinea. New
Guinea Research Unit, Bulletin 54. Port
Moresby.

930. Sinha, D.P.: HAGEN
1969   The Wurup Project in New Guinea Highlands:
Strategies in Planned Change. Oceania 39:
290-297.

931. Skingle, D.C.: FAIWOL, OKSAPMIN and TELEFOL
1970   Some Medicinal Herbs Used by the Natives
of New Guinea. Mankind 7:223-225.

932. Skinner, R.I.: SINASINA
1940   Customs of People in the Mai (Mairifutika)
River Valley. Report to the League of
Nations on the Administration of the
Territory of New Guinea for 1938-39.
Canberra: Government Printer. pp. 21-22.

933. Smith, Marian W.: HAGEN
1950   Additional Materials on Mt. Hagen, New
Guinea. American Anthropologist 52:282.

934. Sorenson, E. Richard: FORE
1971   The Evolving Fore: A Study of Socialization
and Culture Change in the New Guinea
Highlands. Ph.D. Thesis, Stanford,
Stanford University.

935. -----
1972   Socio-Ecological Change among the Fore of
New Guinea. Current Anthropology 13:
349-383 (incl. Comments and Reply).

936. Sorenson, E. Richard and D. Carleton Gajdusek: FORE
1969   Nutrition in the Kuru Region. I. Gardening,
Food Handling, and Diet of the Fore People.
Acta Tropica 26:281-330.

937. Steadman, Lyle B.: HEWA
     1971   Neighbours and Killers: Residence and
            Dominance among the Hewa of New Guinea.
            Ph.D. Thesis, Canberra, The Australian
            National University.

938. Sterly, Joachim: CHIMBU
     1971   Eine krankenbehandlung am oberern Chimbu,
            New Guinea. Ethnomedizin 1:292-293.

939. -----
     1972   Social Context of Epidemic Syphilis in
            the Chimbu District, New Guinea.
            Ethnomedizin 2:311-328.

940. -----
     1973   Krankheiten und krankenbehandlung bei den
            Chimbu im Zentralen hochland von Neu-
            Guinea. Beitrage zur Ethnomedizin,
            Ethnobotanik und Ethnozoologie II.
            Hamburg: Arbeitsgemeinschaft Ethnomedizin.

941. Stöcklin, W.H.: FORE
     1965   Medizin und schwarze magie bei den Fore im
            östlichen hochland Neu-Guineas. In
            Festschrift Alfred Buhler. Basler Beitrage
            zur Geographie und Ethnologie, Ethnologische
            Reihe, Band 2. C.A. Schmitz and R.
            Wildhaber, Eds. Basel. pp. 389-400.

942. -----
     1967   Kuru -- The Laughing Death. Medizinische
            und ethnologische aspekte einer rätselhaffen
            krankheit im hochland Neuguineas. Acta
            Tropica 24:193-224.

943. -----
     1972   Die kurukrankheit in ethnomedizinischer
            sicht. Ethnomedizin 2:91-98.

944. Stöcklin, W.H.: GANATI and SIMBARI
     1968   Kukukuku. Medical Patrol into One of the
            Last Restricted Areas in the New Guinea
            Highlands. Acta Tropica 25:193-216.

945. Stopp, Klaus: HAGEN
     1963   Medicinal Plants of the Mount Hagen People
            (Mbowamb) in New Guinea. Economic Botany
            17:16-22.

946. Stotik, Karl: ENGA
     1970   The Missionary as an Agent of Culture
            Change. In Paul W. Brennan, Ed. (Ref. 240),
            pp. 212-234.

947. Strathern, Andrew J.: HAGEN
      1966a Ceremonial Exchange in the Mount Hagen
             Area. Ph.D. Thesis, Cambridge, Cambridge
             University.

948. -----
      1966b Despots and Directors in the New Guinea
             Highlands. Man, N.S., 1:356-367.

949. -----
      1968   Sickness and Frustration: Variations in
             Two New Guinea Highlands Societies.
             Mankind 6:545-551. (also WIRU).

950. -----
      1969   Kor-nga poklambo or ui mbo? Hagen Magic
             Stones. Archaeology and Physical
             Anthropology in Oceania 4:91-96.

951. -----
      1970a The Female and Male Spirit Cults in Mount
             Hagen. Man, N.S., 5:571-585.

952. -----
      1970b Kiap, Councillor, and Big Man: Role-
             Contrasts in Mount Hagen. In Marion W.
             Ward, Ed. (Ref. 366), pp. 549-567.

953. -----
      1970c Male Initiation in New Guinea Highlands
             Societies. Ethnology 9:373-379.

954. -----
      1970d To Choose a Strong Man: The House of
             Assembly Elections in Mul-Dei, 1968.
             Oceania 41:136-147.

955. -----
      1971a Cargo and Inflation in Mount Hagen.
             Oceania 41:255-265.

956. -----
      1971b Pig Complex and Cattle Complex: Some
             Comparisons and Counterpoints. Mankind
             8:129-136.

957. -----
      1971c The Rope of Moka: Big-Men and Ceremonial
             Exchange in Mount Hagen, New Guinea.
             Cambridge Studies in Social Anthropology,
             No. 4. London: Cambridge University Press.

958. -----
      1972a The Entrepeneurial Model of Social Change:

From Norway to New Guinea. Ethnology 11: 368-379.

959. ----- 1972b One Father, One Blood: Descent and Group Structure among the Melpa People, Mount Hagen, New Guinea. Canberra: The Australian National University Press.

960. ----- 1972c Social Pressures on the Rural Entrepeneur. In Marion W. Ward, Ed. (Ref. 368), pp. 489-503.

961. ----- 1972d The Supreme Court: A Matter of Prestige and Power. Melanesian Law Journal 1(3):23-28.

962. ----- 1973 Political Development and Problems of Social Control in Mt. Hagen. In Ronald J. May, Ed. (Ref. 316), pp. 37-82.

963. ----- 1974a Melpa Land Tenure: Rules and Processes. In Land Tenure in Oceania. Association for Social Anthropology in Oceania, Monograph No. 2. Henry P. Lundsgaarde, Ed. Honolulu: University Press of Hawaii. pp. 18-38.

964. ----- 1974b When Dispute Procedures Fail. In A.L. Epstein, Ed. (Ref. 270), pp. 240-270.

965. Strathern, Andrew J. and A. Marilyn Strathern: HAGEN 1964 Minj Open Electorate: The Campaign in the Dei Council Area. Journal of the Polynesian Society 73:209-211.

966. ----- 1968 Marsupials and Magic: A Study of Spell . Symbolism among the Mbowamb. In Dialectic in Practical Religion. Cambridge Papers in Social Anthropology, No. 5. Edmund R. Leach, Ed. London: Cambridge University Press. pp. 179-202.

967. ----- 1969 Marriage in Melpa. In Robert M. Glasse and Mervyn J. Meggitt, Eds. (Ref. 280), pp. 138-158.

968. ----- 1971 Self-Decoration in Mount Hagen. London:

Duckworth and Toronto: University of
Toronto Press.

969. Strathern, Andrew J.: WIRU
1970 Wiru Penthonyms. Bijdragen tot de Taal-,
Land- en Volkenkunde 126:59-74.

970. -----
1971 Wiru and Daribi Matrilateral Payments.
Journal of the Polynesian Society 80:
449-462. (also MIKARU).

971. Strathern, A. Marilyn: HAGEN
1965 Axe Types and Quarries: A Note on the
Classification of Stone Axe Blades from
the Hagen Area, New Guinea. Journal of
the Polynesian Society 74:182-191.

972. -----
1968a Popokl: The Question of Morality. Mankind
6:553-562.

973. -----
1968b Women's Status in the Mount Hagen Area:
A Study of Marital Relations and Court
Disputes among the Melpa-Speaking Peoples.
Ph.D. Thesis, London, Cambridge University.

974. -----
1969a Stone Axes and Flake Tools: Evaluations
from Two New Guinea Highlands Societies.
Proceedings of the Prehistoric Society
35:311-329. (also WIRU).

975. -----
1969b Why is the Pueraria a Sweet Potato?
Ethnology 8:189-198.

976. -----
1971 Legality or Legitimacy: Hageners' Perception
of the Judicial System. Melanesian Law
Journal 1(2):5-27.

977. -----
1972a Absentee Businessmen: The Reaction at Home
to Hageners Migrating to Port Moresby.
Oceania 43:17-39.

978. -----
1972b Official and Unofficial Courts: Legal
Assumptions and Expectations in a Highlands
Community. New Guinea Research Unit,
Bulletin 47. Port Moresby.

979.   -----
        1972c   Women In Between: Female Roles in a Male
                World, Mount Hagen, New Guinea. New York:
                Seminar Press.

980.   -----
        1974   Managing Information: The Problems of a
                Dispute-Settler (Mount Hagen). In A.L.
                Epstein, Ed. (Ref. 271), pp. 271-316.

981.   Strauss, H. and H. Tischner: HAGEN
        1962   Die Mi-kultur der Hagenberg-stämme im
                östlichen Zentral-Neuguinea. Museum für
                Völkerkunde, Monographien zur Völkerkunde
                III. Hamburg: Kommissionsverlag Cram,
                de Gruyter and Co.

982.   Tischner, Herbert: HAGEN
        1939   Eine ethnographische sammlung aus dem
                östlichen Zentral-Neuguinea (Hagen-Gebirge,
                Wagi-tal, Ramu). Museum für Völkerkunde,
                Mitteilungen, Vol. 21. Hamburg: Friedefischen,
                de Gruyter and Co.

983.   Tomasetti, William E.: CHIMBU
        1966   Community Development and the Chimbu. In
                Eben H. Hipsley, Ed. (Ref. 1659), pp. 85-94.

984.   Turner, Charles V.: SINASINA
        1964a   The "Grease" Complex of New Guinea.
                Practical Anthropology 11:233-234.

985.   -----
        1964b   The Socio-Religious Significance of Baptism
                in Sinasina. Practical Anthropology 11:
                179-180.

986.   -----
        1966   Culture Change and the Sinasina Church.
                Practical Anthropology 13:103-106.

987.   -----
        1968   The Sinasina "Big Man" Complex: A Central
                Culture Theme. Practical Anthropology 15:
                16-23.

988.   -----
        1970   The Sinasina Stone Bowl Cult. Practical
                Anthropology 17:28-32.

989.   Tyler, Michael J.: KARAM
        1961   A Preliminary Note on Herpetological Data
                Obtained from Natives in the Central
                Highlands of New Guinea. British Journal

oi Herpetology 2:219-220.

990. Vayda, Andrew P.: MARING
     1970 On the Nutritional Value of Cannibalism.
           American Anthropologist 72:1462-1463.

991. -----
     1971 Phases of the Process of War and Peace
           among the Marings of New Guinea. Oceania
           42:240. (also see Erratum, 1972, 42:240).

992. -----
     1974 Functions of War. Man, N.S., 9:141, 489.

993. Vayda, Andrew P. and Edwin A. Cook: MARING and NARAK
     1964 Structural Variability in the Bismarck
           Mountain Cultures of New Guinea: A
           Preliminary Report. New York Academy of
           Sciences, Transactions 26:798-803.

994. Vicedom, G.F.: HAGEN
     1938 Ein neuentdecktes volk in Neuguinea:
           Völkerkundliche beobachtungen an der
           bevölkerung des Hagen-berges im ehemals
           Deutschen teil von Neuguinea. Archiv für
           Anthropologie 24:11-44, 190-213.

995. -----
     1962 Junge kirche in Neuguinea. Stuttgart:
           Evangelischer Missionsverlag.

996. Vicedom, G.F. and Herbert Tischner: HAGEN
     1943- Die Mbowamb: Die kultur der Hagenberg-
     1948   stämme im östlichen Zentral-Neuguinea.
            Museum für Völkerkunde und Vorgeschichte,
            Monographien zur Völkerkunde, 3 Vols.
            Hamburg: Friederichsen, de Gruyter and Co.

997. Vincin, D.R.: MIKARU
     1970 Attitudes to Leprosy: Influence on
           Epidemiology and Control. Search 1(5):
           254-255.

998. Waddell, Eric W.: ENGA
     1967 The Dynamics of a New Guinea Highlands
           Agricultural System. Ph.D. Thesis,
           Canberra, The Australian National University.

999. -----
     1972a Agricultural Evolution in the New Guinea
            Highlands. Pacific Viewpoint 13:18-29.

1000. -----
      1972b The Mound Builders: Agricultural Practices,

Environment and Society in the Central
Highlands of New Guinea. American
Ethnological Society, Monograph No. 53.
Seattle: University of Washington Press.

001.   -----
        1973   Raiapu Enga Adaptive Strategies: Structure
                and General Implications. In Harold C.
                Brookfield, Ed. (Ref. 246), pp. 25-54.

002.   Wagner, Merlyn: ENGA
        1970   The Enga Concept of Fear. In Paul W.
                Brennan, Ed. (Ref. 240), pp. 245-318.

003.   Wagner, Roy: MIKARU
        1966   The Curse of Souw: Principles of Daribi
                Clan Definition and Alliance. Ph.D. Thesis,
                Chicago, University of Chicago.

004.   -----
        1967   The Curse of Souw: Principles of Daribi
                Clan Definition and Alliance in New
                Guinea. Chicago: University of Chicago
                Press.

005.   -----
        1969   Marriage among the Daribi. In Robert M.
                Glasse and Mervyn J. Meggitt, Eds. (Ref.
                280), pp. 56-76. (also see Corrections
                in American Anthropologist, 1970, 72:725-
                726 and Oceania, 1969, 40:155).

006.   -----
        1970   Daribi and Foraba Cross-Cousin Terminologies:
                A Structural Comparison. Journal of the
                Polynesian Society 79:91-98. (also FORABA).

007.   -----
        1971   A Problem of Ethnocide: When a Chimbu Meets
                a Karimui. New Guinea 6(2):27-31. (also
                CHIMBU).

008.   -----
        1972a   Comment on E. Richard Sorenson, "Socio-
                Ecological Change among the Fore of New
                Guinea" (Ref. 935). Current Anthropology
                13:376-377.

009.   -----
        1972b   Habu: The Innovation of Meaning in Daribi
                Religion. Chicago: University of Chicago
                Press.

1010. -----
        1972c Mathematical Prediction of Polygamy Rates
               among the Daribi of Karimui Patrol Post,
               Territory of Papua New Guinea. Oceania
               42:205-222.

1011. -----
        1974   Are There Social Groups in the New Guinea
               Highlands? In Frontiers of Anthropology:
               An Introduction to Anthropological
               Thinking. Murray J. Leaf, Ed. New York:
               D. Van Nostrand. pp. 95-122.

1012. Watson, James B.: AGARABE
        1960   A New Guinea "Opening Man." In In the
               Company of Man: Twenty Portraits of
               Anthropological Informants. Joseph B.
               Casagrande, Ed. New York: Harper and Row.
               pp. 127-173.

1013. -----
        1963   Krakatoa's Echo? Journal of the Polynesian
               Society 72:152-155.

1014. -----
        1967   Horticultural Traditions of the Eastern
               New Guinea Highlands. Oceania 38:81-98.
               (also TAIRORA).

1015. -----
        1972   Talking to Strangers. In Crossing Cultural
               Boundaries: The Anthropological Experience.
               Solon T. Kimball and James B. Watson, Eds.
               San Francisco: Chandler. pp. 172-181.

1016. Watson, James B.: GADSUP (data from B.M. DuToit)
        1965   Loose Structure Loosely Construed:
               Groupless Groupings in Gadsup? Oceania
               35:267-271.

1017. Watson, James B.: TAIRORA
        1964   A Previously Unreported Root Crop from the
               New Guinea Highlands. Ethnology 3:1-5.

1018. -----
        1967   Tairora: The Politics of Despotism in a
               Small Society. Anthropological Forum 2:
               53-104. (also see Ronald M. Berndt and
               Peter Lawrence, Eds., Ref. 238, pp. 224-275)

1019. -----
        1970   Society as Organized Flow: The Tairora
               Case. Southwestern Journal of Anthropology
               26:107-124.

020. Watson, James B. and Virginia D. Watson: TAIRORA
     1972   Batainabura of New Guinea. 3 Vols.
             HRAFlex Books, Ethnocentrism Series,
             OJI-005, 006 and 007. New Haven: Human
             Relations Area Files.

021. Watson, Virginia D.: AGARABE
     1955   Pottery in the Eastern Highlands of New
             Guinea. Southwestern Journal of
             Anthropology 11:121-128.

022. -----
     1965   Agarabi Female Roles and Family Structure:
             A Study in Socio-Cultural Change. Ph.D.
             Thesis, Chicago, University of Chicago.

023. Westermann, T.: ENGA
     1968   The Mountain People: Social Institutions
             of the Laiapu Enga. Wapenamanda: Kristen
             Press.

024. White, J. Peter: DUNA
     1968a   Fabricators, Outils Ecailles or Scalar
             Cores? Mankind 6:658-666.

025. -----
     1968b   Ston Naip Bilong Tumbuna. In La Prehistoire:
             Problemes et Tendances. D. de Sonneville-
             Bordes, Ed. Paris: CNRS. pp. 511-515.

026. White, J. Peter and D.H. Thomas: DUNA
     1972   What Mean These Stones? Ethno-Taxonomic
             Models and Archaeological Interpretations
             in the New Guinea Highlands. In Models in
             Archaeology. David L. Clarke, Ed. London:
             Methuen. pp. 275-308.

027. Whiteman, Josephine: CHIMBU
     1965a   Customs and Beliefs Relating to Food,
             Nutrition and Health in the Chimbu Area.
             Tropical and Geographical Medicine 17:
             301-316.

028. -----
     1965b   Girls' Puberty Ceremonies amongst the
             Chimbu. Anthropos 60:410-422.

029. -----
     1966   Social Factors Influencing Health Education
             among the Chimbu. International Journal of
             Health Education 9:8-15.

030. -----
     1972   A Study of Chimbu Conjugal Relationships.

M.A. Thesis, Sydney, University of New South Wales.

1031. -----
    1973   Chimbu Family Relationships in Port
            Moresby. New Guinea Research Unit,
            Bulletin 52. Port Moresby.

1032. Williams, F.E.: AUGU
    1940   Report on the Grasslanders. Territory of
            Papua, Annual Report for 1938-39. Canberra:
            Government Printer. pp. 39-67.

1033. Williams, F.E.: FOI
    1940-   Natives of Lake Kutubu, Papua. Oceania
    1942   11:121-157, 259-294, 374-401; 12:49-74,
            134-154. (also Oceania Monograph No. 6).

1034. -----
    1941   Group Sentiment and Primitive Justice.
            American Anthropologist 43:523-539.

1035. Williams, F.E.: HAGEN
    1937   The Natives of Mount Hagen, Papua: Further
            Notes. Man, Vol. 37, Art. 114, pp. 90-96.

1036. Wirz, Paul: DANI
    1924   Anthropologische und ethnologische
            ergebnisse der Central Neu-Guinea
            Expedition 1921-1922. Nova Guinea 14(1).

1037. Wolfers, Edward P.: HULI
    1971   A Prehistoric Pestle and Mortar from Tari,
            Southern Highlands District, with Some
            Notes on Their Use among the Huli. Papua
            New Guinea Museum Records 1(2):9-12.

1038. Wollaston, A.F.R.: UHUNDUNI
    1912   Pygmies and Papuans: The Stone Age To-Day
            in Dutch New Guinea. London: John Murray.

1039. -----
    1914   An Expedition to Dutch New Guinea.
            Geographical Journal 43:248-273 and map
            ff. p. 364.

1040. Wurm, Helen: GAHUKU
    1961   Sing Sing at Kofuni, Eastern Highlands of
            New Guinea. Australian Territories 1(3):
            26-31.

2. Agriculture and Animal Husbandry Studies

041. Aitchison, T.G.
      1960   The Pig and Its Place in the Impact of the
             New Guinean on Vegetation. In UNESCO
             (Ref. 360), pp. 158-167.
             General discussion of ecological and
             economic dimensions of pig husbandry.

042. Aland, F.P. and D.A. Torlach
      1970   Agricultural Potential. In R. Gerard
             Ward and David A.M. Lea, Eds. (Ref. 49),
             pp. 50-51.
             Brief discussion and mapping of areas
             suitable for agriculture, grazing or
             neither in Papua New Guinea.

043. Anderson, J.L.
      1972   Livestock. In Peter Ryan, Gen. Ed.
             (Ref. 11), Vol. 2, pp. 645-646.
             Discussion of history and present
             administration programs of livestock
             introduction to indigenous villages.

044. Artschwager, E. and E.W. Brandes
      1958   Sugar Cane (Saccharum officinarum L.):
             Origin, Classification and Description
             of Representative Clones. United States
             Department of Agriculture, Agricultural
             Handbook No. 122. Washington, D.C.:
             Government Printing Office.
             Basic reference work on important
             Highlands cultigen.

045. Barrau, Jacques
      1958   Subsistence Ahriculture in Melanesia.
             Bernice P. Bishop Museum Bulletin 219.
             Honolulu.
             Standard reference work and general
             survey of crops, ecology and cultivation
             techniques; includes illustrative
             material from DANI and KAPAUKU of Irian
             Jaya.

046. -----
      1965   L'Humide et le Sec: An Essay on
             Ethnobiological Adaptation to Contrastive
             Environments in the Indo-Pacific Area.
             Journal of the Polynesian Society 74:
             329-346.
             Discussion of wet and dry environments
             in relation to horticulture; includes
             sketch of DANI irrigation techniques.

1047.   Barrie, J.W.
        1956a   Coffee in the Highlands. Papua New Guinea
                Agricultural Journal 11:1-29.
                Description of coffee introduction to
                CHIMBU area.

1048.   -----
        1956b   Population-Land Investigation in the
                Chimbu Sub-district. Papua New Guinea
                Agricultural Journal 11:45-51.
                Brief discussion of population
                pressure and CHIMBU horticulture.

1049.   Brass, L.J.
        1941   Stone Age Agriculture in New Guinea.
                Geographical Review 31:555-569.
                Detailed and illustrated description
                of horticultural techniques of Baliem
                Valley and Pesegem DANI.

1050.   Brookfield, Harold C.
        1958   The Land. In John Wilkes, Ed. (Ref. 13),
                pp. 1-45.
                General survey of resources and
                possibilities for development.

1051.   -----
        1966   An Assessment of Natural Resources. In
                E.K. Fisk, Ed. (Ref. 3), pp. 44-79.
                Similar to Ref. 1050 but based on more
                recent field surveys.

1052.   -----
        1968   New Directions in the Study of Agricultural
                Systems in Tropical Areas. In Evolution
                and Environment. Ellen T. Drake, Ed.
                New Haven: Yale University Press. pp. 413-
                439.
                General discussion of proposals for
                quantitative and systematic studies;
                passing references to CHIMBU.

1053.   -----
        1972   Intensification and Disintensification in
                Pacific Agriculture: A Theoretical Approach.
                Pacific Viewpoint 13:30-48.
                General discussion of study of
                agricultural systems; illustrative
                material from CHIMBU.

1054.   Brown, M. and J.M. Powell
        1972   Frost in the Highlands of Papua New Guinea.
                Science in New Guinea 1(1):45-47.

1055.   -----
         1974   Frost and Drought in the Highlands of
                 Papua New Guinea. Journal of Tropical
                 Geography 38:1-6.
                 Both sources report results of 1972
                 survey of effects of drought and frost
                 on crops in Southern and Western
                 Highlands of Papua New Guinea.

1056.   Burkill, I.H.
         1935   A Dictionary of the Economic Products of
                 the Malay Peninsula. 2 Vols. London:
                 Crown Agents for the Colonies.
                 Standard but slightly dated reference
                 work relevant to most crops and other
                 plants used in New Guinea.

1057.   Cartledge, I.
         1962   Marketing of Coffee from the Territory of
                 Papua and New Guinea. Australian
                 Territories 2(3):23-32.
                 Discussion centering on Goroka and
                 Korofeigu (BENABENA) coffee industry.

1058.   Charles, A.E.
         1972a   Passionfruit Industry. In Peter Ryan,
                 Gen. Ed. (Ref. 11), Vol. 2, pp. 892-894.
                 Description of planting techniques,
                 marketing and present status as cash
                 crop (widely adopted in Highlands).

1059.   -----
         1972b   Pyrethrum Industry. In Peter Ryan, Gen.
                 Ed. (Ref. 11), Vol. 2, pp. 995-997.
                 History of introduction as cash crop
                 in Highlands and discussion of uses and
                 cultivation requirements.

1060.   Cobley, L.
         1956   An Introduction to the Botany of Tropical
                 Crops. London: Longmans, Green.
                 Comprehensive reference work.

1061.   Conroy, W.L.
         1952   Notes on Some Land Use Problems in Papua
                 and New Guinea. Australian Geographer
                 6(2):25-30.
                 Brief discussion; includes material
                 from Wahgi Valley.

1062.   -----
         1960   The Evolution of the Agricultural
                 Environment in Papua and New Guinea. In
                 UNESCO (Ref. 360), pp. 94-97.

Discussion of vegetation changes
resulting from horticulture; illustrated
with material from Sepik and Wahgi
valleys.

1063. Coursey, D.
1968   Yams: An Account of the Nature, Origins,
Cultivation and Utilisation of the Useful
Members of the Dioscoreaceae. New York:
Humanities Press.
Standard reference work on important
Highlands crop.

1064. -----
1972   The Civilizations of the Yam:
Interrelationships of Man and Yams in
Africa and in the Indo-Pacific Region.
Archaeology and Physical Anthropology in
Oceania 7:215-233.
General survey of history and uses of
yams, including New Guinea; extensive
bibliography.

1065. Gillison, A.N.
1972   The Tractable Grasslands of Papua New
Guinea. In Marion W. Ward, Ed. (Ref. 368),
pp. 161-172.
Critical examination of assumptions of
uselessness of grasslands in relation
to horticulture and other human needs.

1066. Grant-Cook, M.
1966   Tea Culture in the Highlands of New
Guinea. Australian Territories 6(1):
13-19.
Discussion of tea cash-cropping in
Garaina and Mount Hagen area.

1067. -----
1969   Tea Industry in Papua and New Guinea.
Australian Territories 9(1):17-21.
Description of tea cash-cropping in
Mount Hagen area.

1068. Haantjens, H.A.
1970a   Agricultural Potential of the Goroka-
Mount Hagen Area. In H.A. Haantjens,
Compiler (Ref. 1069), pp. 146-159.
Classification and description of
suitability of land in area from
Kainantu region to west of Mount Hagen.

1069. ----- (Compiler)
1970b   Lands of the Goroka-Mount Hagen Area,

Territory of Papua and New Guinea. Land
Research Series, No. 27. Melbourne:
Commonwealth Scientific and Industrial
Research Organization.
Collection of papers covering area
from Kainantu region to west of Mount
Hagen.

70. Havel, J.J.
1960a Deflection of Secondary Succession of
Cleared Mid-Mountain Rainforest Sites by
Plantation Tendings. In UNESCO (Ref. 360),
pp. 339-343.
Brief description of regrowth sequence
and dominant species in highland
clearings simulating indigenous
techniques of abandonment and successive
use.

71. -----
1960b Factors Influencing the Establishment of
Ligneous Vegetation in Mid-Mountain Pyro-
and Anthropo-genic Grasslands. In UNESCO
(Ref. 360), pp. 307-312.
Report of study of grasslands in Bulolo
region and Upper Ramu, Asaro, Wahgi
and Mount Hagen areas.

72. Henty, E.E.
1970 Weeds of Coffee in the Central Highlands.
Department of Forests, Division of Botany,
Lae, Botany Bulletin No. 4. Port Moresby:
Government Printer.
Descriptions and drawings of most
common weeds of coffee and subsistence
gardens; suitable for tentative field
identifications.

73. -----
1972 Weeds. In Peter Ryan, Gen. Ed. (Ref. 11),
Vol. 2, pp. 1184-1186.
General discussion and description of
various species and particular crops
most affected.

74. Hill, E.M.
1965 Pyrethrum -- A New Industry for the
Highlands. Australian Territories 5(5):
36-44.
Description of cash-cropping in Mount
Hagen area.

1075. Kimber, A.J.
        1972   The Sweet Potato in Subsistence Agriculture
                Papua and New Guinea Agricultural Journal
                23(3-4):80-102.
                    Discussion of varieties in New Guinea
                    and origin of cultivation.

1076. Laut, P.
        1968   Agricultural Geography. Vol. I. Systems,
                Subsistence and Plantation Agriculture.
                Melbourne: Thomas Nelson.
                    General survey; includes chapter on
                    New Guinea Highlands.

1077. Lea, David A.M.
        1970a   Cash Crop Production by District. In
                R. Gerard Ward and David A.M. Lea, Eds.
                (Ref. 49), pp. 58-59.
                    Brief discussion of history of indigenou
                    cash-cropping; 4 maps show production
                    for two "crops" (coffee and cattle)
                    relevant to Highlands.

1078. -----
        1970b   Staple Crops and Main Sources of Food. In
                R. Gerard Ward and David A.M. Lea, Eds.
                (Ref. 49), pp. 54-55.
                    Brief comments on various staples; map
                    shows areas of principal reliance on
                    each.

1079. -----
        1972   Agriculture, Indigenous. In Peter Ryan,
                Gen. Ed. (Ref. 11), Vol. 1, pp. 10-18.
                    General discussion and survey .

1080. Lea, David A.M. and R. Gerard Ward
        1970   Crop Combinations. In R. Gerard Ward and
                David A.M. Lea, Eds. (Ref. 49), pp. 56-57.
                    General discussion and mapping of
                    various combinations; complements Ref.
                    1078.

1081. McAlpine, J.R.
        1965   Population and Land Use of the Wabag-Tari
                Area. In R.A. Perry et al. (Ref. 1088),
                pp. 125-131.
                    Description of population, settlement
                    and land use for subsistence and
                    commercial production.

1082. -----
        1970   Population and Land Use in the Goroka-

Mount Hagen Area. In H.A. Haantjens,
Compiler (Ref. 1069), pp. 126-145.
Similar in format to Ref. 1081 but
for area indicated.

083. McIntosh, D.H.
1960 The Effect of Man on the Forests of the
Highlands of Eastern New Guinea. In
UNESCO (Ref. 360), pp. 123-126.
Brief discussion of forest/non-forest
ratios and afforestation projects,
based on survey of Upper Ramu, Upper
Lamari, Wahgi, Baiyer and Jimmi
watersheds.

084. Malynicz, George L.
1970 Pig Keeping by the Subsistence
Agriculturalist of the New Guinea
Highlands. Search 1(5):201-204.
Brief discussion of pig husbandry
based on literature.

085. Massal, Emile and Jacques Barrau
1956 Food Plants of the South Sea Islands.
South Pacific Commission, Technical Paper
No. 94. Noumea.
Standard reference work on staple
foods, cultivated and wild.

086. Millar, Andree
1972 Ornamental Plants. In Peter Ryan, Gen.
Ed. (Ref. 11), Vol. 2, pp. 873-876.
General discussion and description of
ornamental garden plants; oriented
toward garden hobbyists but includes
information on plants traditionally
cultivated.

087. Norris, K.R., J.L. Anderson and N.J. Talbot
1972 Livestock Pests. In Peter Ryan, Gen. Ed.
(Ref. 11), Vol. 2, pp. 646-650.
Description of major arthropod pests
and internal parasites, primarily with
reference to cattle, but also pigs,
poultry and dogs.

088. Perry, R.A. et al.
1965 General Report on Lands of the Wabag-Tari
Area, Territory of Papua and New Guinea,
1960-61. Land Research Series No. 15.
Melbourne: Commonwealth Scientific and
Industrial Research Organization.
Collection of papers covering area
from Wabag (Western Highlands) to Lake

Kutubu area of Southern Highlands.

1089. Purdy, D.J.
      1972   Cattle Industry. In Peter Ryan, Gen. Ed.
              (Ref. 11), Vol. 1, pp. 137-141.
              History of introduction and progress
              of administration efforts; discussion
              of potential problems in relation to
              indigenous land tenure systems.

1090. Reynders, J.J.
      1961   Some Remarks about Shifting Cultivation in
              Netherlands New Guinea. Netherlands
              Journal of Agricultural Science 9(1):

1091. -----
      1962   Shifting Cultivation in the Star Mountains
              Area. Nova Guinea (Anthropology) 3:45-73.
              Both sources describe indigenous
              horticulture in STAR MOUNTAINS, Irian
              Jaya.

1092. Rutherford, G.K.
      1964   The Soils and Land Use of the Area Occupied
              by the Enga of the New Guinea Highlands.
              Canadian Geographer 8:142-146.
              Analysis of soils and description of
              horticultural practices of ENGA of
              Lai Valley.

1093. Rutherford, G.K. and R.A. Perry
      1965   Land Use Capability of the Wabag-Tari Area.
              In R.A. Perry et al. (Ref. 1088), pp. 132-
              136.
              Discussion of factors limiting more
              intensive land use and assessment of
              regional potential.

1094. Schindler, A.J.
      1952   Land Use by Natives of Aiyura Village,
              Central Highlands, New Guinea. South
              Pacific 6:302-307.
              General description of horticultural
              system of village of TAIRORA-speakers.

1095. -----
      1959   Pyrethrum in the Highlands of New Guinea.
              Papua and New Guinea Agricultural Journal
              12:1-8.
              Brief discussion of potential as cash
              crop.

096. Shand, R.T.
     1972a Coffee Industry. In Peter Ryan, Gen. Ed.
           (Ref. 11), Vol. 1, pp. 192-195.
           General discussion of cultivation
           requirements, history of introduction
           to Highlands, marketing systems and
           prospects.

097. -----
     1972b Tea Industry. In Peter Ryan, Gen. Ed.
           (Ref. 11), Vol. 2, pp. 1119-1120.
           Brief discussion similar in coverage
           to Ref. 1096.

098. Simmonds, N.W.
     1959 Bananas. London: Longmans, Green.
          Standard reference work on important
          Highlands crop.

099. Straatmans, W.
     1967 Ethnobotany of New Guinea in its Ecological
          Perspective. Journal d'Agriculture
          Tropicale et de Botanique Appliquée 14(1-2):
          1-20.
                    * * * * *

100. Szent-Ivany, J.J.H.
     1972 Insect Pests of Agriculture and Forestry.
          In Peter Ryan, Gen. Ed. (Ref. 11), Vol. 1,
          pp. 559-564.
          Description and drawings of major pests,
          discussed in relation to subsistence
          and cash crops affected.

101. Walker, D.
     1966 Vegetation of the Lake Ipea Region, New
          Guinea Highlands. I. Forest, Grassland
          and "Garden." Journal of Ecology 54:
          503-533.
          Detailed description of vegetation,
          including succession composition in
          fallow garden plots of ENGA.

102. Womersley, John S.
     1972a Crop Plants. In Peter Ryan, Gen. Ed.
           (Ref. 11), Vol. 1, pp. 222-232.
           Description of distribution and uses
           of crops including most recently
           introduced fruits and vegetables.

103. Yen, Douglas E.
     1972 Ethnobotany. In Peter Ryan, Gen. Ed.
          (Ref. 11), Vol. 1, pp. 380-384.
          General discussion of man-flora relations.

Since a large number of the sources listed in this section are published in a long-standing and continuing series abbreviation will be employed in this part of the bibliography. The Linguistic Circle of Canberra (LCC), affiliated with The Australian National University, produces four series: Series A, Occasional Papers; Series B, Monographs; Series C, Books; and Series D, Special Publications, all of which carry the additional title of Pacific Linguistics. An abbreviated entry might read LCC, PL, A12:1-10, which would indicate pp. 1-10 in Occasional Paper No. 12 of this publication series. Where no page numbers are provided the source consists of the entire volume indicated.

A. General Surveys and Comparative Studies

1104. Bee, Darlene
        1965   Comparative and Historical Problems in
                East New Guinea Highland Languages. In
                Papers in New Guinea Linguistics, LCC,
                PL, A6:1-37. (also see Howard P.
                McKaughan, Ed., Ref. 1122, pp. 739-768).
                Comparison of selected features and
                suggestion of historical relationships
                among AGARABE, AUYANA, AWA, BINUMARIEN,
                GADSUP, TAIRORA and USURUFA.

1105. Bee, Darlene and Alan Pence
        1962   Toward Standardization of a Survey Word
                List for Papua and New Guinea. In Summer
                Institute of Linguistics (Ref. 1125),
                pp. 64-75.
                Suggested list of 190 words and phrases
                in English, Neo-Melanesian and Police
                Motu for initial word-list compilation
                in field research.

1106. Bromley, H. Myron
        1967   The Linguistic Relationships of Grand
                Valley Dani: A Lexicostatistical
                Classification. Oceania 37:286-308.
                Calculation of cognate percentages and
                resulting classification of DANI, DEM,
                JALÉ and WANO.

1107. Capell, Arthur
        1948-   Distribution of Languages in the Central
        1949   Highlands, New Guinea. Oceania 19:104-
                129, 234-253, 349-377.

Comprehensive, but now dated, survey of
phonetics, grammar and vocabularies,
based on author's field research;
superseded by more recent field surveys
listed below.

08. -----
1954 A Linguistic Survey of the Southwestern
Pacific. South Pacific Commission,
Technical Paper No. 70. Noumea.
General survey by administrative
district with maps and extensive
bibliography.

09. ----- (Ed.)
1962 A Linguistic Survey of the Southwestern
Pacific. (New and Revised Ed.) South
Pacific Commission, Technical Paper
No. 136. Noumea.
Updated version of Ref. 1108, including
information from unpublished sources.

10. -----
1969 A Survey of New Guinea Languages. Sydney:
Sydney University Press.
Comprehensive survey, emphasizing
phonologies, of both Austronesian and
Non-Austronesian languages; includes
sixteen detailed maps of distribution
and boundaries of known Non-Austronesian
languages.

11. -----
1972 Languages. In Peter Ryan, Gen. Ed.
(Ref. 11), Vol. 2, pp. 610-617.
General sketch of distribution and
structure, comparing "Melanesian,"
"Papuan" and "Polynesian" languages;
includes classification of "Papuan"
languages.

12. Dye, W., Patricia Townsend and William Townsend
1968 The Sepik Hill Languages: A Preliminary
Report. Oceania 39:146-156.
Survey and comparison, including HEWA
and UMAIROF.

13. Elson, B.F. (Ed.)
1964 Verb Studies in Five New Guinea Languages.
Publications in Linguistics and Related
Fields, No. 10. Norman, Okla.: Summer
Institute of Linguistics.
Collection of papers by S.I.L. workers,
mostly on Highlands languages.

1114.   Franklin, Karl J.
        1968   Languages of the Gulf District: A Preview.
                In Papers in New Guinea Linguistics, LCC,
                PL, A16:18-44.
                        Preliminary survey including Angan,
                        FASU, FOI, MIKARU, PAWAIA, TURAMA AND
                        KIKORI RIVERS FAMILY and lowland
                        languages.

1115.   Healey, Alan
        1964   The Ok Language Family in New Guinea.
                Ph.D. Thesis, Canberra, The Australian
                National University.
                        Comprehensive survey and classification
                        of languages of extreme western highlands
                        of Papua New Guinea and extreme eastern
                        highlands of Irian Jaya; includes BIMIN,
                        FAIWOL, KAWOL, MIANMIN, NGALUM, SETAMAN,
                        SIBIL, TELEFOL, TIFAL and WAGARABAI.

1116.   Hooley, Bruce A.
        1964   A Brief History of New Guinea Linguistics.
                Oceania 35:26-44.
                        History of linguistic research in New
                        Guinea as a whole, beginning with word
                        lists of 17th Century explorers;
                        includes extensive bibliography.

1117.   Larson, Gordon F. and Mildred O. Larson
        1972   The Ekagi-Wodani-Moni Language Family of
                West Irian. Irian 1(3):80-95.
                        Survey sketch of KAPAUKU, MONI and
                        WODA.

1118.   Laycock, Donald C. and C.L. Voorhoeve
        1971   History of Research in Papuan Languages.
                In Thomas A. Sebeok, Ed. (Ref. 1124),
                pp. 509-540.
                        Brief history and survey of research
                        on Non-Austronesian languages of New
                        Guinea; includes large bibliography.

1119.   Longacre, Robert E.
        1972a   Hierarchy and Universality of Discourse
                Constituents in New Guinea Languages:
                Discussion. Washington,D.C.: Georgetown
                University Press.

1120.   -----
        1972b   Hierarchy and Universality of Discourse
                Constituents in New Guinea Languages:
                Texts. Washington, D.C.: Georgetown
                University Press.

Both sources report analyses and
comparisons of AUYANA, CHIMBU, OKSAPMIN
and other languages.

1121. McKaughan, Howard P.
       1964   A Study of Divergence in Four New Guinea
              Languages. In James B. Watson, Ed. (Ref.
              373), pp. 98-120. (also see Howard P.
              McKaughan, Ed., Ref. 1122, pp. 694-738).
              Comparison and lexicostatistical
              analysis of AUYANA, AWA, GADSUP, OYANA
              and TAIRORA.

1122. ----- (Ed.)
       1973   The Languages of the Eastern Family of the
              East New Guinea Highland Stock.
              Anthropological Studies in the Eastern
              Highlands of New Guinea, Vol. 1. Seattle:
              University of Washington Press.
              Collection of papers, most previously
              published, on several Highlands
              languages; includes section introductions
              by McKaughan.

1123. Pike, Eunice V.
       1964   The Phonology of New Guinea Highlands
              Languages. In James B. Watson, Ed. (Ref.
              373), pp. 121-132.
              Survey and comparison of phonology of
              twenty-five Highlands languages and
              others in New Guinea.

1124. Sebeok, Thomas A. (Ed.)
       1971   Current Trends in Linguistics, Vol. 8:
              Linguistics in Oceania. 2 Parts.
              The Hague: Mouton.
              Collection of papers including two on
              relevant New Guinea languages.

1125. Summer Institute of Linguistics (Members)
       1962   Studies in New Guinea Linguistics.
              Oceania Linguistic Monograph No. 6.
              Sydney.
              Collection of papers, mostly on
              Highlands languages.

1126. Trefry, David
       1965   A Comparative Study of Kuman and Pawaian:
              Non-Austronesian Languages of New Guinea.
              M.A. Thesis, Sydney, University of Sydney.

1127. -----
       1969   A Comparative Study of Kuman and Pawaian:
              Non-Austronesian Languages of New Guinea.

LCC, PL, B13.
Second is published version of Ref.
1126; both report extended comparison
of CHIMBU and PAWAIA.

1128. Voorhoeve, C.L.
1968   The Central and South New Guinea Phylum:
A Report on the Language Situation in
South New Guinea. In Papers in New Guinea
Linguistics, LCC, PL, A16:1-17.
Comparative and taxonomic essay dealing
largely with lowlands languages but
including BOSAVI, FASU and TELEFOL.

1129. Wurm, Stefan (Stephen) A.
1960   The Changing Linguistic Picture of New
Guinea. Oceania 31:121-136.
Survey of recent field research with
tentative sketch of East New Guinea
Highland Stock.

1130. -----
1961a   The Linguistic Situation in the Highlands
Districts of Papua and New Guinea.
Australian Territories 1(2):14-23.
Survey of recent work and detailed
outline and map of East New Guinea
Highland Stock.

1131. -----
1961b   Map of the Languages of Eastern, Western,
and Southern Highlands, Territory of Papua
and New Guinea. LCC, PL, C13.
Colored map showing distribution of
languages of East New Guinea Highland
Stock.

1132. -----
1961c   New Guinea Languages. Current Anthropology
2:114-116.
Condensed version of Ref. 1133.

1133. -----
1962   The Languages of the Eastern, Western and
Southern Highlands, Territory of Papua and
New Guinea. In Arthur Capell (Ref. 1109),
pp. 105-128.
Survey of East New Guinea Highland Stock
languages with remarks on common
features; bibliography organized by
language, including unpublished sources.

1134. -----
       1964a Australian New Guinea Highlands Languages
              and the Distribution of Their Typological
              Features. In James B. Watson, Ed.,
              (Ref. 373), pp. 77-97.
              Survey of major phonological features
              of languages of East New Guinea Highland
              Stock with suggested classification
              based on lexicostatistics.

1135. -----
       1964b Phonological Diversification in Australian
              New Guinea Highlands Languages. LCC, PL,
              B2.
              Extensive phonological comparisons of
              languages of East New Guinea Highland
              Stock.

1136. -----
       1964c Recent Developments in Linguistic Studies
              on the Australian New Guinea Mainland.
              In Papers in New Guinea Linguistics, LCC,
              PL, A4:1-17.
              Survey of recent research, much of it
              in Highlands areas.

1137. -----
       1964d Recent Linguistic Studies on the New
              Guinea Mainland. Australian Territories
              4(5):21-30.
              Survey of recent field research; map
              showing fifty-one languages (most in
              Highlands) studied as of early 1960's.

1138. -----
       1965a The Language Situation in New Guinea.
              Hemisphere 9(6):8-13.
              Overview of New Guinea languages,
              written for general audience.

1139. -----
       1965b Recent Comparative and Typological Studies
              in Papuan Languages in Australian New
              Guinea. Lingua 15:373-399.
              Comprehensive survey including all
              Highlands languages with maps of
              distribution of various stocks.

1140. -----
       1970a Indigenous Languages. In R. Gerard Ward
              and David A.M. Lea, Eds. (Ref. 49), pp. 16-19.
              Brief taxonomic essay with two maps
              showing phyla, stocks and families for
              Papua New Guinea only.

1141. -----
         1970b Lingue Franche. In R. Gerard Ward and
                David A.M. Lea, Eds. (Ref. 49), pp. 20-21.
                Brief notes on major and minor lingue
                franche in Papua New Guinea; map
                shows areas of substantial numbers of
                speakers of each.

1142. -----
         1971a New Guinea Highlands Pidgin: Course
                Materials. LCC, PL, D3.
                Analysis and manual of Neo-Melanesian,
                with sections on phonology and grammar
                including copious examples.

1143. -----
         1971b The Papuan Linguistic Situation. In
                Thomas A. Sebeok, Ed. (Ref. 1124),
                pp. 541-657.
                Comprehensive survey of research done
                through 1969; detailed classification
                and discussion of Non-Austronesian
                languages of all of New Guinea.

1144. -----
         1971c A Thousand Languages. In Peter Hastings,
                Ed. (Ref. 5), pp. 74-88.
                General survey with classification of
                languages for whole island; includes
                distribution maps.

1145. -----
         1972a Languages, Call. In Peter Ryan, Gen. Ed.
                (Ref. 11), Vol. 2, p. 617.
                Brief characterization of use of
                shouting to communicate.

1146. -----
         1972b Pidgin English. In Peter Ryan, Gen. Ed.
                (Ref. 11), Vol. 2, pp. 902-905.
                General discussion of prevalence,
                distribution and characteristics of
                Neo-Melanesian.

1147. Wurm, Stephen A. and Donald C. Laycock
         1961   The Question of Language and Dialect in
                New Guinea. Oceania 32:128-143.
                General discussion of problems of
                classification; includes examples from
                languages of East New Guinea Highland
                Stock.

1148. ----- (Eds.)
       1970   Pacific Linguistic Studies in Honour of
              Arthur Capell. LCC, PL, C13.
              Festschrift to Capell including a few
              papers of direct relevance to Highlands
              languages.

1149. Z'Graggen, J.A.
       1971   Classificatory and Typological Studies in
              Languages of the Madang District. LCC,
              PL, C19.
              Comparison and classification, mostly
              of lowland languages but including
              KARAM.

B. Specific Language Descriptions and Analyses

1150. Aufenanger, Heinrich: GENDE and BIYOM
       1952   Vokabular und grammatik der Gende-sprache
              in Zentral-Neuguinea. Micro-Bibliotheca
              Anthropos, 1.

1151. Aufenanger, Heinrich: SIANE
       1956   R.F. Salisbury's Vocabulary of the Siane
              Language of the Eastern Highlands of New
              Guinea. Anthropos 51:1064-1066.

1152. Aufenanger, Heinrich: WAHGI
       1953a Textproben der Nondugl-sprache (Zentral-
              Neuguinea). Anthropos 48:569-577.

1153. -----
       1953b Vokabular und grammatik der Nondugl-sprache
              in Zentral-Neuguinea. Micro-Bibliotheca
              Anthropos, 5.

1154. Bee, Darlene, Lorna Luff and Jean Goddard: AGARABE
       1973   Notes on Agarabi Phonology. In Howard P.
              McKaughan, Ed. (Ref. 1122), pp. 414-423.

1155. Bee, Darlene: USURUFA
       1965a A Profile of Usarufa Constructions.
              Anthropological Linguistics 7(9):90-114.

1156. -----
       1965b Usarufa: A Descriptive Grammar. Ph.D.
              Thesis, Bloomington, Indiana University.
              (also see Howard P. McKaughan, Ed.,
              Ref. 1122, pp. 225-323).

135

1157. \-\-\-\-\-
       1965c   Usarufa Distinctive Features and Phonemes.
               (M.A. Thesis, Bloomington, Indiana
               University). In Papers in New Guinea
               Linguistics, LCC, PL, A6:39-68. (also
               see Howard P. McKaughan, Ed., Ref. 1122,
               pp. 204-224).

1158. \-\-\-\-\-
       1972   Phonological Interference between Usarufa
               and Pidgin English. Kivung 5:69-95.

1159. \-\-\-\-\-
       1973   Usarufa Text. In Howard P. McKaughan, Ed.
               (Ref. 1122), pp. 390-400.

1160. Bee, Darlene and Kathleen Barker Glasgow: USURUFA
       1962   Usarufa Tone and Segmental Phonemes. In
               Summer Institute of Linguistics (Ref. 1125),
               pp. 111-127. (also see Howard P. McKaughan,
               Ed. Ref. 1122, pp. 190-203).

1161. Biggs, Bruce: KARAM
       1963   A Non-Phonemic Central Vowel Type in
               Karam, a "Pygmy"-Language of the Schrader
               Mountains, Central New Guinea.
               Anthropological Linguistics 5(4):13-17.

1162. Blowers, Bruce L.: GAWIGL
       1970   Kaugel Phonemic Statement. In Papers in
               New Guinea Linguistics, LCC, PL, A26:1-12.

1163. Blowers, Bruce L. and Ruth Blowers: GAWIGL
       1970   Kaugel Verb Morphology. In Papers in New
               Guinea Linguistics, LCC, PL, A25:37-60.

1164. Bolinger, Dwight: KARAM (data from A. Pawley)
       1969   The Sound of the Bell. Kivung 2(3):2-7.

1165. Bromley, H. Myron: DANI
       1961   The Phonology of Lower Grand Valley Dani:
               A Comparative and Structural Study of
               Skewed Phonemic Patterns. Verhandelingen
               van het Koninklijk Instituut voor Taal-,
               Land- en Volkenkunde, Deel 34.
               's-Gravenhage: Martinus Nijhoff.

1166. \-\-\-\-\-
       1972a   The Grammar of Lower Grand Valley Dani in
               Discourse Perspective. Ph.D. Thesis, New
               Haven, Yale University.

1167. \-\-\-\-\-
       1972b   The Grammar of Lower Grand Valley Dani in

Discourse Perspective. Irian 1:112-114.

168. Bunn, Gordon and Ruth Bunn: SINASINA
     1970   Golin Phonology. In Papers in New Guinea
             Linguistics, LCC, PL, A23:1-7.

169. Burce, Willard L.: ENGA
     1963   An Investigation Preliminary to Translating
             the Gospel of Mark into the Enga Language.
             Ph.D. Thesis, St. Louis, Concordia Seminary.

170. -----
     1965   Sentence Structures in Mark: Greek and Enga.
             The Bible Translator 16:128-141.

171. Burgmann, Arnold: CHIMBU (data from A. Schäfer)
     1953   A. Schäfer's vokabular der Chimbu-sprache
             in Zentral-Neuguinea. Anthropos 48:268-273.

172. Burgmann, Arnold: GENDE (data from H. Aufenanger)
     1953   H. Aufenanger's vokabular und grammatik
             der Gende-sprache in Zentral-Neuguinea.
             Anthropos 48:263-267.

173. Burgmann, Arnold: WAHGI (data from H. Aufenanger)
     1953   H. Aufenanger's vokabular und grammatik
             der Nondugl-sprache in Zentral-Neuguinea.
             Anthropos 48:616-620.

174. Cochrane, Anne: HEWA
     1968   Notes on Yoliapi. Kivung 1(3):134-145.

175. Cook, Edwin A.: NARAK
     1966   Narak: Language or Dialect? Journal of the
             Polynesian Society 75:437-444.

176. -----
     1967   A Preliminary Statement of Narak Spatial
             Diexis. Anthropological Linguistics 9(6):
             1-29.

177. Crotty, John: ENGA
     1951   First Dictionary of Tchaga (=Enga) Language,
             Central Highlands, New Guinea. Anthropos
             46:933-963.

178. Deibler, Ellis W., Jr.: GAHUKU
     1964   The Application of Matrix to the Gahuku
             Verbs. In Papers in New Guinea Linguistics,
             LCC, PL, A3:17-26.

179. -----
     1967   Gahuku Verb Structure. Ph.D. Thesis, Ann
             Arbor, University of Michigan.

1180. ------
        1968a Translating from Basic Structure. The
               Bible Translator 19(1):14-16.

1181. ------
        1968b Trends in Tagmemics. Kivung 1(3):153-163.

1182. ------
        1969   Sememics and Translation. Kivung 2(1):
               13-18.

1183. ------
        1971   Uses of the Verb "To Say" in Gahuku.
               Kivung 4(2):101-110.

1184. Doble, Marion L.: KAPAUKU
        1950   Transliteration in Kapauku. The Bible
               Translator 1(2):133-135.

1185. ------
        1960   Kapauku-Malayan-Dutch-English Dictionary.
               Verhandelingen van het Koninklijk Instituut
               voor Taal-, Land- en Volkenkunde.
               's-Gravenhage: Martinus Nijhoff.

1186. ------
        1962   Essays on Kapauku Grammar. Nieuw-Guinea
               Studien 6:152-155, 211-218, 279-298.

1187. ------
        1963   Grace and Justification Linked in Kapauku.
               The Bible Translator 14(1):37-39.

1188. Franklin, Joice: KEWA
        1965   Kewa II: Higher Level Phonology.
               Anthropological Linguistics 7(5):84-88.

1189. Franklin, Karl J.: KEWA
        1964   Kewa Verb Morphology. In B.F. Elson, Ed.
               (Ref. 1113), pp. 100-130.

1190. ------
        1965   Kewa Clause Markers. Oceania 35:272-285.

1191. ------
        1967   Kewa Sentence Structure. In Papers in New
               Guinea Linguistics, LCC, PL, A13:27-59.

1192. ------
        1968   The Dialects of Kewa. LCC, PL, B10.

1193. ------
        1969   A Grammar and Dialect Study of Kewa. Ph.D.
               Thesis, Canberra, The Australian National

University.

1194.   -----
         1971a   A Grammar of Kewa, New Guinea. LCC, PL,
                 C16.

1195.   -----
         1971b   Tagmemics and Tagmemic Rules. Linguistics
                 70:25-44.

1196.   Franklin, Karl J. and Joice Franklin: KEWA
         1962   Kewa I: Phonological Asymmetry.
                 Anthropological Linguistics 4(7):29-37.

1197.   Frantz, Chester I.: GADSUP
         1962   Grammatical Categories as Indicated by
                 Gadsup Noun Affixes. In Summer Institute
                 of Linguistics (Ref. 1125), pp. 44-63.
                 (also see Howard P. McKaughan, Ed., Ref.
                 1122, pp. 424-438).

1198.   Frantz, Chester I. and Marjorie E. Frantz: GADSUP
         1966   Gadsup Phoneme and Toneme Units. In
                 Papers in New Guinea Linguistics, LCC, PL,
                 A7:1-11. (also see Howard P. McKaughan,
                 Ed., Ref. 1122, pp. 406-413).

1199.   Frantz, Chester I. and Howard P. McKaughan: GADSUP
         1964   Gadsup Independent Verb Affixes. In
                 B.F. Elson, Ed. (Ref. 1113), pp. 84-99.
                 (also see Howard P. McKaughan, Ed., Ref.
                 1122, pp. 439-449).

1200.   Goddard, Jean: AGARABE
         1967   Agarabi Narratives and Commentary. In
                 Papers in New Guinea Linguistics, LCC, PL,
                 A13:1-25. (also see Howard P. McKaughan,
                 Ed., Ref. 1122, pp. 450-468).

1201.   Haiman, John: YAGARIA
         1972   Ablaut in the Hua Verb. Oceanic
                 Linguistics 11(1):32-46.

1202.   Hamp, Eric P.: WAHGI (data from L. Luzbetak)
         1958   Wahgi (New Guinea) Prosodic Phonemes.
                 Oceania 29:62-64.

1203.   Harnsworth, Joan: NARAK
         1972   Narak Noun Possession and Morphophonemic
                 Rules. Anthropological Linguistics 14(2):
                 46-61.

1204.   Healey, Alan: TELEFOL
         1964   Telefol Phonology. LCC, PL, B3.

1205.   Healey, Phyllis M.:   TELEFOL
        1964   Teléfóól Quotative Clauses.   In Papers in
                New Guinea Linguistics, LCC, PL, A3:27-34.

1206.   -----
        1965a   Levels, Constituent Strings, and Agreement
                in Telefol Syntax.   Ph.D. Thesis, Canberra,
                The Australian National University.

1207.   -----
        1965b   Telefol Clause Structure.   In Papers in
                New Guinea Linguistics, LCC, PL, A5:1-26.

1208.   -----
        1965c   Telefol Noun Phrases.   LCC, PL, B4.

1209.   -----
        1965d   Telefol Verb Phrases.   In Papers in New
                Guinea Linguistics, LCC, PL, A5:27-53.

1210.   -----
        1966   Levels and Chaining in Telefol Sentences.
                LCC, PL, B5.

1211.   Irwin, Barry: SINASINA
        1974   Salt-Yui Grammar.   LCC, PL, B35.

1212.   James, Dorothy S.:   SIANE
        1966   Siane Morphophonemics.   M.A. Thesis,
                Urbana, University of Illinois.

1213.   -----
        1968   Towards an Ethnic Hymnody.   Practical
                Anthropology 16:34-38.

1214.   -----
        1970   Embedding and Coordinating Transforms in
                Siane.   In Stephen A. Wurm and Donald C.
                Laycock, Eds. (Ref. 1148), pp. 1095-1125.

1215.   James, Dorothy S. and Ramona Lucht: SIANE
        1962   Phonemes of Siane.   Te Reo 5:12-16.

1216.   Kerr, Harland B.:   TAIRORA
        1973   Subject Morphemes in the Tairora Verb
                Complex: Obura Dialect.   In Howard P.
                McKaughan, Ed. (Ref. 1122), pp. 598-624.

1217.   Lang, Adrienne: ENGA
        1971   Nouns and Classificatory Verbs in Enga
                (New Guinea): A Semantic Study.   Ph.D.
                Thesis, Canberra, The Australian National
                University.

1218. -----
    1973   Enga Dictionary, with English Index.
            LCC, PL, C20.

1219. Lang, Ranier: ENGA
    1970   Enga Questions: Structural and Semantic
            Studies. Ph.D. Thesis, Canberra, The
            Australian National University.

1220. Larson, Gordon F.: MONI
    1958a   Preliminary Studies in the Moni Language.
            Bijdragen tot de Taal-, Land- en
            Volkenkunde 114:406-431.

1221. -----
    1958b   Verb and Hierarchical Structures in Moni
            Narration. M.A. Thesis, Ann Arbor,
            University of Michigan.

1222. Lawrence, Helen: OKSAPMIN
    1972   Viewpoint and Location in Oksapmin.
            Anthropological Linguistics 14:311-316.

1223. Lawrence, Marshall: OKSAPMIN
    1971   Oksapmin Clause Structure. Kivung 4(2):
            111-132.

1224. -----
    1972a   Oksapmin Sentence Structure. In Papers
            in New Guinea Linguistics, LCC, PL,
            A34:17-46.

1225. -----
    1972b   Structure and Function of Oksapmin Verbs.
            Oceanic Linguistics 11(1):47-66.

1226. Lloyd, Richard G.: BARUA
    1969   Gender in a New Guinea Language: Baruya
            Nouns and Noun Phrases. In Papers in New
            Guinea Linguistics, LCC, PL, A22:25-67.

1227. Lloyd, Richard G. and Alan Healey: BARUA
    1970   Baruya Phonemes: A Problem in
            Interpretation. Linguistics 60:33-48.

1228. Loeweke, Eunice and Jean May: FASU
    1966   Fasu Grammar. Anthropological Linguistics
            8(6):17-33.

1229. Longacre, Robert E.: FORE (data from G. Scott)
    1970   Paragraph and Sentence Structure in New
            Guinea Highlands Languages. Kivung 3:
            150-163.

1230. Loving, Aretta and Howard P. McKaughan: AWA
      1964   Awa Verbs. Part II. The Internal Structure
              of Dependent Verbs. In B.F. Elson, Ed.
              (Ref. 1113), pp. 31-44. (also see Howard
              P. McKaughan, Ed., Ref. 1122, pp. 56-64).

1231. Loving, Richard E.: AWA
      1966   Awa Phonemes, Tonemes, and Tonally
              Differentiated Allomorphs. In Papers in
              New Guinea Linguistics, LCC, PL, A7:23-32.
              (also see Howard P. McKaughan, Ed., Ref.
              1122, pp. 10-18).

1232. -----
      1973a   The Dialects of Awa. In Howard P.
              McKaughan, Ed. (Ref. 1122), pp. 6-9.

1233. -----
      1973b   An Outline of Awa Grammatical Structures.
              In Howard P. McKaughan, Ed. (Ref. 1122),
              pp. 65-87.

1234. Loving, Richard E. and Aretta Loving: AWA
      1962   A Preliminary Survey of Awa Noun Suffixes.
              In Summer Institute of Linguistics (Ref.
              1125), pp. 28-43. (also see Howard P.
              McKaughan, Ed., Ref. 1122, pp. 19-30).

1235. Loving, Richard E. and Howard P. McKaughan: AWA
      1964   Awa Verbs. Part I. The Internal Structure
              of Independent Verbs. In B.F. Elson, Ed.
              (Ref. 1113), pp. 1-30. (also see Howard P.
              McKaughan, Ed., Ref. 1122, pp. 36-55).

1236. Luzbetak, Louis J.: WAHGI
      1956   Middle Wahgi Phonology and Standardization
              of Orthographies in the New Guinea
              Highlands. Oceania Linguistic Monograph
              No. 2. Sydney.

1237. McCarthy, Joy: KANITE
      1965   Clause Chaining in Kanite. Anthropological
              Linguistics 7(5):59-70.

1238. McKaughan, Howard P.: AUYANA
      1973   Auyana Texts. In Howard P. McKaughan, Ed.
              (Ref. 1122), pp. 324-389.

1239. McKaughan, Howard P. and Doreen Marks: AUYANA
      1973   Notes on Auyana Phonology and Morphology.
              In Howard P. McKaughan, Ed. (Ref. 1122),
              pp. 181-189.

1240. McKaughan, Howard P.: AWA
       1973 Awa Texts. In Howard P. McKaughan, Ed.
             (Ref. 1122), pp. 88-175.

1241. McKaughan, Howard P. and Aretta Loving: AWA
       1973 Possessive Prefixes Occurring with
             Inalienable Awa Nouns. In Howard P.
             McKaughan, Ed. (Ref. 1122), pp. 31-35.

1242. McKaughan, Howard P.: GADSUP
       1973 Gadsup Texts. In Howard P. McKaughan,
             Ed. (Ref. 1122), pp. 469-512.

1243. McKaughan, Howard P.: TAIRORA
       1966 Sequences of Clauses in Tairora. Oceanic
             Linguistics 5(1):1-12. (also see Howard
             P. McKaughan, Ed., Ref. 1122, pp. 588-597).

1244. May, Jean and Eunice Loeweke: FASU
       1965 The Phonological Hierarchy in Fasu.
             Anthropological Linguistics 7(5):89-97.

1245. Nicholson, Ruth and Ray Nicholson: FORE
       1962 Fore Phonemes and Their Interpretation.
             In Summer Institute of Linguistics (Ref.
             1125), pp. 128-148.

1246. Oatridge, Des and Jennifer Oatridge: BINUMARIEN
       1966 Phonemes of Binumarien. In Papers in New
             Guinea Linguistics, LCC, PL, A7:13-21.
             (also see Howard P. McKaughan, Ed., Ref.
             1122, pp. 517-522).

1247. Oatridge, Des, Jennifer Oatridge and Alan Healey:
       BINUMARIEN
       1973 Binumarien Noun Affixes. In Howard P.
             McKaughan, Ed. (Ref. 1122), pp. 557-560.

1248. Pawley, Andrew: KARAM
       1966 The Structure of Karam: A Grammar of a
             New Guinea Highlands Language. Ph.D.
             Thesis, Auckland, University of Auckland.

1249. -----
       1969 Transformational Grammar and the Native
             Speaker: Some Elementary Issues. Kivung
             2(2):2-36.

1250. -----
       1970 Are Emic Dictionaries Possible? An
             Experiment with Karam, a New Guinea
             Highlands Language. Kivung 3(1):8-16.

1251. Pike, Kenneth L.: FORE (data from G. Scott)
      1963 Theoretical Implications of Matrix
            Permutation in Fore (New Guinea).
            Anthropological Linguistics 5(8):1-23.

1252. Pike, Kenneth L. and Graham K. Scott: FORE
      1963 Pitch Accent and Non-Accented Phrases
            in Fore (New Guinea). Zeitschrift für
            Phonetik, Sprachwissenschaft und
            Kommunikationsforschung 16:179-189.

1253. Pilch, H.: FORE (data from G. Scott)
      1970 Pike-Scott's Analyses of Fore
            Supra-segmentals. Kivung 3(2):133-142.

1254. Renck, G.L.: YAGARIA
      1967 A Tentative Statement of the Phonemes of
            Yagaria. In Papers in New Guinea
            Linguistics, LCC, PL, A12:19-48.

1255. Rule, Joan: MENDI
      1965 A Comparison of Certain Phonemes of the
            Languages of the Mendi and Nembi Valleys,
            Southern Highlands, Papua. Anthropological
            Linguistics 7(5):98-105.

1256. Salisbury, Richard F.: SIANE
      1956a An Outline Grammar and Word List of the
            Siane Language of the Eastern Highlands
            of New Guinea. Micro-Bibliotheca
            Anthropos Monographs. Fribourg.

1257. -----
      1956b The Siane Language of the Eastern Highlands
            of New Guinea. Anthropos 51:447-480.

1258. -----
      1956c Vocabulary of the Siane Language of the
            Eastern Highlands of New Guinea. Micro-
            Bibliotheca Anthropos, No. 24.

1259. -----
      1962 Notes on Bilingualism and Linguistic
            Change in New Guinea. Anthropological
            Linguistics 4(7):1-13.

1260. Schäfer, Alfons: CHIMBU
      1953 Vokabular der Chimbu-sprache in Zentral-
            Neuguinea. Micro-Bibliotheca Anthropos,
            No. 2.

1261. Scott, Graham K.: FORE
      1963 The Dialects of Fore. Oceania 33:280-286.

1262. -----
1968   Fore Final Verbs. In Papers in New Guinea
        Linguistics, LCC, PL, A16:45-62.

1263. -----
1973   Higher Levels of Fore Grammar. LCC, PL,
        B23.

1264. Stap, P.A.M. van der: DANI
      1966a   Outline of Dani Morphology. Ph.D. Thesis,
               Amsterdam, University of Amsterdam.

1265. -----
1966b   Outline of Dani Morphology. Verhandelingen,
         Koninklijk Instituut voor Taal-, Land- en
         Volkenkunde, Deel 48. 's-Gravenhage:
         Martinus Nijhoff.

1266. Steinkraus, Walter: TIFAL
      1969   Tifal Phonology Showing Vowel and Tone
              Neutralizations. Kivung 2(1):57-66.

1267. Steltenpool, J.: KAPAUKU
      1969   Ekagi-Dutch-English-Indonesian Dictionary.
              The Hague: Martinus Nijhoff.

1268. Strange, David: ASARO
      1973   Indicative and Subjunctive in Upper Asaro.
              Linguistics 110:82-97.

1269. Strange, Gladys Neeley: ASARO
      1965   Nominal Elements in Upper Asaro.
              Anthropological Linguistics 7(5):71-79.

1270. Stringer, Mary and Joyce Hotz: WAFFA
      1971a   The Occurrence and Co-occurrence of Waffa
               Noun Suffixes. Te Reo 14:49-62. (also
               see Howard P. McKaughan, Ed., Ref. 1122,
               pp. 547-556).

1271. -----
1971b   Waffa Phonemes. Te Reo 14:42-48. (also
         see Howard P. McKaughan, Ed., Ref. 1122,
         pp. 523-529).

1272. Swick, J.: CHUAVE
      1966   Chuave Phonological Hierarchy. In Papers
              in New Guinea Linguistics, LCC, PL, A7:
              33-48.

1273. Vincent, Alex: TAIRORA
      1973a   Notes on Tairora Noun Morphology. In
               Howard P. McKaughan, Ed. (Ref. 1122),
               pp. 530-546.

145

1274. ------
          1973b Tairora Texts. In Howard P. McKaughan,
                 Ed. (Ref. 1122), pp. 625-688.

1275. ------
          1973c Tairora Verb Structure. In Howard P.
                 McKaughan, Ed. (Ref. 1122), pp. 561-587.

1276. Vincent, Alex and Lois Vincent: TAIRORA
          1962   Introductory Notes on Tairora Verb
                 Morphology and Syntax. In Summer Institute
                 of Linguistics (Ref. 1125), pp. 4-27.

1277. Young, Robert A.: BENABENA
          1964   The Primary Verb in Bena-Bena. In B.F.
                 Elson, Ed. (Ref. 1113), pp. 45-83.

1278. ------
          1971   The Verb in Bena-Bena: Its Form and
                 Function. LCC, PL, B18.

1279. Young, Robert A. and Rosemary Young: BENABENA
          1965   The Three Dimensional Classification
                 System of Bena-Bena Nouns. Anthropological
                 Linguistics 7(5):80-83.

1280. Young, Rosemary: BENABENA
          1962   The Phonemes of Kanite, Kamano, Benabena,
                 and Gahuku. In Summer Institute of
                 Linguistics (Ref. 1125), pp. 90-110.
                 (also GAHUKU, KAMANO and KANITE).

1281. ------
          1968   Words Under a Bushel. Practical
                 Anthropology 15:213-216.

PART IV   PREHISTORY

. General Surveys and Reconstructions

282.   Allen, F.J. ("Jim")
        1970   Excavations of Prehistoric Sites. In
                R. Gerard Ward and David A.M. Lea, Eds.
                (Ref. 49), p. 97.
                Very brief survey of excavations since
                1959; map shows distribution of sites
                in Papua New Guinea, eight of which
                are in Highlands areas.

283.   -----
        1972   The First Decade in New Guinea
                Archaeology. Antiquity, Vol. 46, No.
                183, pp. 180-190.
                Broad survey of excavations since
                1959 and interpretive syntheses.

284.   Barrau, Jacques
        1960   The Selection, Domestication and
                Cultivation of Food Plants in Tropical
                Oceania in the Pre-European Era. In
                UNESCO (Ref. 360), pp. 67-72.
                Brief discussion of wild plant foods
                available to pre-horticultural
                populations for eventual domestication.

285.   ----- (Ed.)
        1963   Plants and the Migrations of Pacific
                Peoples: A Symposium. Honolulu:
                Bishop Museum Press.
                Collection of papers relevant to
                reconstructions of settlement and
                prehistory of Pacific in general;
                some papers specifically relate to
                Highlands prehistory.

286.   -----
        1965a   Histoire et préhistoire horticales de
                l'Oceanie tropicale. Journal de la
                Société des Océanistes 21:55-78.
                Similar to Ref. 1287 but more detailed
                discussion of banana, sugar cane,
                sweet potato, taro and yams.

1287.   -----
        1965b   Witnesses of the Past: Notes on Some
                Food Plants of Oceania. Ethnology 4:
                282-294.
                Detailed discussion of distribution

and characteristics of probable early
food sources, especially Cordyline,
Pueraria and yams.

1288. Brookfield, Harold C. and J. Peter White
1968 Revolution or Evolution in the Prehistory
of the New Guinea Highlands: A Seminar
Report. Ethnology 7:43-52.
Report of results of symposium held
to evaluate "sweet potato revolution"
hypothesis (see James B. Watson ref's.
below).

1289. Bulmer, Ralph N.H.
1971 The Role of Ethnography in Reconstructing
the Prehistory of Melanesia. In Roger C.
Green and M. Kelly, Eds. (Ref. 1299), pp.
36-44.
Discussion of various ways ethnographic
evidence is directly relevant to
proposed reconstructions; passing
references to Highlands societies.

1290. Bulmer, Susan
1969 Archaeological Fieldwork in Papua and New
Guinea to 1969. Man in New Guinea 1(5):
8-14.
Brief survey of field research to
1969, including Highlands sites;
includes complete bibliography.

1291. -----
1975 Settlement and Economy in Prehistoric
Papua New Guinea: A Review of the
Archaeological Evidence. Journal de la
Société des Océanistes 31(46):7-75.
Comprehensive survey of evidence for
initial settlement and prehistoric
subsistence economies in Highlands,
Lowlands and Island Melanesia.

1292. Bulmer, Susan and Ralph N.H. Bulmer
1964 The Prehistory of the Australian New
Guinea Highlands. In James B. Watson,
Ed. (Ref. 373), pp. 39-76.
General survey of excavations to early
1960's and tentative synthesis of
information from both archaeological
and non-archaeological sources;
outlines general typological and
chronological sequence.

293. Golson, Jack
1968   Archaeological Prospects for Melanesia.
<u>In</u> Prehistoric Culture in Oceania: A
Symposium. I. Yawata and Y.H. Sinoto,
Eds. Honolulu: Bishop Museum Press.
pp. 3-14.
General survey of excavations,
interpretations and research
priorities, especially regarding New
Guinea Highlands.

294. -----
1971   Both Sides of the Wallace Line: Australia,
New Guinea and Asian Prehistory.
Archaeology and Physical Anthropology in
Oceania 6:124-144.
General discussion of stone implements,
pottery and evidence of horticulture,
with probable interpretations; includes
Highlands data.

295. -----
1972a Land Connections, Sea Barriers and the
Relationship of Australia and New Guinea
Prehistory. <u>In</u> Bridge and Barrier: The
Natural and Cultural History of Torres
Strait. Department of Biogeography and
Geomorphology, Publication BG3. D. Walker,
Ed. Canberra: The Australian National
University. pp. 375-397.
General discussion including synthesis
of New Guinea data, especially from
Highlands excavations.

1296. -----
1972b The Pacific Islands and Their Prehistoric
Inhabitants. <u>In</u> R. Gerard Ward, Ed.
(Ref. 369), pp. 5-33.
General survey including New Guinea.

1297. -----
1972c Prehistory. <u>In</u> Peter Ryan, Gen. Ed.
(Ref. 11), Vol.2, pp. 961-970.
General reconstruction suggested;
extensive bibliography.

1298. -----
1972d The Remarkable History of Indo-Pacific
Man: Missing Chapters from Every World
Prehistory. Journal of Pacific History
7:5-25. (also see Search, 1972, 3(1-2):
13-21).
General discussion including New Guinea
with brief consideration of Wahgi Valley

149

excavations.

1299. Green, Roger C. and M. Kelly (Eds.)
      1971   Studies in Oceanic Culture History, Vol. 2.
              Pacific Anthropological Records, No. 11.
              Honolulu: Bishop Museum Press.
              Collection of papers including some
              directly relevant to New Guinea.

1300. Howells, William
      1973   The Pacific Islanders. New York: Charles
              Scribner's Sons.
              General but detailed survey and
              evaluation of various reconstructions
              of settlement of Pacific including New
              Guinea; includes extensive bibliography.

1301. Keleny, G.P.
      1960   Notes on the Origin and Introduction of
              the Basic Food Crops of the New Guinea
              People. In UNESCO (Ref. 360), pp. 76-85.
              Discussion of probable origin and
              duration in New Guinea of banana,
              coconut, corn, sago, sweet potato, taro,
              tobacco and yams, with some mention of
              recent introductions.

1302. -----
      1962   The Origin and Introduction of the Basic
              Food Crops of the New Guinea People.
              Papua and New Guinea Agricultural Journal
              15(1-2):7-13.
              Same as Ref. 1301.

1303. Mitton, R.D.
      1972   Stone as a Cultural Factor in the Central
              and Eastern Highlands. Irian 1(3):4-11.
              Discussion of need for research into
              prehistory of Irian Jaya.

1304. O'Brien, Patricia J.
      1972   The Sweet Potato: Its Origin and Dispersal.
              American Anthropologist 74:342-365.
              Comprehensive survey of literature
              including extended discussion of New
              Guinea Highlands "sweet potato
              revolution."

1305. Robbins, Ross G.
      1960   The Anthropogenic Grasslands of Papua and
              New Guinea. In UNESCO (Ref. 360), pp. 313-
              329.
              Detailed description of grassland
              formation and succession related to

horticulture; speculations on
settlement history indicated by
grassland patterns.

306. -----
1963　Correlations of Plant Patterns and
Population Migration into the Australian
New Guinea Highlands. In Jacques Barrau,
Ed. (Ref. 1284), pp. 45-59.
Comparison of various reconstructions
of Highlands settlement in relation to
gradient of grassland formations.

307. -----
1969　Plant History in Melanesia. In The History
of Melanesia (Ref. 289), pp. 477-491.
Discussion of plant geography and
ethnobotany with implications for
prehistory.

308. -----
1972　Vegetation and Man in the Southwest Pacific
and New Guinea. In R. Gerard Ward, Ed.
(Ref. 369), pp. 74-90.
General discussion, similar to Ref's.
1306 and 1307.

309. Shutler, Mary Elizabeth and Richard Shutler, Jr.
1967　Origins of the Melanesians. Archaeology
and Physical Anthropology in Oceania 2:
91-99.
General discussion of probable
settlement of Melanesia, including New
Guinea.

310. Shutler, Richard, Jr.
1971　Pacific Radiocarbon Dates: An Overview.
In Roger C. Green and M. Kelly, Eds.
(Ref. 1299), pp. 13-27.
Includes brief discussion of New
Guinea, including Highlands.

311. Shutler, Richard, Jr. and Mary Elizabeth Shutler
1975　Oceanic Prehistory. Menlo Park: Cummings.
Broad survey including brief
discussion of New Guinea Highlands.

312. Sorenson, E. Richard and Peter E. Kenmore
1974　Proto-Agricultural Movement in the
Eastern Highlands of New Guinea. Current
Anthropology 15:67-73.
Proposed reconstruction of introduction
and spread of horticulture in Eastern
Highlands; based on blood group genetics

151

and vegetation changes.

1313. Troughton, Ellis
        1971 The Early History and Relationships of
              the New Guinea Highlands Dog (Canis
              hallstromii). Linnaean Society of New
              South Wales, Proceedings 96(2):93-98.
              Discussion of probable duration of
              domesticated dog in New Guinea with
              implications for prehistory.

1314. Walker, D.
        1970 The Changing Vegetation of the Montane
              Tropics. Search 1(5):217-221.
              Description of vegetation patterns
              for past 5,000 years in Mount Hagen
              region.

1315. Warner, J.N.
        1962 Sugar Cane: An Indigenous Papuan
              Cultigen. Ethnology 1:405-411.
              Discussion of botanical classification
              and probable origin of cultivated forms
              of sugar cane in New Guinea.

1316. Watson, James B.
        1965a From Hunting to Horticulture in the New
              Guinea Highlands. Ethnology 4:295-309.
              Reconstruction of hypothetical pre-
              Ipomoean (sweet potato) "revolution,"
              with general survey of Highlands
              evidence.

1317. ------
        1965b The Significance of a Recent Ecological
              Change in the Central Highlands of New
              Guinea. Journal of the Polynesian
              Society 74:438-450.
              Similar to Ref. 1316, but stressing
              social and cultural evidence.

1318. ------
        1972 Comment on E. Richard Sorenson, "Socio-
              Ecological Change among the Fore of New
              Guinea" (Ref. 935). Current Anthropology
              13:377-378.
              General discussion of "sweet potato
              revolution" hypothesis in relation to
              Sorenson's suggestions.

1319. White, J. Peter
        1968 Studies of Prehistory in the New Guinea
              Highlands. Australian Natural History.
              16(3):83-86.

General discussion and survey of recent
research.

320. -----
      1971a New Guinea and Australian Prehistory: The
             "Neolithic Problem." In Aboriginal Man
             and Environment in Australia. D.J.
             Mulvaney and J. Golson, Eds. Canberra:
             The Australian National University Press.
             pp. 182-195.
             General discussion of settlement of New
             Guinea, including discussion of
             Highlands horticulture.

321. -----
      1971b New Guinea: The First Phase in Oceanic
             Settlement. In Roger C. Green and M. Kelly,
             Eds. (Ref. 1299), pp. 45-52.
             General discussion of prehistory of
             New Guinea, including some Highlands
             sites.

322. Wurm, Stephen A.
      1966   Language and Agriculture in New Guinea.
             New Scientist 31(506):216-218.
             Correlation of linguistic evidence with
             suggested reconstructions of prehistory
             from anthropology, archaeology and
             botany.

323. Yen, Douglas E.
      1960   The Sweet Potato in the Pacific: The
             Propagation of the Plant in Relation to
             Its Distribution. Journal of the
             Polynesian Society 69:368-375.
             Detailed analysis of development of
             varieties, probable conditions and
             time required, with implications for
             antiquity of horticulture.

324. -----
      1963   Sweet Potato Variation and Its Relation
             to Human Migration in the Pacific. In
             Jacques Barrau, Ed. (Ref. 1284), pp. 93-
             117.
             Similar to Ref. 1323.

1325. -----
      1968   Natural and Human Selection in the Pacific
             Sweet Potato. In Evolution and
             Environment. Ellen T. Drake, Ed. New
             Haven: Yale University Press. pp. 387-412.
             Similar to Ref's. 1323 and 1324.

1326. -----
1971   The Development of Agriculture in Oceania.
        In Roger C. Green and M. Kelly, Eds.
        (Ref. 1299), pp. 1-12.
        Similar to Ref. 1327.

1327. -----
1973   The Origins of Oceanic Agriculture.
        Archaeology and Physical Anthropology in
        Oceania 8:68-85.
            General discussion of movement of major
            contemporary crops into Pacific from
            Asia in relation to archaeological
            evidence; suggests prehistoric sequence
            of occupation and subsistence.

1328. -----
1974   The Sweet Potato and Oceania: An Essay in
        Ethnobotany. Bernice P. Bishop Museum,
        Bulletin 236. Honolulu.
            Comprehensive survey of evidence
            regarding sweet potato in Pacific;
            includes extended discussions of New
            Guinea prehistory and early horticulture.

1329. Yen, Douglas E. and Jocelyn M. Wheeler
      1968   Introduction of Taro into the Pacific:
              The Indications of Chromosome Numbers.
              Ethnology 7:259-267.
                  Cytological investigations indicating
                  Asian origin of taro; discussion of
                  possible pathways of entry and
                  distribution in Pacific, including
                  New Guinea.

B. Archaeological Site Reports and Topical Studies

1330. Adam, Leonhard
      1946   Comments on Some Recent Contributions to
              the Prehistory of New Guinea. Mankind 3:
              252-258.
                  Discussion of various stone objects
                  from Middle Ramu Highlands region near
                  Atemble.

1331. -----
      1947   Some Uncommon Perforated Stone Implements
              from the Morobe and Mt. Hagen Areas.
              Mankind 3:345-351.
                  Description of stone discs and club
                  heads, not precisely identified as to
                  provenience.

1332.   Allen, F.J. ("Jim")
        1970a   A Collection of Flaked Stone Artefacts
                from the Western Highlands. Papua New
                Guinea Museum, Records 1:47-53.
                Description of surface collection
                from Upper Kaugel Valley.

1333.   -----
        1970b   Prehistoric Agricultural Systems in the
                Wahgi Valley: A Further Note. Mankind 7:
                177-183.
                Report on excavations and finds at
                Kuk and Manton sites near Mount Hagen.

1334.   Bartlett, H.K.
        1964   Flint Implements Found near Nipa, Central
                Papuan Highlands (with Comments by Norman
                B. Tindale). South Australian Museum,
                Records 14:669-673.
                Description of surface finds in Nembi
                River area.

1335.   Bulmer, Susan
        1964a   Prehistoric Stone Implements from the
                New Guinea Highlands. Oceania 34:246-
                268.
                Survey of implements from Kainantu
                area, Kaironk Valley and excavations
                at Kiowa (Wahgi Valley) and Yuku
                (Baiyer Valley).

1336.   -----
        1964b   Radiocarbon Dates from New Guinea.
                Journal of the Polynesian Society 73:
                327-328.
                Dates for materials from Kiowa rock
                shelter excavations (Wahgi Valley).

1337.   -----
        1966a   Pig Bone from Two Archaeological Sites in
                the New Guinea Highlands. Journal of the
                Polynesian Society 75:504-505.
                Description and radiocarbon dates from
                Kiowa and Yuku sites.

1338.   -----
        1966b   The Prehistory of the Australian New
                Guinea Highlands: A Discussion of
                Archaeological Field Survey and
                Excavations, 1959-60. M.A. Thesis,
                Auckland, University of Auckland.
                Detailed description of materials
                from Kiowa and Yuku sites.

1339. Bulmer, Susan and William C. Clarke
       1970   Two Stone Spear or Dagger Heads from the
              Bismarck Mountains, New Guinea. Papua
              New Guinea Museum, Records 1:42-46.
              Description of surface finds near
              Simbai River.

1340. Bulmer, Susan and William Tomasetti
       1970   A Stone Replica of a Bronze Socketed Axe
              from the Eastern Highlands of Australian
              New Guinea. Papua New Guinea Museum,
              Records 1:38-41.
              Description of surface find at Bomai
              (Chimbu District).

1341. England, Peter
       1946   The Ramu Stones: Notes on Stone Carvings
              Found in the Annanberg - Atemble Area,
              Ramu Valley, New Guinea. Mankind 3:233-
              236.
              Description of stone discs, mortars
              and carved figure from Middle Ramu
              hills.

1342. Fischer, Hans
       1968   Archaeologische funde und beobachtungen
              vom Tauri-oberlauf Neuguineas.
              Abhandlungen und Berichte des Staatlichen
              Museums für Völkerkunde, Dresden, 28:73-80.
              Brief description of surface finds in
              Upper Tauri River region.

1343. Flenley, J.
       1967   The Present and Former Vegetation of the
              Wabag Region of New Guinea. Ph.D. Thesis,
              Canberra, The Australian National
              University.
              Description and analysis of present
              flora and reconstruction of vegetation
              changes through palynological analysis.

1344. -----
       1972   The Evidence of the Quaternary Vegetation
              Change in New Guinea. In The Quaternary
              Era in Malesia. Department of Geography,
              University of Hull, Miscellaneous Series,
              No. 13. P. Ashton and M. Ashton, Eds.
              pp. 99-108.
              Discussion similar to part of Ref. 1343.

1345. Goldman, Philip
       1965   A Remarkable Stone Figure from the New
              Guinea Highlands. Journal of the
              Polynesian Society 74:78-79.

156

Description of stone carving found
in cave in Ambum Valley (Western
Highlands District).

1346. Golson, Jack, R.J. Lampert, J.M. Wheeler and W.R.
        Ambrose
        1967   A Note on Carbon Dates for Horticulture
               in the New Guinea Highlands. Journal of
               the Polynesian Society 76:369-371.
               Discussion of dates of materials from
               Manton site near Mount Hagen.

1347. Heider, Karl G.
        1967   An Unusual Carved Stone from Mount Hagen,
               New Guinea. Archaeology and Physical
               Anthropology in Oceania 2:188-189.
               Description of surface find from
               garden near Mount Hagen.

1348. Hope, G.S.
        1973   The Vegetation History of Mount Wilhelm,
               Papua New Guinea. Ph.D. Thesis, Canberra,
               The Australian National University.
               Detailed description and analysis of
               prehistoric vegetation changes based
               on palynological investigations.

1349. Lampert, R.J.
        1967   Horticulture in the New Guinea Highlands -
               C14 Dating. Antiquity, Vol. 41, No. 164,
               pp. 307-309.
               Report of dates from open site near
               Mount Hagen.

1350. McCarthy, Frederick D.
        1936   A Prehistoric Mortar from New Guinea.
               Australian Museum Magazine 6(4):111.

1351. ------
        1944   Some Unusual Stone Artifacts from Australia
               and New Guinea. Australian Museum Records
               21:264-266.

1352. ------
        1949   Some Prehistoric and Recent Stone
               Implements from New Guinea. Australian
               Museum Records 22:155-163.
               Descriptions of surface garden finds
               from Benabena, Mount Hagen area, Wahgi
               Valley and lowland areas.

1353. MacKay, Roy D.
        1970   Rock-Shelter Paintings in Nambaiyufa,
               Chimbu District, New Guinea. Papua New

157

Guinea Museum and Art Gallery, Annual
Report of the Trustees, pp. 7-18. Port
Moresby.
Description as indicated.

1354.   Miles, G.P.L.
        1935   A Stone Pestle and Mortar from the Upper
                Ramu River. Man, Vol. 35, Art. 201,
                p. 185.
                Description of stone implements found
                in Infuntera Creek in 1933.

1355.   Polach, H.A., J. Golson, J.F. Lovering and J.J. Stipp
        1968   A.N.U. Radiocarbon Date List II.
                Radiocarbon 10:179-199.
                Includes dates for materials from
                Batari Cave (Middle Lamari River),
                Kafiavana (Asaro Valley), Manton site
                (Mount Hagen) and Lake Birip (Wabag).

1356.   Powell, Jocelyn M.
        1970a   The History of Agriculture in the New
                Guinea Highlands. Search 1(5):199-200.
                Brief discussion of implications of
                excavations near Mount Hagen.

1357.   -----
        1970b   The Impact of Man on the Vegetation of the
                Mt. Hagen Region, New Guinea. Ph.D.
                Thesis, Canberra, The Australian National
                University.
                Detailed description of results of
                palynological studies of changes in
                vegetation over several millenia.

1358.   -----
        1973   Man and Flora in Papua New Guinea.
                Australian Natural History 17:305-310.
                General discussion, similar to Ref.
                1356.

1359.   -----
        1974   A Note on Wooden Gardening Implements of
                the Mt. Hagen Region, New Guinea. Papua
                New Guinea Museum, Records 4:21-28.
                Brief discussion as indicated.

1360.   Pretty, Graeme L.
        1964   Stone Objects Excavated in New Guinea.
                Man, Vol. 64, Art. 138, p. 117.
                Brief report on surface finds from
                Nondugl.

361. -----
        1968   Two More Prehistoric Stone Artefacts from
                Western Papua. South Australian Museum,
                Records 15:693-697.
                Description of engraved boulder from
                Olsobip and stone bowl from Mt. Bosavi
                region.

362. Stijn, Matthaus van
        1953-   Vier altertumliche steinartefakte vom
        1955   Wahgi River in Zentral-Neuguinea.
                Anthropos 48:971-976.
                Description of prehistoric stone
                artifacts found near Banz, Bundi,
                Dirima, Kup, Mingende, Minj, Mount
                Hagen, Nondugl and other locations.

363. White, J. Peter
        1965a   Archaeological Excavations in New Guinea:
                An Interim Report. Journal of the
                Polynesian Society 74:40-56.
                Description of some results of
                excavations at Aibura (Kainantu area)
                and Niobe (Chuave region).

364. -----
        1965b   An Archaeological Survey in Papua-New
                Guinea. Current Anthropology 6:334-335.
                Very brief report on sites in Ref.
                1363.

365. -----
        1967   Taim Bilong Bipo: Investigations Towards
                a Prehistory of the Papua-New Guinea
                Highlands. Ph.D. Thesis, Canberra, The
                Australian National University.
                Detailed description and analysis of
                excavations at Aibura and Batari Caves
                (Lamari River), Kafiavana (Asaro Valley)
                and Niobe, near Chuave.

366. -----
        1969a   Rock Paintings from the Strickland River,
                Western Highlands, New Guinea. Papua and
                New Guinea Scientific Society,
                Transactions 10:1-7.
                Description as indicated.

367. -----
        1969b   Typologies for Some Prehistoric Flaked
                Stone Artefacts of the Australian New
                Guinea Highlands. Archaeology and
                Physical Anthropology in Oceania 4:18-46.

Analysis of materials from three Lamari
River shelter-sites.

1368. -----
        1972   Ol Tumbuna: Archaeological Excavations
                in the Eastern Central Highlands, Papua
                New Guinea. Department of Prehistory,
                Research School of Pacific Studies, Terra
                Australis, 2. Canberra: The Australian
                National University.
                Detailed description and analysis;
                published version of Ref. 1365.

1369. White, J. Peter and Carmel White
        1964   A New Frontier in Archaeology: Rock Art
                in Papua-New Guinea. The Illustrated
                London News, 14 Nov., Vol. 245, pp. 775-
                777.
                Brief discussion including photographs
                and notes on five cave and shelter
                sites in Lamari River region of
                Eastern Highlands.

A. Human Biology and Population Genetics

1370. Barnicot, N.A. and Jekabs Kariks
        1960   Haptoglobin and Transferrin Variants in
               Peoples of the New Guinea Highlands.
               Medical Journal of Australia 2:859-861.
               (ASARO, CHIMBU, FORE and SINASINA).

1371. Baumgarten, A., Eugene Giles and C.C. Curtain
        1967   Distribution of the Group Specific (Gc)
               Serum Component in the Populations of
               the Markham Valley, New Guinea. American
               Journal of Physical Anthropology 26:79-83.
               (WAFFA and lowlanders).

1372. -----
        1968   The Distribution of Haptoglobin and
               Transferrin Types in Northeast New Guinea.
               American Journal of Physical Anthropology
               29:29-37.
               (BINUMARIEN, WAFFA and lowlanders).

1373. Bennett, J.H.
        1961   Haptoglobin Types in Natives from the
               Kuru Region and Other Parts of Melanesia.
               British Medical Journal 2:428-429.
               (FORE and others).

1374. Bennett, J.H., C.O. Auricht, A.J. Gray, R.L. Kirk
        and L.Y.C. Lai
        1961   Haptoglobin and Transferrin Types in the
               Kuru Region of Australian New Guinea.
               Nature, 7 Jan., 189:68-69.
               (FORE).

1375. Blackburn, C.R.M. and R.W. Hornabrook
        1969   Haptoglobin Gene Frequencies in the People
               of the New Guinea Highlands. Archaeology
               and Physical Anthropology in Oceania 4:
               56-63.
               (AUYANA, CHIMBU, FORE, GIMI, KEIGANA
               and KYAKA ENGA).

1376. Blake, N.M., R.L. Kirk, E. Pryke and P. Sinnett
        1969   Lactate Dehydrogenase Electrophoretic
               Variant in a New Guinea Highlands
               Population. Science, 14 Feb., 163:701-702.
               (ENGA).

1377. Booth, P.B.
       1968   A Further Example of Sub-group A$_2$ in a
              Melanesian. Papua and New Guinea Medical
              Journal 11(1):22.
              (MENYA).

1378. -----
       1971   A Review of the Gerbich Blood Group System
              in Papua New Guinea. Papua and New Guinea
              Medical Journal 14(3):74-76.
              (various districts including Highlands).

1379. Booth, P.B. and R.W. Hornabrook
       1972   Weak I^r Red Cell Antigen in Melanesians:
              Family and Population Studies. Human
              Biology in Oceania 1:306-309.
              (East Sepik, Madang and Morobe
              Districts).

1380. Booth, P.B., K. McLoughlin, R.W. Hornabrook and
       A. MacGregor
       1972   The Gerbich Blood Group System in New
              Guinea: III. The Madang District, the
              Highlands, the New Guinea Islands, and
              the South Papuan Coast. Human Biology
              in Oceania 1:267-272.
              (various districts including Highlands).

1381. Broek, A.J.P. van den
       1913a Das skelett eines Pesechem. Ein Beitrag
              zur Anthropologie der Papuanen von
              Niederlandisch Sudwest-Neu-Guinea.
              Nova Guinea 7:281-353.
              (Pesegem DANI).

1382. -----
       1913b Zur anthropologie des bergstammes Pesegem
              im innern von Niederlandisch-Neu-Guinea.
              Nova Guinea 7:233-276.
              (Pesegem DANI)

1383. Buchbinder, Georgeda
       1973   Maring Microadaptation: A Study of
              Demographic, Nutritional, Genetic, and
              Phenotypic Variation among the Simbai
              Valley Maring of Australian New Guinea.
              Ph.D. Thesis, New York, Columbia University.
              (MARING).

1384. Buchbinder, Georgeda and Peggy Clarke
       1971   The Maring People of the Bismarck Ranges
              of New Guinea: Some Physical and Genetic
              Characteristics. Human Biology in Oceania
              1:121-133.   (MARING).

1385. Champness, L.T., Olga Kooptzoff and R.J. Walsh
       1960   A Study of the Population Near Aiome, New
              Guinea. Oceania 29:294-304.
              (KARAM).

1386. Cotes, J.E., J.R. Adam, H.R. Anderson, V.F. Kay,
       J.M. Patrick and M.J. Saunders
       1972   Lung Function and Exercise Performance
              of Young Adult New Guineans. Human
              Biology in Oceania 1:316-317.
              (YAGARIA and Karkar Island).

1387. Cotter, Helen and R.J. Walsh
       1958   Haemoglobin Values in Some Pacific
              Native Groups. Medical Journal of
              Australia 2:603-605.
              (Anga, CHIMBU and lowlanders).

1388. Craggs, E.M., Olga Kooptzoff and R.J. Walsh
       1958   The Blood Groups of the Kukukuku.
              Oceania 29:67-70.
              (probably MENYA).

1389. Curtain, C.C.
       1964   A Structural Study of Abnormal
              Haemoglobins Occurring in New Guinea.
              Australian Journal of Experimental Biology
              and Medical Science 42:89-97.
              (various Highlanders).

1390. Curtain, C.C., D.C. Gajdusek, C. Kidson, J.G.
       Gorman, L.T. Champness and R. Rodrigue
       1965a Haptoglobins and Transferrins in Melanesia:
              Relation to Hemoglobin, Serum Haptoglobin
              and Serum Ion Levels in Population Groups
              in Papua-New Guinea. American Journal of
              Physical Anthropology 23:363-379.
              (AGARABE, AUYANA, ENGA, FOI, FORE,
              GADSUP, GIMI, HULI, KANITE, MENDI,
              TAIRORA, USURUFA and YAGWOIA).

1391. ------
       1965b Serum Pseudocholinesterase Levels and
              Variants in the Peoples of Papua and New
              Guinea. American Journal of Tropical
              Medicine and Hygiene 14:671-677.
              (same as in Ref. 1390).

1392. ------
       1965c A Study of the Serum Proteins of the
              Peoples of Papua and New Guinea. American
              Journal of Tropical Medicine and Hygiene
              14:678-690.
              (same as in Ref. 1390).

1393. Curtain, C.C., D.C. Gajdusek, Denise O'Brien and
       R.M. Garruto
       1974   Congenital Defects of the Central Nervous
              System Associated with Hyperendemic Goiter
              in a Neolithic Highland Society of Western
              New Guinea. IV. Serum Proteins and
              Haptoglobins, Transferrins and Hemoglobin
              Types in Goitrous and Adjacent Non-Goitrous
              Western Dani Populations. Human Biology
              46:331-338.
              (Mulia and Swart Valley DANI).

1394. Curtain, C.C., D.C. Gajdusek and V. Zigas
       1961   Studies on Kuru. II. Serum Proteins in
              Natives from the Kuru Region of New Guinea.
              American Journal of Tropical Medicine and
              Hygiene 10:92-109.
              (FORE, GIMI, KANITE, KEIGANA, YAGARIA,
              YATE and USURUFA; compared with other
              Highlanders).

1395. Curtain, C.C., C. Kidson, D.C. Gajdusek and J.G.
       Gorman
       1962   Distribution Pattern, Population Genetics
              and Anthropological Significance of
              Thalassemia and Abnormal Hemoglobins in
              Melanesia. American Journal of Physical
              Anthropology 20:475-483.
              (ENGA, GADSUP, GIMI, KAMANO, SIMBARI,
              TAIRORA and USURUFA; compared with
              various lowlanders).

1396. Curtain, C.C., Erna von Loghem, A. Baumgarten,
       T. Golab, J.G. Gorman, C.F. Rutgers and C. Kidson
       1971   The Ethnological Significance of the
              Gamma-globulin (Gm) Factors in Melanesia.
              American Journal of Physical Anthropology
              34:257-271.
              (CHIMBU, ENGA and WAHGI; compared with
              lowlanders).

1397. Curtain, C.C., A. Baumgarten, J.G. Gorman, C. Kidson,
       L.T. Champness, R. Rodrigue and D.C. Gajdusek
       1965   Cold Haemagglutinins: Unusual Incidence
              in Melanesian Populations. British Journal
              of Haematology 11:471-479.
              (AGARABE, AUYANA, ENGA, FOI, FORE,
              GADSUP, GIMI, HULI, KANITE, MENDI,
              MENYA, TAIRORA and USURUFA; compared
              with lowlanders).

1398. Doran, Gregory A. and Leonard Freedman
       1974   Metrical Features of the Dentition and
              Arches of Populations from Goroka and

Lufa, Papua New Guinea. Human Biology
46:583-594.
(ASARO and YAGARIA; compared with other
Highlanders, lowlanders and others).

399. Dunn, Diane, Olga Kooptzoff, A.V.G. Price and
R.J. Walsh
1956 The Blood Groups of a Third Series of
New Guinea Natives from Port Moresby.
Oceania 27:56-63.
(includes MENYA).

400. Fox, R.H., A.J. Hackett, Patricia M. Woodward,
G.M. Budd and A.L. Hendrie
1972 A Study of Temperature Regulation in New
Guinea People. Human Biology in Oceania
1:310-315.
(YAGARIA and Karkar Island).

401. Freedman, Leonard and N.W.G. Macintosh
1965 Stature Variation in Western Highland
Males of East New Guinea. Oceania 35:
286-304.
(ENGA, GAWIGL, HULI, IPILI and MENDI).

402. Garruto, R.M., D.C. Gajdusek and J. ten Brink
1974 Congenital Defects of the Central Nervous
System Associated with Hyperendemic Goiter
in a Neolithic Highland Society of Western
New Guinea. III. Serum and Urinary Iodine
Levels in Goitrous and Adjacent Non-
Goitrous Populations. Human Biology 46:
311-329.
(Mulia and Swart Valley DANI, FORE,
MONI, TAIRORA, UHUNDUNI and Bellona
Island).

1403. Giles, Eugene
1966 Physical Anthropology in the Markham
Valley. Ph.D. Thesis, Cambridge, Mass.,
Harvard University.
(includes WAFFA).

1404. -----
1970 Culture and Genetics. In Current Directions
in Anthropology: A Special Issue. American
Anthropological Association, Bulletins,
Vol. 3, No. 3, Part 2. Ann Fischer, Ed.
pp. 87-98.
(includes WAFFA).

1405 Giles, Eugene, Eugene Ogan and A.G. Steinberg
1965 Gamma Globulin Factors (Gm and Inv) in New

165

Guinea: Anthropological Significance.
Science, 26 Nov., 150:1158-1160.
(BINUMARIEN and WAFFA; compared with
Bougainville and others).

1406. Giles, Eugene, E. Ogan, R.J. Walsh and M.A. Bradley
1966 Blood Group Genetics of Natives of the
Morobe District and Bougainville,
Territory of New Guinea. Archaeology
and Physical Anthropology in Oceania 1:
135-154.
(BINUMARIEN and WAFFA; compared with
Bougainville and others).

1407. Giles, Eugene, R.J. Walsh and M.A. Bradley
1966 Micro-Evolution in New Guinea: The Role
of Genetic Drift. New York Academy of
Sciences, Annals 134:655-665.
(WAFFA).

1408. Giles, Eugene, E.S. Wyber and R.J. Walsh
1970 Micro-Evolution in New Guinea: Additional
Evidence for Genetic Drift. Archaeology
and Physical Anthropology in Oceania 5:
60-71.
(WAFFA; compared with lowlanders).

1409. Graydon, J.J., N.M. Semple, R.T. Simmons and
S. Franken
1958 Blood Groups in Pygmies of the Wissel
Lakes in Netherlands New Guinea (with
Anthropological Notes by H.J.T. Bijlmer).
American Journal of Physical Anthropology
16:149-171.
(KAPAUKU).

1410. Gusinde, Martin
1958 Somatological Investigation of the Pygmies
in the Schrader Mountains of New Guinea.
American Philosophical Society, Yearbook
for 1957, pp. 270-274. Philadelphia.
(KARAM).

1411. ------
1961 Somatology of the Ayom Pygmies of New
Guinea. American Philosophical Society,
Proceedings 105:394-411.
(KARAM).

1412. Harvey, R.G.
1971 The "Red-Skins" of Lufa Sub-District:
Further Observations on the Distinctive
Skin Pigmentation of Some New Guinea
Indigenes. Human Biology in Oceania 1:

103-113.
(YAGARIA).

1413. Hungerford, D.A., E. Giles and C.G. Creech
1965   Chromosome Studies of Eastern New Guinea
        Natives. Current Anthropology 6:107-110.
        (WAMPUR and lowlanders).

1414. Kariks, Jekabs
1961   Serum Protein Values in New Guinea Highland
        Natives. Medical Journal of Australia 2:
        305-307.
        (ASARO).

1415. Kariks, Jekabs and J. Clatworthy
1960   Serum Bilirubin Values in Healthy Goroka
        Natives. Papua and New Guinea Medical
        Journal 4:67-70.
        (ASARO).

1416. Kariks, Jekabs, Olga Kooptzoff, M. Steed, H. Cotter
      and R.J. Walsh
1960   A Study of Some Physical Characteristics
        of the Goroka Natives, New Guinea.
        Oceania 30:225-236.
        (ASARO, BENABENA, GAHUKU, SIANE and
        YAGARIA).

1417. Kenrick, K.G.
1967   Gc-Aborigine in a New Guinea Population.
        Acta Genetica et Statistica Medica 17:
        222-225.
        (CHIMBU).

1418. Kirk, R.L.
1965   Population Genetic Studies of the
        Indigenous Peoples of Australia and New
        Guinea. In Progress in Medical Genetics
        IV. A.G. Steinberg and A.G. Bearn, Eds.
        New York: Grune and Stratton. pp. 202-241.
        General survey of genetics research.

1419. -----
1966   Population Genetic Studies in Australia
        and New Guinea. In The Biology of Human
        Adaptability. P.T. Baker and J.S. Weiner,
        Eds. Oxford: Clarendon Press. pp. 395-
        430.
        General survey, similar to Ref. 1418.

1420. Kitchin, F. David, A.G.Bearn, M. Alpers and
      D.C. Gajdusek
1972   Genetic Studies in Relation to Kuru. III.
        Distribution of the Inherited Serum Group-

Specific Protein (Gc) Phenotypes in New
Guineans: An Association of Kuru and the
GcAb Phenotype. American Journal of
Human Genetics 24(6), Suppl., S72-S85.
(AUYANA, BARUA, ENGA, FORE, GIMI,
HULI, KEIGANA, MENDI, MENYA, SIMBARI
and UHUNDUNI; compared with others).

1421. Lai, L.Y.C.
1966   Hereditary Red Cell Acid Phosphatase
        Types in Australian White and New Guinea
        Native Populations. Acta Genetica et
        Statistica Medica 16:313-320.
        (CHIMBU and OKSAPMIN; compared with
        lowlanders).

1422. Littlewood, Robert A.
1966   Isolate Patterns in the Eastern Highlands
        of New Guinea. Journal of the Polynesian
        Society 75:95-106.
        (AUYANA, AWA, GADSUP and TAIRORA).

1423. ------
1972a   Comment on E. Richard Sorenson, "Socio-
        Ecological Change among the Fore of New
        Guinea" (Ref. 935). Current Anthropology
        13:375-376.
        (AWA).

1424. ------
1972b   Physical Anthropology of the Eastern
        Highlands of New Guinea. Anthropological
        Studies in the Eastern Highlands of New
        Guinea, Vol. 2. Seattle: University of
        Washington Press.
        (AUYANA, AWA, GADSUP and TAIRORA).

1425. Livingstone, Frank B.
1963   Blood Groups and Ancestry: A Test Case
        from the New Guinea Highlands. Current
        Anthropology 4:541-542.
        (AGARABE, ASARO, AUYANA, BENABENA,
        FORE, GADSUP, GAHUKU, GIMI, TAIRORA
        and USURUFA).

1426. McCullogh, J.M. and Eugene Giles
1970   Human Cerumen Types in Mexico and New
        Guinea: A Humidity-Related Polymorphism
        in "Mongoloid" Peoples. Nature, 2 May,
        226:460-462.
        (WAFFA; compared with lowlanders and
        others).

427. MacGregor, A. and R.W. Hornabrook
      1971   Haemoglobin Concentration, Packed Cell
             Volume and Reticulocyte Count of Cord
             Blood in New Guinea Highlanders. Papua
             and New Guinea Medical Journal 14:43-45.
             (ASARO, CHIMBU and KAMANO).

428. McHenry, Henry and Eugene Giles
      1971   Morphological Variation and Heritability
             in Three Melanesian Populations: A
             Multivariate Approach. American Journal
             of Physical Anthropology 35:241-254.
             (WAFFA).

429. Macintosh, N.W.G.
      1960   A Preliminary Note on Skin Colour in the
             Western Highland Natives of New Guinea.
             Oceania 30:279-293.
             (ENGA and HAGEN).

430. Macintosh, N.W.G., R.J. Walsh and Olga Kooptzoff
      1958   The Blood Groups of the Native
             Inhabitants of the Western Highlands,
             New Guinea. Oceania 28:173-198.
             (ENGA, HULI and MENDI).

431. MacLennan, R., M. Bradley and R.J. Walsh
      1967   The Blood Group Pattern at Oksapmin,
             Western Highlands, New Guinea. Archaeology
             and Physical Anthropology in Oceania 2:
             57-61.
             (DUNA, OKSAPMIN and TELEFOL).

432. MacLennan, R., Olga Kooptzoff and R.J. Walsh
      1960   A Survey of the Blood Groups and
             Haemoglobin Values of the Natives in the
             Mount Hagen Area, New Guinea. Oceania 30:
             313-320.
             (GAWIGL, HAGEN and KANDAWO).

433. Malcolm, L.A., P.B. Booth and L.L. Cavalli-Sforze
      1971   Intermarriage Patterns and Blood Group
             Gene Frequencies of the Bundi People of
             the New Guinea Highlands. Human Biology
             43:187-199.
             (GENDE; compared with ASARO, CHIMBU,
             MARING, WAHGI and others).

434. Morris, P.J., A. Ting, M. Alpers and M. Simons
      1970   Leukocyte Antigens in New Guinea. Search
             1(5):259-260.
             (FORE).

169

1435. Munro, R.R.
       1966   Histological Aspects of Skin Pigmentation
               in Indigenes of the Territory of Papua-
               New Guinea. Archaeology and Physical
               Anthropology in Oceania 1:119-134.
               (HAGEN and TELEFOL; compared with
               lowlanders and others).

1436. Nijenhuis, L.E.
       1961   Blood Group Frequencies in the Upper Digul
               and Muyu Districts and in the Star Mountains
               of Netherlands New Guinea. Nova Guinea
               1:1-14.
               (STAR MOUNTAINS; compared with
               lowlanders).

1437. Plato, C.C. and D.C. Gajdusek
       1972   Genetic Studies in Relation to Kuru. IV.
               Dermatoglyphics of the Fore and Anga
               Populations of the Eastern Highlands of
               New Guinea. American Journal of Human
               Genetics 24(6), Suppl., S86-S94.
               (FORE, GENATI, KEIGANA and SIMBARI;
               compared with KARAM and lowlanders).

1438. Powell, Keith C., Monasse Soatt and Kathleen Booth
       1970   Survey of Blood Folate, Haemoglobin and
               Blood Groups in a Group of Sepik
               Villagers. Papua and New Guinea Medical
               Journal 13:56-58.
               (TELEFOL and lowlanders).

1439. Rieckmann, K.H., Olga Kooptzoff and R.J. Walsh
       1961   Blood Groups and Haemoglobin Values in
               the Telefolmin Area, New Guinea.
               Oceania 31:296-304.
               (TELEFOL; compared with CHIMBU,ENGA,
               HAGEN, WAHGI and lowlanders).

1440. Russell, D.A., S.C. Wigley, D.R. Vincin, G.C. Scott,
       P.B. Booth and R.T. Simmons
       1971   Blood Groups and Salivary ABH Secretions
               among the Inhabitants of the Karimui
               Plateau and Adjoining Areas of the New
               Guinea Highlands. Human Biology in
               Oceania 1:79-89.
               (MIKARU).

1441. Semple, N.N., R.T. Simmons, J.J. Graydon, G. Randmae
       and D. Jamieson
       1956   Blood Group Frequencies in Natives of the
               Central Highlands of New Guinea, and in
               the Bainings of New Britain. Medical
               Journal of Australia 2:365-371.

(ASARO, CHIMBU, HAGEN, WAHGI and
various lowlanders and others).

442. Serjeantson, J., L.Y.C. Lai, A. Baumgarten and
C.C. Curtain
1973   Blood Group, Erythrocyte Acid, Phosphatase,
Serum Group Specific Component, Haptoglobin
and Transferrin Gene Frequencies amongst
the Gogodara (Balimo), Kuman (Minj) and
Enga (Laiagam) Peoples of New Guinea.
Human Biology in Oceania 2:139-146.
(ENGA, WAHGI and lowlanders).

443. Simmons, R.T. and D.C. Gajdusek
1962   Blood Group Genetical Studies on Kuru-
Afflicted Natives of the Eastern Highlands
of New Guinea, and Comparisons with
Unaffected Neighboring Tribes in Papua-New
Guinea. Bibliotheca Haematologica 13:255-259.
(AGARABE, AUYANA, AWA, FORE, GADSUP,
GANATI, GIMI, KAMANO, KANITE, KEIGANA,
PAWAIA, SIMBARI, SINASINA, TAIRORA and
USURUFA).

444. Simmons, R.T., D.C. Gajdusek, J.G. Gorman, C. Kidson
and R.W. Hornabrook
1967   Presence of the Duffy Blood Group Gene Fy[b]
Demonstrated in Melanesians. Nature,
18 March, 213:1148-1149.
(Anga, CHIMBU, DANI, ENGA, FORE,
KAPAUKU and lowlanders).

445. Simmons, R.T., J.J. Graydon, C.C. Curtain and
A. Baumgarten
1968   Blood Group Genetic Studies in Laiagam,
and Mt. Hagen (Lepers) New Guinea.
Archaeology and Physical Anthropology in
Oceania 3:49-54.
(ENGA and various others).

446. Simmons, R.T., J.J. Graydon, D.C. Gajdusek, M. Alpers
and R.W. Hornabrook
1972   Genetic Studies in Relation to Kuru. II.
Blood Group Genetic Patterns in Kuru
Patients and Population of the Eastern
Highlands of New Guinea. American Journal
of Human Genetics 24(6), Suppl., S39-S71.
(same as in Ref. 1443).

447. Simmons, R.T., J.J. Graydon, V. Zigas, Lois L. Baker
and D.C. Gajdusek
1961a Studies on Kuru. V. A Blood Group
Genetical Survey of the Kuru Region and
Other Parts of Papua-New Guinea. American

Journal of Tropical Medicine and Hygiene
10:639-664.
(same as in Ref. 1443).

1448. -----
1961b Studies on Kuru. VI. Blood Groups in
Kuru. American Journal of Tropical
Medicine and Hygiene 10:665-668.
(same as in Ref. 1443).

1449. Simons, M.J., C.W. Binns, L.A. Malcolm and E.H. Yap
1972 Australia Antigen Frequencies in Two
Groups of Highland New Guineans. Papua
and New Guinea Medical Journal 15:91-97.
(ENGA and GENDE).

1450. Sinnett, Peter F., N.M. Blake, R.L. Kirk, L.Y.C. Lai
and R.J. Walsh
1970 Blood, Serum Protein and Enzyme Groups
among Enga-Speaking People of the Western
Highlands, New Guinea, with an Estimate
of Genetic Distance between Clans.
Archaeology and Physical Anthropology in
Oceania 5:236-252.
(ENGA).

1451. Steinberg, Arthur G., D.C. Gajdusek and M. Alpers
1972 Genetic Studies in Relation to Kuru. V.
Distribution of Human Gamma Globulin
Allotypes in New Guinea Populations.
American Journal of Human Genetics 24(6),
Suppl., S95-S110.
(BOSAVI, FAIWOL, FORE, HULI, PAWAIA,
SIMBARI and USURUFA; compared with
lowlanders and others).

1452. Vines, A.P. and P.B. Booth
1965 Highlanders of New Guinea and Papua: A
Blood Group Survey. Oceania 35:208-217.
(CHIMBU, CHUAVE, HAGEN, HULI, KAMANO,
MENDI, POLOPA and WIRU).

1453. Walsh, R.J.
1972a Human Genetics. In Peter Ryan, Gen. Ed.
(Ref. 11), Vol. 1, pp. 540-543.
General discussion of population
genetics research and clinical
conditions of genetic origin (e.g.,
"red skins" and albinism).

1454. -----
1972b Physical Anthropology. In Peter Ryan,
Gen. Ed. (Ref. 11), Vol. 2, pp. 896-901.
Very general survey with passing

references to specific locales,
including Highlands.

1455.   Walsh, R.J., Helen Cotter and N.W.G. Macintosh
        1959   Haemoglobin Values of Natives in the
               Western Highlands, New Guinea. Medical
               Journal of Australia 1:834-836.
               (ENGA, HULI, MENDI and others).

1456.   Walsh, R.J., J.L. Jameson and Olga Kooptzoff
        1960   Blood Groups and Haemoglobin Values of
               Natives from Minj, New Guinea. Oceania
               31:77-82.
               (WAHGI; compared with others).

1457.   Walsh, R.J., T.G.C. Murrell and Margaret A. Bradley
        1966   A Medical and Blood Group Survey of the
               Lake Kopiago Natives. Archaeology and
               Physical Anthropology in Oceania 1:57-66.
               (DUNA and HEWA).

1458.   Watson, James B., V. Zigas, Olga Kooptzoff and
        R.J. Walsh
        1961   The Blood Groups of Natives in Kainantu,
               New Guinea. Human Biology 33:25-41.
               (AGARABE, AUYANA, GADSUP, GIMI,
               OYANA, TAIRORA and USURUFA).

1459.   Wolstenholme, J. and R.J. Walsh
        1967   Heights and Weights of Indigenes of the
               Western Highlands District, New Guinea.
               Archaeology and Physical Anthropology in
               Oceania 2:220-226.
               (ENGA and HAGEN).

1460.   Wood-Jones, F.
        1936   Skulls from the Purari Plateau, New
               Guinea. Journal of Anatomy 70:405-409.
               (unidentified except as from a "high
               inland plateau"; references to
               Chinnery, Spinks and Taylor suggest
               BENABENA).

B. Demographic Studies

1461.   Becroft, T.C., J.M. Stanhope and P.M. Burchett
        1969   Mortality and Population Trends among the
               Kyaka Enga, Baiyer Valley. Papua and New
               Guinea Medical Journal 12(2):48-55.
               (KYAKA ENGA).

173

1462. Brewer, K.R.W. and A.J. Whittington
       1969   The 1966 Census of Papua and New Guinea.
              Australian External Territories 9(2):2-14.
              Discussion of field trials and conduct
              of census; not statistical summary.

1463. Couvee, L.M.J.
       1962   Marriage, Obstetrics, and Infant Mortality
              among the Kapauku in the Central Highlands,
              West New Guinea. Tropical and Geographical
              Medicine 14:325-333.
              (KAPAUKU).

1464. Kaa, D.J. van de
       1970   Estimates of the Vital Rates and Future
              Growth. In People and Planning in Papua
              and New Guinea. New Guinea Research Unit,
              Bulletin 34, pp. 1-23. Port Moresby.
              Projection of likely population growth
              in decade of 1970's.

1465. -----
       1971   The Demography of Papua and New Guinea's
              Indigenous Population. Ph.D. Thesis,
              Canberra, The Australian National
              University.
              General survey based largely on 1966
              census; includes many detailed
              analyses and specialized tables.

1466. -----
       1972   Population. In Peter Ryan, Gen. Ed.
              (Ref. 11), Vol. 2, pp. 945-953.
              General survey based on 1966 census
              and other sources; discusses
              demography and distribution of
              population, with map.

1467. McArthur, Norma
       1966   The Demographic Situation. In E.K. Fisk,
              Ed. (Ref. 3), pp. 103-114.
              General discussion of difficulties of
              censusing and lack of detailed records
              available.

1468. Stanhope, J.M.
       1970   Patterns of Fertility and Mortality in
              Rural New Guinea. In People and Planning
              in Papua and New Guinea. New Guinea
              Research Unit, Bulletin 34, pp. 24-41.
              Port Moresby.
              General discussion including most
              districts with details on Baiyer
              River (KYAKA ENGA).

1469. Ward, R. Gerard
       1970   Distribution and Density of Population.
               In R. Gerard Ward and David A.M. Lea,
               Eds. (Ref. 49), pp. 8-11.
               Two maps showing population
               distribution in Papua New Guinea
               and rural population density,
               based on 1966 census; general
               discussion of patterns illustrated
               by maps.

C. Medical Research

        A substantial body of literature has been produced
over the past fifteen years regarding the disease known
as kuru, confined to several ethnolinguistic groups in the
Eastern Highlands of New Guinea. The most complete
bibliography for all sources, anthropological and medical,
is that produced by two of the principal researchers, D.C.
Gajdusek and M.P. Alpers (Ref. 1522 below) and which is
presently being updated and revised. The reader is
referred to that document for a more complete listing than
is provided here.
        Many of the works arising from the kuru research have
already been listed above and additional sources are given
below. Those papers which are clinical or strictly medical
in substance are not included here; I have attempted to
include all of those sources which would be of direct
interest to anthropologists without pretending completeness.
Furthermore since many of the references deal with a small
number of ethnolinguistic groups which are directly affected
by the disease I have avoided repetition of the names of
those groups by simply annotating with a "KURU" designation.
The groups in question are: AUYANA, FORE, GIMI, KAMANO,
KANITE, KEIGANA, USURUFA, YAGARIA and YATE; reference
numbers of these sources are included in the appropriate
sections of the Ethnolinguistic Group Index.

1470. Adam, A.
       1969   Deficiencies of Red-Green Vision among
               Some Populations of Mainland Papua and
               New Guinea. Papua and New Guinea Medical
               Journal 12(4):113-120.
               Includes all mainland districts,
               including Highlands.

1471. Adams, D.D., T.H. Kennedy, J.C. Choufoer and
       A. Querido
       1968   Endemic Goiter in Western New Guinea. III.
               Thyroid Stimulation Activity of Serum
               from Severely Iodine-Deficient People.
               Journal of Clinical Endocrinology and

Metabolism 28:685-692.
(Mulia DANI).

1472. Adels, B. and D.C. Gajdusek
1963   Survey of Measles Patterns in New Guinea,
Micronesia and Australia: with a Report
of New Virgin Soil Epidemics and the
Demonstration of Susceptible Primitive
Populations by Serology. American
Journal of Hygiene 77:317-343.
(AWA, DANI, FORE, MENYA, SIMBARI,
STAR MOUNTAINS, TAIRORA and others).

1473. Alpers, Michael P.
1965   Epidemiological Changes in Kuru, 1957 to
1963. In Slow, Latent and Temperate
Virus Infections. National Institute of
Neurological Disease and Blindness,
Monographs, No. 2. D.C. Gajdusek, C.J.
Gibbs, Jr. and M. Alpers, Eds. Washington:
Government Printing Office. pp. 65-82.
("KURU").

1474. ------
1966   Kuru. In A Manual of Tropical Medicine.
(Fourth Ed.). G.W. Hunter, W.W. Frye and
J.C. Swartzwelder, Eds. Philadelphia:
W.B. Saunders. pp. 646-650.
("KURU").

1475. ------
1968   Kuru: Implications of Its Transmissibility
for the Interpretation of Its Changing
Epidemiological Pattern. In The Central
Nervous System: Some Experimental Models
of Neurological Diseases. International
Academy of Pathology, Monograph No. 9.
O.T. Bailey and D.E. Smith, Eds. Baltimore:
Williams and Wilkins. pp. 234-251.
("KURU").

1476. ------
1969   Kuru. In Virus Diseases and the Nervous
System: A Symposium. C.W.M. Whitty, J.T.
Hughes and F.O. MacCallum, Eds. Oxford:
Blackwell. pp. 83-97.
("KURU")

1477. ------
1970   Kuru in New Guinea: Its Changing Pattern
and Etiological Elucidation. American
Journal of Tropical Medicine and Hygiene
19:133-137.
("KURU").

1478.   Alpers, Michael P. and D.C. Gajdusek
        1965   Changing Patterns of Kuru: Epidemiological
                Changes in the Period of Increasing
                Contact of the Fore People with Western
                Civilization. American Journal of
                Tropical Medicine and Hygiene 14:852-879.
                ("KURU").

1479.   Arter, W.J., G.M. Stathers, M.H. Mah, C.R.B.
        Blackburn and V.J. McGovern
        1968   Liver Disease in the Highland Populations
                of the Territory of Papua and New Guinea.
                I. Observations on Liver Biopsies from
                Persons Selected in Field Surveys.
                Tropical and Geographical Medicine 20:
                202-216.
                (CHIMBU, FORE and KYAKA ENGA).

1480.   Barmes, D.E.
        1972   Dental Health. In Peter Ryan, Gen. Ed.
                (Ref. 11), Vol. 1, pp. 243-246.
                General discussion of factors related
                to caries rates, periodontal disease
                and malocclusion and relationship to
                betel-chewing and smoking.

1481.   Barnes, Robert
        1963   Two Cases of Pre-eclampsia and One of
                Eclampsia in the Highlands of New Guinea.
                Medical Journal of Australia 2:884-886.
                (Kundiawa Hospital; probably CHIMBU).

1482.   -----
        1966   Epidemiology of 1964-1965 Influenza
                Outbreak in the Sepik District. Papua
                and New Guinea Medical Journal 9:127-132.
                (includes FAIWOL, OKSAPMIN and TELEFOL).

1483.   Benfante, R.J., R.D. Traub, K.A. Lim, J. Hooks,
        L.J. Gibbs, Jr. and D.C. Gajdusek
        1974   Immunological Reactions in Kuru: Attempts
                to Demonstrate Serological Relationships
                between Kuru and Other Known Infectious
                Agents. American Journal of Tropical
                Medicine and Hygiene 23:476-488.
                ("KURU").

1484.   Bennett, J.H.
        1960   Kuru and Sporadic Tremor Syndromes in New
                Guinea. Lancet, 6 Feb., 1:339.
                (FORE only).

1485.   -----
        1962a   Population and Family Studies on Kuru.
                Eugenics Quarterly 9:59-68.
                (FORE, GIMI, KANITE and KEIGANA only).

1486.   -----
        1962b   Population Studies in the Kuru Region of
                New Guinea. Oceania 33:24-46.
                (AGARABE, FORE, GIMI, KAMANO, KANITE
                and KEIGANA).

1487.   Bennett, J.H., B.W. Gabb and Carolyn R. Dertel
        1966   Further Changes of Pattern in Kuru.
                Medical Journal of Australia 1:379-386.
                (FORE, GIMI, KANITE and KEIGANA only).

1488.   Bennett, J.H., A.J. Gray and C.O. Auricht
        1959   The Genetical Study of Kuru. Medical
                Journal of Australia 2:505-508.
                (FORE, GIMI, KANITE and KEIGANA only).

1489.   Bennett, J.H., F.A. Rhodes and H.N. Robson
        1958   Observations on Kuru. I. A Possible
                Genetic Basis. Australasian Annals of
                Medicine 7:269-275.
                (FORE only).

1490.   -----
        1959   A Possible Genetic Basis for Kuru.
                American Journal of Human Genetics 11:
                169-187.
                (FORE only).

1491.   Black, Robert H.
        1954   A Malaria Survey of the People Living on
                the Minj River in the Western Highlands
                of New Guinea. Medical Journal of
                Australia 2:782-787.
                (WAHGI).

1492.   -----
        1972   Malaria. In Peter Ryan, Gen. Ed. (Ref.
                11), Vol. 2, pp. 679-684.
                Sketch of history of surveys and
                attempts to control; discussion of
                vectors, recent incidence and clinical
                features.

1493.   Blackburn, C.R.B., W.J. Arter, P. Burchett,
        T. Murrell, A. Radford, K. Meehan, M. Ma and V.J.
        McGovern
        1966   Hepatomegaly: An Epidemiological Study in
                the Eastern and Western Highlands Districts
                of New Guinea. Papua and New Guinea

Medical Journal 9:21-26.
(CHIMBU and KYAKA ENGA).

94. Blackburn, C.R.B. and M.H. Ma
1971a   Skin Reactions of Natives in the Western
Highlands of New Guinea to an Antigen
Prepared from Dirofilaria immitis.
Tropical and Geographical Medicine 23:
272-277.
(CHIMBU, KYAKA ENGA and Trobriands).

95. -----
1971b   Skin Reactions of Natives in the Western
Highlands of New Guinea to a Schistosoma
mansoni Antigen. Tropical and Geographical
Medicine 23:278-281.
(KYAKA ENGA and Trobriands).

96. -----
1972   Hepatomegaly in Papua New Guinea: Progress
Report on a Long Term Study. Papua and
New Guinea Medical Journal 15(2):84-90.
(CHIMBU, KYAKA ENGA and Trobriands).

97. Booth, Kathleen
1970   Leukaemia in the Territory of Papua and
New Guinea. Papua and New Guinea Medical
Journal 13:81-83.
(various unidentified Highlanders).

98. Boughton, Clement R.
1970   Clinical Observations on Immunity in
Leprosy. Search 1(5):256-258.
(MIKARU).

99. Bowler, D.P.
1972   Child Health. In Peter Ryan, Gen. Ed.
(Ref. 11), Vol. 1, pp. 154-156.
General discussion of infant mortality
rates, commonest causes of death and
various government services available.

500. Burnet, F.M.
1965a   Appendix to: The Changing Face of Kuru.
Lancet, 29 May, 1:1141-1142.
("KURU").

501. -----
1965b   Kuru -- The Present Position. Papua and
New Guinea Medical Journal 8(1):3-7.
("KURU").

502. -----
1971   Reflections on Kuru. Human Biology in

Oceania 1:3-9.
("KURU").

1503. -----
       1972   Kuru. In Peter Ryan, Gen. Ed. (Ref. 11),
               Vol. 1, pp. 586-588.
               ("KURU").

1504. Buttfield, I.H., B.S. Hetzel and R.W. Hornabrook
       1968   Kuru: The Endocrine Status. Australasian
               Annals of Medicine 17:20-22.
               ("KURU").

1505. Choufoer, J.C., M. van Rhijn, A.A.H. Kassenaar and
       A. Querido
       1963   Endemic Goiter in Western New Guinea:
               Iodine Metabolism in Goitrous and Non-
               Goitrous Subjects. Journal of Clinical
               Endocrinology and Metabolism 23:1203-1217.
               (Mulia DANI).

1506. Choufoer, J.C., M. Van Rhijn and A. Querido
       1965   Endemic Goiter in Western New Guinea. II.
               Clinical Picture, Incidence and
               Pathogenesis of Endemic Cretinism.
               Journal of Clinical Endocrinology and
               Metabolism 25:385-402.
               (Mulia DANI).

1507. Cleary, G.J. and C.R.B. Blackburn
       1968   Air Pollution in Native Huts in the
               Highlands of New Guinea. Archives of
               Environmental Health 17:785-794.
               (CHIMBU and KYAKA ENGA).

1508. DuToit, Brian M.
       1965   Medicine and Anthropology. South African
               Journal of Science 61(2):55-60.
               (includes discussion of endemic goiter
               among Mulia DANI).

1509. Egerton, J.R.
       1966   Bacteriology of Enteritis Necroticans in
               New Guinea Highlanders. Papua and New
               Guinea Medical Journal 9:55-59.
               (ASARO, CHIMBU, CHUAVE, DUNA, ENGA,
               HULI and KYAKA ENGA).

1510. Ewers, W.H.
       1972   Parasites of Man in Papua-New Guinea.
               South East Asian Journal of Tropical
               Medicine and Public Health 3(1):79-86.
               (General discussion).

511. Ewers, W.H. and W.T. Jeffrey
      1971   Parasites of Man in Niugini. Port
             Moresby: Jacaranda Press.
             Detailed description of parasites
             and discussion of related diseases.

512. Fenner, Frank
      1972   Viral Infections. In Peter Ryan, Gen.
             Ed. (Ref. 11), Vol. 2, pp. 1174-1176.
             Brief discussion of smallpox, measles,
             chickenpox, influenza, poliomyelitis
             and dengue fever, several of which are
             endemic in Highlands areas.

513. Fischer, Ann and John L. Fischer
      1960   Aetiology of Kuru. Lancet, 25 June,
             1:1417-1418.
             General discussion and argument against
             genetic aetiology.

514. -----
      1961   Culture and Epidemiology: A Theoretical
             Investigation of Kuru. Journal of Health
             and Human Behavior 2:16-25.
             Expanded discussion of genetic and
             other possible etiologies.

515. Fisher, S.
      1956   A Serological Survey on a Group of Natives
             of the Wabag Area of the Western Highlands
             of New Guinea for Diphtheria Antitoxin
             and Antibody to Haemophilus Pertussis.
             Medical Journal of Australia 2:405-408.
             (ENGA).

516. Fortune, Reo F.
      1960   Statistics of Kuru. Medical Journal of
             Australia 1:764-765.
             (FORE only).

517. Gajdusek, D. Carleton
      1958   Kuru: An Acute Degenerative Neurological
             Disorder in Melanesian Natives. American
             Neurological Association, Transactions,
             pp. 156-158.
             ("KURU").

518. -----
      1962a Congenital Defects of the Central Nervous
             System Associated with Hyperendemic Goiter
             in a Neolithic Highland Society of
             Netherlands New Guinea. I. Epidemiology.
             Pediatrics 29:345-363.
             (Mulia DANI).

1519. -----
       1962b Kuru: An Appraisal of Five Years of
              Investigation. Eugenics Quarterly 9:
              69-74.
              ("KURU").

1520. -----
       1963   Kuru. Royal Society of Tropical Medicine
              and Hygiene, Transactions 57:151-169.
              ("KURU").

1521. -----
       1964   Factors Governing the Genetics of Primitive
              Human Populations. Cold Spring Harbor
              Symposia on Quantitative Biology 29:121-
              135.
              ("KURU").

1522. Gajdusek, D. Carleton and Michael P. Alpers
       1970   Bibliography of Kuru. (Rev. Ed.).
              Bethesda, Md.: National Institute of
              Neurological Diseases and Stroke,
              National Institutes of Health.
                    Comprehensive and annotated; organized
                    by subject including medical research,
                    anthropology, linguistics and natural
                    history of kuru region.

1523. Gajdusek, D. Carleton and Lucy H. Reid
       1961   Studies on Kuru. IV. The Kuru Patterns in
              Moke, a Representative Fore Village.
              American Journal of Tropical Medicine and
              Hygiene 10:628-638.
              (FORE only).

1524. Gajdusek, D.C., E.R. Sorenson and Judith Meyer
       1970   A Comprehensive Cinema Record of
              Disappearing Kuru. Brain 93:65-76.
              ("KURU").

1525. Gajdusek, D.C. and Vincent Zigas
       1957   Degenerative Disease of the Central Nervous
              System in New Guinea. The Endemic
              Occurrence of "Kuru" in the Native
              Population. New England Journal of
              Medicine 257:974-978.
              ("KURU").

1526. -----
       1959   Kuru. Clinical, Pathological and
              Epidemiological Study of an Acute
              Progressive Degenerative Disease of the
              Central Nervous System among Natives of
              the Eastern Highlands of New Guinea.

American Journal of Medicine 26:442-469.
("KURU").

527. Gajdusek, D.C., V. Zigas and J. Baker
      1961   Studies on Kuru. III. Patterns of Kuru
             Incidence: Demographic and Geographic
             Epidemiological Analysis. American
             Journal of Tropical Medicine and Hygiene
             10:599-627.
             ("KURU" and AWA, PAWAIA, SIMBARI and
             TAIRORA).

528. Garner, M.F. and R.W. Hornabrook
      1968   Treponematosis in the Eastern Highlands
             of New Guinea. World Health Organization,
             Bulletin 38:189.
             (AUYANA and FORE).

529. -----
      1970a 1968 Survey of Treponematosis in the
             Eastern Highlands of New Guinea. British
             Journal of Venereal Disease 46:13-17.
             (AUYANA, FORE, GIMI and KEIGANA).

530. -----
      1970b Treponematosis in New Guinea. Papua and
             New Guinea Medical Journal 13:53-55.
             (AUYANA, FORE, GIMI and KEIGANA).

531. -----
      1973   Treponematosis in Papua New Guinea. A
             Review of Surveys Undertaken between 1964
             and 1972. Papua New Guinea Medical
             Journal 16:189-193.
             (AUYANA, FORE, GIMI and KEIGANA).

532. Garner, M.F., R.W. Hornabrook and J.L. Backhouse
      1972   Treponematosis along the Highlands Highway.
             Papua New Guinea Medical Journal 15:139.
             (various locations from Kainantu to
             Mount Hagen).

533. Giblin, W.E.
      1954   "Daraprim" in the Whagi (sic) Valley of
             New Guinea. Medical Journal of Australia
             1:9-10.
             (unidentified government hospital at
             "east end of Whagi Valley").

534. Glasse, Robert M.
      1961   A "Kuru" Bibliography. Oceania 31:294-295.
             Brief list of early sources on kuru
             research.

1535.   Gorman, J.G. and Chev Kidson
         1962   Distribution Pattern of an Inherited
                 Trait, Red Cell Enzyme Deficiency in New
                 Guinea and New Britain. American Journal
                 of Physical Anthropology 20:347-356.
                 (AUYANA, AWA, DANI, FORE, GADSUP,
                 MENYA, TAIRORA and YATE; also
                 lowlanders and island Melanesians).

1536.   Hansman, David, Lorraine Devitt, Helen Miles and
         Ian Riley
         1974   Pneumococci Relatively Insensitive to
                 Penicillin in Australia and New Guinea.
                 Medical Journal of Australia 2:353-356.
                 (ASARO, HULI, YAGARIA and others).

1537.   Harland, P.S.E.G.
         1967   Kuru, Rainfall and Nutrition. Lancet,
                 9 Dec., 2:1259.
                 Suggested relationship of kuru to
                 nutrition and seasonality of crops.

1538.   Harvey, R.G.
         1971   Anomaloscope Testing of the Colour Vision
                 of a New Guinea Highland Population.
                 Human Biology in Oceania 1:144-149.
                 (YAGARIA).

1539.   Hausfeld, R.G.
         1970   An Anthropological Method for Measuring
                 Exposure to Leprosy in a Leprosy-Endemic
                 Population at Karimui, New Guinea. World
                 Health Organization, Bulletin 43:863-877.
                 (MIKARU).

1540.   Hetzel, Basil S.
         1971   The History of Endemic Cretinism. In
                 Basil S. Hetzel and Peter O.D. Pharoah,
                 Eds. (Ref. 1542), pp. 5-8.
                 General discussion, including Papua
                 New Guinea and Irian Jaya.

1541.   -----
         1972   Goitre and Cretinism. In Peter Ryan,
                 Gen. Ed. (Ref. 11), Vol. 1, pp. 498-499.
                 Brief discussion of relationship to
                 diet and soil; includes distribution
                 map.

1542.   Hetzel, Basil S. and Peter O.D. Pharoah (Eds.)
         1971   Endemic Cretinism. Institute of Human
                 Biology, Monograph Series, No. 2.
                 Goroka.
                 Collection of papers, some dealing

with Highlands societies.

543. Hill, E.M.
1966   Leprosy in the New Guinea Highlands.
Australian Territories 6(4):25-33.
Discussion of incidence and attempts
at control by Administration.

544. Hoffman, N.E. and J.D. Mathews
1968   Gastro-Intestinal Disease in New Guinea.
Medical Journal of Australia 1:153.
(FORE).

545. Hornabrook, R.W.
1966   Kuru -- Some Misconceptions and Their
Explanation. Papua and New Guinea Medical
Journal 9(1):11-15.
General discussion of theories of
etiology.

546. -----
1968   Kuru -- A Subacute Cerebellar Degeneration.
The Natural History and Clinical Features.
Brain 91:53-74.
General discussion.

547. -----
1970   The Auyana Head Nodders. Papua and New
Guinea Medical Journal 13(3):90-92.
Discussion of "essential tremor,"
regarded by AUYANA as sorcery-caused.

548. -----
1971   Neurological Aspects of Endemic Cretinism
in Eastern New Guinea. In Basil S. Hetzel
and Peter O.D. Pharoah, Eds. (Ref. 1542),
pp. 105-107.
(KARAM).

549. -----
1972   Syphilis. In Peter Ryan, Gen. Ed.
(Ref. 11), Vol. 2, pp. 1108-1109.
Description of symptoms and course of
disease; brief suggestions regarding
epidemiology and relation to social
change.

1550. Hornabrook, R.W. and E.J. Field
1969   Clinical and Pathological Findings in
Kuru. Lancet, 15 March, 1:576.
General discussion.

1551.   Hornabrook, R.W. and D. Moir
        1970   Kuru Epidemiological Trends.   Lancet,
                5 Dec., 2:1175-1179.
                General discussion.

1552.   Hotchin, J.
        1966   Kuru as a Persisting Tolerated Infection.
                Lancet, 2 July, 2:28-31.
                · Suggested etiology.

1553.   Ivinskis, V., Olga Kooptzoff, R.J. Walsh and
        Diane Dunn
        1956   A Medical and Anthropological Study of
                the Chimbu Natives of the Central
                Highlands of New Guinea.   Oceania 27:
                143-157.
                (CHIMBU).

1554.   Kariks, Jekabs
        1960   Kwashiorkor in the Highlands of New
                Guinea.   Papua and New Guinea Medical
                Journal 4(1):5-18.
                (ASARO).

1555.   -----
        1962   Some Observations on Serum Protein Levels
                in Kwashiorkor and Their Changes during
                Treatment.   Medical Journal of Australia
                2:411-414.
                (ASARO).

1556.   -----
        1972   Yaws.   In Peter Ryan, Gen. Ed. (Ref. 11),
                Vol. 2, pp. 1227-1230.
                Description of symptoms (including
                photographs), transmission, prevalence
                and control measures.

1557.   Kidson, Chev
        1961a   Deficiency of Glucose-6-Phosphate
                Dehydrogenase: Some Aspects of the Trait
                in People of Papua-New Guinea.   Medical
                Journal of Australia 2:506-509.
                (unidentified Highlanders in Kainantu
                region; compared with lowlanders and
                island Melanesians).

1558.   -----
        1961b   Erythrocyte Glucose-6-Phosphate
                Dehydrogenase Deficiency in New Guinea and
                New Britain.   Nature, 17 June, 190:1120-
                1121.
                (unidentified Highlanders in Kainantu
                region and New Britain).

186

1559. -----
          1965   Kuru as a Model of Hormonally Programmed
                  Central Nervous Degeneration. Lancet,
                  23 Oct., 2:830-831.
                  General discussion.

1560. Kidson, Chev and D.C. Gajdusek
          1962   Congenital Defects of the Central Nervous
                  System Associated with Hyperendemic Goiter
                  in a Neolithic Highland Society of
                  Netherlands New Guinea. II. Glucose-6-
                  Phosphate Dehydrogenase in the Mulia
                  Population. Pediatrics 29:364-368.
                  (Mulia DANI).

1561. Kidson, Chev and J.G. Gorman
          1962   Contribution of Red Cell Enzyme Deficiency
                  Trait to an Understanding of Genetic
                  Relationships between Melanesian and
                  Other Populations. American Journal of
                  Physical Anthropology 20:357-363.
                      (AUYANA, AWA, DANI, FORE, GADSUP,
                      MENYA, TAIRORA and YATE; compared
                      with lowlanders, island Melanesians
                      and world distribution).

1562. Kiloh, L.G. and J.E. Cawte
          1972   Mental Health. In Peter Ryan, Gen. Ed.
                  (Ref. 11), Vol. 2, pp. 759-763.
                      Discussion of traditional patterns of
                      mental illness, transitional patterns
                      with urbanization and organic patterns.

1563. Ma, M.H., C.R.B. Blackburn, V.J. McGovern,
       P. Burchett and W.J. Arter
          1968   Liver Disease in the Highland Populations
                  of the Territory of Papua and New Guinea.
                  II. Histological Observations on Liver
                  Tissues of Patients in Hospital.
                  Tropical and Geographical Medicine 20:
                  307-316.
                      (ASARO, CHIMBU and KYAKA ENGA).

1564. McArthur, Norma
          1964   The Age Incidence of Kuru. Annals of
                  Human Genetics 27:341-352.
                      ("KURU").

1565. -----
          1972   Cross-Currents: The Statistics of Kuru.
                  Human Biology in Oceania 1:289-298.
                      ("KURU").

187

1566. McMahon, J.E.
        1973-   Malaria Endemicity amongst the Semi-
        1974   Nomadic People of the Karimui Area of
                 Papua New Guinea. Papua New Guinea
                 Medical Journal 17:99-107.
                 (MIKARU).

1567. McMillan, Bruce and A. Kelly
        1967   Ovale Malaria in Eastern New Guinea.
                 Tropical and Geographical Medicine 19:
                 172-176.
                 (CHIMBU).

1568. McMillan, Bruce, A. Kelly and J.C. Walker
        1971   Prevalence of Hymenolepis diminuta
                 Infection in Man in the New Guinea
                 Highlands. Tropical and Geographical
                 Medicine 23:390-392.
                 (ASARO, HAGEN, HULI and KYAKA ENGA).

1569. Maddocks, Ian and Luke Rovin
        1965   A New Guinea Population in which Blood
                 Pressure Appears to Fall as Age Advances.
                 Papua and New Guinea Medical Journal 8:
                 17-21.
                 (CHIMBU).

1570. Malaria Branch, Department of Public Health, Port
        Moresby
        1970   Malaria. In R. Gerard Ward and David A.M.
                 Lea, Eds. (Ref. 49), p. 28.
                 Very brief discussion; distribution map
                 indicates occasional epidemic areas in
                 Highlands.

1571. Malcolm, L.A.
        1969   Child Mortality and Disease Pattern: Recent
                 Changes in the Bundi Area. Papua and New
                 Guinea Medical Journal 12:13-17.
                 (GENDE).

1572. Mathews, John D.
        1965   The Changing Face of Kuru. An Analysis of
                 Pedigrees Collected by R.M. Glasse and
                 Shirley Glasse and of Recent Census Data.
                 Lancet, 29 May, 1:1138-1141.
                 ("KURU").

1573. -----
        1967a   The Epidemiology of Kuru. Papua and New
                 Guinea Medical Journal 10(3):76-82.
                 ("KURU").

1574. -----
       1967b Kuru, Rainfall and Nutrition. Lancet,
              25 Nov., 2:1147.
              Critique of Harland (Ref. 1537).

1575. -----
       1967c A Transmission Model for Kuru. Lancet,
              15 April, 1:821-825.
              Suggested etiology.

1576. Mathews, John D., R.M. Glasse and S. Lindenbaum
       1968   Kuru and Cannibalism. Lancet, 24 Aug.,
              2:449-452.
              Discussion of proposed etiology.

1577. Metselaar, D.
       1959a Een malaria survey in de Baliem Vallei.
              Nieuw-Guinea Studien 3:101-118.
              (DANI).

1578. -----
       1959b Malaria Control in Netherlands New
              Guinea. South Pacific Commission,
              Quarterly Bulletin 9(1):33-35.
              General discussion of administration
              control in Irian Jaya.

1579. -----
       1959c Two Malaria Surveys in the Central
              Mountains of Netherlands New Guinea.
              American Journal of Tropical Medicine
              and Hygiene 8:364-367.
              (DANI compared with WAHGI).

1580. Murrell, T.G.C.
       1966a Pig-Bel -- Case Reports. Papua and New
              Guinea Medical Journal 9:68-71.
              (ASARO, CHIMBU, ENGA and KAMANO).

1581. -----
       1966b Some Epidemiological Features of Pig-
              Bel. Papua and New Guinea Medical
              Journal 9:39-50.
              (ASARO, CHIMBU, ENGA, HAGEN, HULI,
              KYAKA ENGA, MENDI and WAHGI).

1582. Murrell, T.G.C., J.R. Egerton, Anita Rampling,
       Janet Samels and P.D. Walker
       1966   The Ecology and Epidemiology of the
              Pig-bel Syndrome in Man in New Guinea.
              Journal of Hygiene 64:375-396.
              (ASARO, CHIMBU, CHUAVE, DUNA, ENGA,
              HULI and KYAKA ENGA).

189

1583. Murrell, T.G.C. and L. Roth
       1963   Necrotizing Jejunitis: A Newly Discovered
               Disease in the Highlands of New Guinea.
               Medical Journal of Australia 1:61-69.
                 (ASARO, CHIMBU, CHUAVE, DUNA, ENGA,
                 HULI and KYAKA ENGA).

1584. Murrell, T.G.C., L. Roth, J.R. Egerton, Janet Samels
       and P.D. Walker
       1966   Pig-bel: Enteritis Necroticans: A Study
               in Diagnosis and Management. Lancet,
               29 Jan., 1:217-222.
                 Definition and classification as disease
                 of small bowel; based on laboratory
                 analyses of 210 cases.

1585. Neumann, Meta A., D.C. Gajdusek and V. Zigas
       1964   Neuropathologic Findings in Exotic
               Neurologic Disorders among Natives of the
               Highlands of New Guinea. Journal of
               Neuropathology and Experimental Neurology
               23:486-507.
                 (AGARABE, FORE, HULI, KAMANO, KANITE
                 and MENDI).

1586. Paine, Brenda G.
       1971   Growth and Development. In Basil S.
               Hetzel and Peter O.D. Pharoah, Eds.
               (Ref. 1542), pp. 94-100.
                 Endemic cretinism among HAGEN.

1587. -----
       1973   Pertussis in the Highlands -- A Clinical
               Review. Papua New Guinea Medical Journal
               16:36-41.
                 (patients in Mount Hagen hospital).

1588. Papua New Guinea Institute of Medical Research
       1974   A Bibliography of Medical and Human
               Biological Research of Papua New Guinea.
               Goroka: Institute of Human Biology.

1589. Parkinson, A.D.
       1973-   Malaria in Papua New Guinea 1973. Papua
       1974   New Guinea Medical Journal 17:8-16.
                 General survey.

1590. Peters, W.
       1959   Liver Enlargement and Malaria in New
               Guinea. Tropical and Geographical
               Medicine 11:219-222.
                 (ENGA and lowlanders).

1591. Peters, W. and S.H. Christian
      1960   Studies on the Epidemiology of Malaria in
             New Guinea. Parts IV,V and VI. Unstable
             Highland Malaria. Royal Society of
             Tropical Medicine and Hygiene, Transactions
             54:529-548.
             (WAHGI).

1592. Peters, W., S.H. Christian and J.L. Jameson
      1958   Malaria in the Highlands of Papua and
             New Guinea. Medical Journal of Australia
             2:409-416.
             (ASARO, CHIMBU, CHUAVE, ENGA, HAGEN,
             HULI, KYAKA ENGA, MIKARU, SINASINA
             and WAHGI; also lowlanders).

1593. Pharoah, P.O.D.
      1971a Endemic Cretinism in New Guinea. Papua
             and New Guinea Medical Journal 14:115-119.
             (KARAM).

1594. -----
      1971b Epidemiological Studies of Endemic
             Cretinism in the Jimi River Valley in
             New Guinea. In Basil S. Hetzel and
             Peter O.D. Pharoah, Eds. (Ref. 1542),
             pp. 109-116.
             (KARAM).

1595. Ponsford, Joan, Maureen Larkin, D.C. Dorman and
      N.F. Stanley
      1955   Virus Antibodies in New Guinea Natives.
             Australian Journal of Science 18(2):
             64-65.
             (ENGA).

1596. Querido, A.
      1971   The Epidemiology of Cretinism. In Basil
             S. Hetzel and Peter O.D. Pharoah, Eds.
             (Ref. 1542), pp. 9-18.
             General discussion including New
             Guinea.

1597. Reid, Sophie
      1972   Skin Diseases. In Peter Ryan, Gen. Ed.
             (Ref. 11), Vol. 2, pp. 1039-1042.
             Brief discussions of albinism,
             inflammations, infections, nutritional
             deficiencies, callogen diseases and
             neoplastic conditions.

1598. Rhodes, F.A. and S.E.J. Anderson
      1970   An Outbreak of Treponematosis in the
             Eastern Highlands. Papua and New Guinea

Medical Journal 13:49-52.
(unidentified Highlanders in Goroka
hospital; probably ASARO).

1599. Riley, I.D.
1973 Pneumonia in Papua New Guinea. Papua and
New Guinea Medical Journal 16:9-14.
(HULI, KYAKA ENGA and lowlanders).

1600. Roth, L.
1966 Diagnosis and Management of Pig-Bel.
Papua and New Guinea Medical Journal 9:
51-54.
General discussion.

1601. Rountree, Phyllis M.
1956 Staphylococci Harboured by People in
Western Highlands of New Guinea. Lancet,
19 May, 1:719-720.
(ENGA).

1602. Rountree, Phyllis M., Mary Beard, W.J. Arter and
Ann Woolcock
1967 Further Studies on the Nasal Flora of
People of Papua-New Guinea. Medical
Journal of Australia 1:967-969.
(CHIMBU, FORE, KYAKA ENGA and
Trobriands).

1603. Rountree, Phyllis M. and P.K. Littlewood
1964 The Nasal Flora of the Auyana People in
the Eastern Highlands of New Guinea.
Medical Journal of Australia 2:336-337.
(AUYANA).

1604. Russell, D.A.
1960 Leprosy in Papua and New Guinea. Papua
and New Guinea Medical Journal 4:49-54.
(ENGA, FORE, HULI and KYAKA ENGA).

1605. Scragg, R.F.R.
1972 Medical Demography. In Peter Ryan, Gen.
Ed. (Ref. 11), Vol. 2, pp. 740-746.
General survey of demographic studies
and mortality figures.

1606. Shlimovitz, Nathan
1946 Leprosy: A Report of Nine Cases among
Natives of the Mount Hagen Area in New
Guinea. Medical Journal of Australia 1:
369-370.
(HAGEN).

607. Sinnett, Peter F. and Albert Solomon
      1968   Physical Fitness in a New Guinea Highland
              Population. Papua and New Guinea
              Medical Journal 11(2):56-59.
              (ENGA).

608. Sinnett, Peter F. and H.M. Whyte
      1973a   Epidemiological Studies in a Highland
              Population of New Guinea: Environment,
              Culture, and Health Status. Human Ecology
              1:245-277.
              (ENGA).

609. -----
      1973b   Epidemiological Studies in a Total
              Highland Population, Tukisenta, New Guinea:
              Cardiovascular Disease and Relevant
              Clinical, Electrocardiographic, Radiological
              and Biochemical Findings. Journal of
              Chronic Diseases 26:265-290.
              (ENGA).

610. Smith, M. and F.S. Smith
      1968   The Problem of Vesico-Vaginal Fistula in
              the New Guinea Highlands. Papua and New
              Guinea Medical Journal 11:19-21.
              (unidentified patients in Goroka
              hospital).

611. Spencer, Terence E.T., Margaret Spencer, M.T.
      Jemesen and J.W.J. Tommerup
      1956   Malaria in the Mount Hagen Area. Papua
              and New Guinea Medical Journal 1:110-113.
              (HAGEN).

612. Stanbury, John B.
      1971   The Patterns of Endemic Cretinism. In
              Basil S. Hetzel and Peter O.D. Pharoah,
              Eds. (Ref. 1542), pp. 19-28.
              (Mulia DANI).

613. Standfast, H.A.
      1972   Medical Entomology. In Peter Ryan, Gen.
              Ed. (Ref. 11), Vol. 2, pp. 746-748.
              Brief discussions of insects (by order)
              of medical importance and related
              diseases.

614. Stanhope, J.M.
      1968   Blood Pressures of the Tinam-Aigram
              People near Simbai, Madang District.
              Papua and New Guinea Medical Journal
              11(2):60-61.
              (KARAM).

1615. Stanley, N.F.
      1972   Burkitt's Lymphoma. In Peter Ryan, Gen.
             Ed. (Ref. 11), Vol. 1, pp. 127-129.
             Childhood cancer rare in Highlands;
             discussion of distribution, probable
             role of viruses and incidence.

1616. Tommerup, J.W.J.
      1955   Diary and Summary of a Medical Patrol in
             the Wabaga Sub-District of the Western
             Highlands. Papua and New Guinea Medical
             Journal 1:69-73.
             (ENGA).

1617. Venkatachalam, P.S. and V. Ivinskis
      1957   Kwashiorkor in New Guinea. Medical Journal
             of Australia 1:275-277.
             (ASARO and CHIMBU).

1618. Vines, A.P.
      1972   Disease Prevalence (Morbidity). In Peter
             Ryan, Gen. Ed. (Ref. 11), Vol. 1, pp. 258-
             266.
             General discussion of distribution
             and prevalence of numerous major
             diseases and mention of diseases
             absent in New Guinea.

1619. Wallace, Gordon D., V. Zigas and D.C. Gajdusek
      1974   Toxoplasmosis and Cats in New Guinea.
             American Journal of Tropical Medicine and
             Hygiene 23:8-14.
             (Mulia DANI, FORE, KEIGANA, USURUFA
             and lowlanders).

1620. Ward, Hugh
      1958   Infectious Disease in the Western Highlands
             of New Guinea. Oceania 28:199-203.
             (ENGA, HULI and MENDI).

1621. Whyte, H.M.
      1958   Body Fat and Blood Pressure of Natives in
             New Guinea. Australasian Annals of
             Medicine 7:36-46.
             (CHIMBU).

1622. Wigley, S.C.
      1970   Tuberculosis. In R. Gerard Ward and
             David A.M. Lea, Eds. (Ref. 49), p. 26.
             Very brief discussion with map; none
             shown in Highlands but reported to be
             locally occurring resulting from
             contact with coastal peoples.

1623. -----
       1972   Pneumonia and Other Non-Tuberculous Lung
               Diseases. In Peter Ryan, Gen. Ed.
               (Ref. 11), Vol. 2, pp. 914-916.
               Discussion of epidemiology and
               frequency, especially in urban areas.

1624. Wigley, S.C. and D.A. Russell
       1972   Leprosy and Tuberculosis. In Peter
               Ryan, Gen. Ed. (Ref. 11), Vol.2, pp.
               640-644.
               Discussion of distribution and
               current attempts to treat and control.

1625. Wilkey, I.S. and D.G. Johnson
       1971   Vulval Ulceration due to Herpes Infection.
               Papua and New Guinea Medical Journal 14:
               27-30.
               (patients in Goroka, Mount Hagen and
               Kainantu hospitals).

1626. Wilkey, I.S. and G. Sutherland
       1971   A Case of Congenital Syphilis in New
               Guinea. Papua and New Guinea Medical
               Journal 14:50-51.
               (CHIMBU).

1627. Williams, Nancy M.
       1969   Additional Kuru Bibliography. Oceania 39:
               236-237.
               Supplement to R.M. Glasse (Ref. 1534);
               now both superseded by D.C. Gajdusek
               and M.P. Alpers (Ref. 1522).

1628. Wilson, Keith, V. Zigas and D.C. Gajdusek
       1959   New Tremor Syndromes Occurring Sporadically
               in Natives of the Wabag-Laiagam-Kmndep
               Region of the Western Highlands of
               Australian New Guinea. Lancet, 31 Oct.,
               2:699-702.
               (ENGA).

1629. Wisseman, C.L., Jr., D.C. Gajdusek, F.D. Schofield
       and E.C. Rosenzweig
       1964   Arthropod-Borne Virus Infections of
               Aborigines Indigenous to Australasia.
               A Preliminary Report. World Health
               Organization, Bulletin 30:211-219.
               (also in Papua and New Guinea Medical
               Journal, 1964, 7(1):12-18).
               (DANI, ENGA, FORE, MENYA, PAWAIA and
               Kainantu region).

1630. Woolcock, Ann J., M.H. Colman and C.R.B. Blackburn
  1973 Chronic Lung Disease in Papua New Guinea
    and Australian Populations. Papua and
    New Guinea Medical Journal 16(1):29-35.
    (KYAKA ENGA and Trobriands).

1631. Yelland, L.C.
  1955 Tari Sub-District Patrols: Numbers 1,2,
    and 3 from January to June, 1954. Papua
    and New Guinea Medical Journal 1(1):29-32.
    (HULI).

1632. Zigas, Vincent
  1970 Kuru in New Guinea: Discovery and
    Epidemiology. American Journal of
    Tropical Medicine and Hygiene 19:130-132.
    ("KURU").

1633. -----
  1973 Hookworm Anaemia in the Southern Highlands.
    Papua and New Guinea Medical Journal
    16(1):51-53.
    (HULI).

1634. Zigas, Vincent and D.C. Gajdusek
  1957 Kuru: Clinical Study of a New Syndrome
    Resembling Paralysis Agitans in Natives of
    the Eastern Highlands of Australian New
    Guinea. Medical Journal of Australia 2:
    745-754.
    ("KURU").

1635. -----
  1959 Kuru: Clinical, Pathological and
    Epidemiological Study of a Recently
    Discovered Acute Progressive Degenerative
    Disease of the Central Nervous System
    Reaching "Epidemic" Proportions among
    Natives of the Eastern Highlands of New
    Guinea. Papua and New Guinea Medical
    Journal 3(1):1-24.
    ("KURU").

D. Development and Nutrition Studies

1636. Bailey, K.V.
  1962 Peanut Feeding for Infants and Toddlers.
    Papua and New Guinea Medical Journal 6(1):
    30-31.
    (CHIMBU).

1637. -----
　　　1963a　Malnutrition in New Guinean Children and
　　　　　　　its Treatment with Solid Peanut Foods.
　　　　　　　Journal of Tropical Pediatrics and
　　　　　　　African Child Health 9(2):35-43.
　　　　　　　(CHIMBU).

1638. -----
　　　1963b　Nutrition in New Guinea. Food and
　　　　　　　Nutrition Notes and Reviews 20(7-8):
　　　　　　　89-96.
　　　　　　　(CHIMBU).

1639. -----
　　　1963c　Nutritional Status of East New Guinean
　　　　　　　Populations. Tropical and Geographical
　　　　　　　Medicine 15:389-402.
　　　　　　　(CHIMBU, KYAKA ENGA, SINASINA and
　　　　　　　Maprik lowlanders).

1640. -----
　　　1963d　Premastication of Infant Foods in New
　　　　　　　Guinea Highlands. South Pacific
　　　　　　　Commission, Technical Information
　　　　　　　Circular 61(1):1-3.
　　　　　　　(CHIMBU).

1641. -----
　　　1963e　Team Studies Infant Nutrition in New
　　　　　　　Guinea Highlands. South Pacific
　　　　　　　Commission, Quarterly Bulletin 13(1):
　　　　　　　38-40.
　　　　　　　(CHIMBU).

1642. -----
　　　1964a　Growth of Chimbu Infants in the New
　　　　　　　Guinea Highlands. Journal of Tropical
　　　　　　　Pediatrics and African Child Health
　　　　　　　10(1):3-16.
　　　　　　　(CHIMBU, KYAKA ENGA and others).

1643. -----
　　　1964b　Nutritional Oedema in the Chimbu, New
　　　　　　　Guinea Highlands. Tropical and
　　　　　　　Geographical Medicine 16:33-42.
　　　　　　　(CHIMBU).

1644. -----
　　　1965　Quantity and Composition of Breast Milk
　　　　　　in Some New Guinea Populations. Journal
　　　　　　of Tropical Pediatrics and African Child
　　　　　　Health 11(2):35-49.
　　　　　　(CHIMBU, KYAKA ENGA and Maprik).

1645. -----
       1966   Protein Malnutrition and Peanut Foods in
               the Chimbu. In Eben H. Hipsley, Ed.
               (Ref. 1659), pp. 2-30.
               (CHIMBU).

1646. -----
       1968   Composition of New Guinea Highland Foods.
               Tropical and Geographical Medicine 20:
               141-146.
               (CHIMBU).

1647. -----
       1972   Malnutrition. In Peter Ryan, Gen. Ed.
               (Ref. 11), Vol. 2, pp. 684-688.
               Brief sketch of systematic surveys
               conducted since 1947; description of
               clinical features and discussion of
               causes and treatment.

1648. Bailey, K.V. and J. Whiteman
       1963   Dietary Studies in the Chimbu (New Guinea
               Highlands). Journal of Tropical Geography
               and Medicine 15:377-388.
               (CHIMBU).

1649. Barnes, Robert
       1963   A Comparison of Growth Curves of Infants
               from Two Weeks to 20 Months in Various
               Areas of the Chimbu Subdistrict of the
               Eastern Highlands of New Guinea. Medical
               Journal of Australia 2:262-266.
               (CHIMBU).

1650. Becroft, Thelma C. and K.V. Bailey
       1965   Supplementary Feeding Trial in New Guinea
               Highlands Infants. Journal of Tropical
               Pediatrics and African Child Health 11(2):
               28-34.
               (KYAKA ENGA).

1651. Couvée, L.M.J.
       1962   The Nutritional Condition of the Kapaukus
               in the Central Highlands of Netherlands
               New Guinea. II. Clinical and Haematological
               Data. Tropical and Geographical Medicine
               14:314-324.
               (KAPAUKU).

1652. Couvée, L.M.J., D.H. Nugteren and R. Luyken
       1962   The Nutritional Condition of the Kapaukus
               in the Central Highlands of Netherlands
               New Guinea. I. Biochemical Examinations.
               Tropical and Geographical Medicine 14:27-32.
               (KAPAUKU).

1653. Dickie, J. and D.S. Malcolm
       1940   Note on a Salt Substitute Used by One of
               the Inland Tribes of New Guinea. Journal
               of the Polynesian Society 49:144-147.
               Analysis of sample collected by Reo
               Fortune in 1930's among KAMANO.

1654. Gajdusek, D. Carleton, R.M. Garruto and R. Dedecker
       1974   Congenital Defects of the Central Nervous
               System Associated with Hyperendemic Goiter
               in a Neolithic Highland Society of
               Western New Guinea. V. A Note on Birth
               Weights and Infantile Growth Rates in the
               Mulia Population. Human Biology 46:339-
               344.
                   (Mulia DANI).

1655. Hamilton, Lucy (also see Reid, Lucy H.)
       1955   Indigenous versus Introduced Vegetables
               in the Village Dietary. Papua and New
               Guinea Agricultural Journal 10:54-57.
                   (FORE).

1656. -----
       1960   An Experiment to Observe the Effect of
               Eating Substances called ereriba Leaves
               and agara Bark. Papua and New Guinea
               Scientific Society, Transactions 1:16-18.

1657. Hipsley, Eben H.
       1965a   Energy Utilisation by New Guineans, Social
               and Economic Significance. Food and
               Nutrition Notes and Reviews 22(9-10):
               101-106.
                   (CHIMBU).

1658. -----
       1965b   Food in Relation to Other Needs of Man,
               the Example of New Guinea. Food and
               Nutrition Notes and Reviews 22(9-10):
               91-100.
                   (CHIMBU).

1659. ----- (Ed.)
       1966   An Integrated Approach to Nutrition and
               Society: The Chimbu Case. New Guinea
               Research Unit, Bulletin No. 9. Port
               Moresby.
                   Collection of papers, all dealing with
                   CHIMBU.

1660. -----
       1967   The Relation between Energy Utilisation
               and Food Production -- The Examples of

New Guinea and Australia. Food and
Nutrition Notes and Reviews 24(1-2):6-13.
(CHIMBU; compared with Australians).

1661. Hipsley, Eben H. and Nancy Kirk
1965 Studies of the Dietary Intake and Energy
Expenditure of New Guineans. South
Pacific Commission, Technical Paper 147.
Noumea.
(CHIMBU and lowlanders).

1662. Jelliffe, D.B. and I. Maddocks
1964 Notes on Ecologic Malnutrition in the New
Guinea Highlands. Clinical Pediatrics 3:
432-438.
Generalized discussion of diet,
malnutrition, deficiency diseases and
maternal depletion syndromes.

1663. MacKay, S.R.
1960 Growth and Nutrition of Infants in the
Western Highlands of New Guinea. Medical
Journal of Australia 1:452-459.
(ENGA and KYAKA ENGA).

1664. Malcolm, L.A.
1966 The Age of Puberty in the Bundi People.
Papua and New Guinea Medical Journal
9(1):16-20.
(GENDE).

1665. ------
1968 Genesis and Variation: A Study in the
Growth and Development of the Bundi People
of the New Guinea Highlands. M.A. Thesis,
Otago, University of Otago.
(GENDE).

1666. ------
1969a Determination of the Growth Curve of the
Kukukuku People of New Guinea from Dental
Eruption in Children and Adult Height.
Archaeology and Physical Anthropology in
Oceania 4:72-78.
(MENYA; compared with CHIMBU, GENDE,
KARAM and others).

1667. ------
1969b Growth and Development of the New Guinea
Child. Papua and New Guinea Journal of
Education 6(1):23-32.
(GENDE).

1668. -----
       1970a   Growth and Development in New Guinea: A
               Study of the Bundi People of the Madang
               District. Institute of Human Biology,
               Monograph Series, No. 1. Goroka.
               (GENDE).

1669. -----
       1970b   The Growth and Development of the Bundi
               Child of the New Guinea Highlands. Human
               Biology 42:293-328.
               (GENDE; compared with others).

1670. -----
       1970c   Growth, Malnutrition and Mortality in the
               Infant and Toddler of the Asai Valley of
               the New Guinea Highlands. American Journal
               of Clinical Nutrition 23:1090-1095.
               (KARAM).

1671. -----
       1970d   Growth of the Under Three Year Old New
               Guinea Child. Journal of Tropical
               Pediatrics 16(2):53-61.
               (GENDE and others).

1672. -----
       1970e   Growth Retardation in a New Guinea Boarding
               School and Its Response to Supplementary
               Feeding. British Journal of Nutrition 24:
               297-305.
               (GENDE).

1673. -----
       1972   Child Growth and Development. In Peter
               Ryan, Gen. Ed. (Ref. 11), Vol. 1, pp. 153-
               154.
               General discussion of growth patterns;
               no specific cases mentioned.

1674. Malcolm, L.A., E. Balasubramaniam and G. Edwards
       1973   Effect of Protein Supplementation on the
               Hair of Chronically Malnourished New
               Guinea School Children. American Journal
               of Clinical Nutrition 26:479-481.
               (GENDE).

1675. Malcolm, L.A. and B. Bue
       1970   Eruption Times of Permanent Teeth and the
               Determination of Age in New Guinean
               Children. Tropical and Geographical
               Medicine 22:307-312.
               (GENDE, KYAKA ENGA and lowlanders).

1676. Morishita, Harumi
      1969   Physique and Physical Performance of
             the Primary School Children in the
             Central Highland of New Guinea.
             Archaeology and Physical Anthropology in
             Oceania 4:123-128.
             (CHIMBU).

1677. Norgan, N.G., Anna Ferro-Luzzi and J.V.G.A. Durnin
      1972   An Investigation of a Nutritional Enigma:
             Studies on Coastal and Highland
             Populations in New Guinea. Human Biology
             in Oceania 1:318-319.
             (YAGARIA and Karkar Island).

1678. Oomen, H.A.P.C.
      1958   Nutrition and Environment of the Papuan
             Child. Tropical and Geographical Medicine
             10:337-340.
             (CHIMBU and lowlanders).

1679. -----
      1959   Poor-food Patterns in New Guinea. Nieuw-
             Guinea Studien 3:35-46.
             (CHIMBU and lowlanders).

1680. -----
      1971   Ecology of Human Nutrition in New Guinea:
             Evaluation of Subsistence Patterns.
             Ecology of Food and Nutrition 1:3-18.
             Analysis of staple foods among CHIMBU,
             GENDE and KYAKA ENGA.

1681. Oomen, H.A.P.C. and M.W. Corden
      1970   Metabolic Studies in New Guineans: Nitrogen
             Metabolism in Sweet Potato Eaters. South
             Pacific Commission, Technical Paper 163.
             Noumea.
             (KYAKA ENGA).

1682. Oomen, H.A.P.C. and S.H. Malcolm
      1958   Nutrition and the Papuan Child: A Study in
             Human Welfare. South Pacific Commission,
             Technical Paper 118. Noumea.
             (CHIMBU).

1683. Oomen, H.A.P.C., W. Spoon, J.E. Heesterman, J. Ruinard
      R. Luyken and P. Slump
      1961   The Sweet Potato as the Staff of Life of
             the Highland Papuan. Journal of Tropical
             Geography and Medicine 13(1):55-66.
             General discussion using samples from
             Wissel Lakes KAPAUKU.

684. Reid, Lucy H. and D. Carleton Gajdusek (also see
      Hamilton, Lucy)
          1969   Nutrition in the Kuru Region. II. A
                  Nutritional Evaluation of Traditional
                  Fore Diet in Moke Village in 1957.
                  Acta Tropica 26:331-345.
                  (FORE).

685. Ross, John A.
          1966   Introducing Peanut Butter into Chimbu
                  Infant Diet. In Eben H. Hipsley, Ed.
                  (Ref. 1659), pp. 95-103.
                  (CHIMBU).

686. Shand, R.T.
          1966   Nutrition and Economic Progress in the
                  Chimbu. In Eben H. Hipsley, Ed. (Ref.
                  1659), pp. 67-84.
                  (CHIMBU).

687. Sinnett, Peter F.
          1972   Nutrition in a New Guinea Highlands
                  Community. Human Biology in Oceania 1:
                  299-305.
                  (ENGA).

688. Sinnett, Peter F., G. Keig and W. Craig
          1973   Nutrition and Age-Related Changes in the
                  Body Build of Adults: Studies in a New
                  Guinea Highland Community. Human Biology
                  in Oceania 2:50-62.
                  (ENGA).

689. Symons, P.
          1969   Some Observations of the Bundi Research
                  Project. New Guinea Psychologist 1(2):
                  21-22.
                  Discussion of mental development in
                  relation to slow physical growth of
                  GENDE.

690. Temgwe, N.
          1966   Experiences of Peanut Feeding in the
                  Chimbu District. In Eben H. Hiplsey, Ed.
                  (Ref. 1659), pp. 104-108.
                  (CHIMBU).

691. Venkatachalam, P.S.
          1962   A Study of the Diet, Nutrition and Health
                  of the People of the Chimbu Area (New
                  Guinea Highlands). Territory of Papua
                  and New Guinea, Department of Public
                  Health, Monograph No. 4. Port Moresby.
                  (CHIMBU).

1692. Wills, Pamela A.
         1958   Salt Consumption by Natives of the
                 Territory of Papua and New Guinea.
                 Philippine Journal of Science 87:169-177.
                   Analyses of salt samples from CHIMBU,
                   KAMANO, KAPAUKU, MENYA and TELEFOL,
                   with notes on preparation techniques.

PART VI PHYSICAL ENVIRONMENT

A. Geology, Geomorphology and Soils

693. Bik, M.J.
1967   Structural Geomorphology and
Morphoclimatic Zonation in the Central
Highlands, Australian New Guinea. In
Landform Studies from Australia and New
Guinea. J.N. Jennings and J.A. Mabbutt,
Eds. Canberra: The Australian National
University Press. pp. 26-47.
Detailed description of region from
Lake Kutubu to Mt. Giluwe in Southern
Highlands, including Mendi and Waga
Valleys and Kandep Plains.

694. Brooks, J.A.
1965   Earthquake Activity and Seismic Risk in
Papua and New Guinea. Bureau of Mineral
Resources, Geological and Geophysical
Report No. 74. Canberra.
General survey including Highlands
regions.

695. Brown, M.J.F.
1970   Landforms. In R. Gerard Ward and David
A.M. Lea, Eds. (Ref. 49), pp. 38-39.
Brief physiographic descriptions and
mapping of major landform types.

696. Denham, David
1970   Earthquakes. In R. Gerard Ward and
David A.M. Lea, Eds. (Ref. 49), pp. 36-37.
Discussion and mapping of zones of
major and minor seismic activity;
includes several Highlands locations.

697. Dow, D.B. and F.E. Dekker
1964   The Geology of the Bismarck Mountains,
New Guinea. Bureau of Mineral Resources,
Geological and Geophysical Report No. 76.
Canberra.
Description of topography, stratigraphy
and geological history; classification
and description of major formations.

698. Dow, D.B. and M.D. Plane
1965   The Geology of the Kainantu Goldfields.
Bureau of Mineral Resources, Geological
and Geophysical Report No. 79. Canberra.
Similar to Ref. 1697 in format, but

205

includes region from eastern edge of
Highlands at Kassam Pass to Henganofi
area.

1699. Freeman, C.
1973 Scientific Bibliographies for New Guinea.
Science in New Guinea 1(2):32-36.
Annotated list including geology,
fauna, flora and medicine.

1700. Haantjens, H.A.
1970a Geologic and Geomorphic History of the
Goroka-Mount Hagen Area. In H.A. Haantjens,
Compiler (Ref. 1069), pp. 19-23.
Brief discussion of pre-Pleistocene
geology and geomorphology of region
covered.

1701. -----
1970b New Guinea Soils: Their Formation, Nature,
and Distribution. Search 1(5):233-238.
General survey.

1702. -----
1970c Soils. In R. Gerard Ward and David A.M.
Lea, Eds. (Ref. 49), pp. 40-41.
Description and mapping of various
soil associations.

1703. -----
1970d Soils of the Goroka-Mount Hagen Area. In
H.A. Haantjens, Compiler (Ref. 1069),
pp. 80-103.
Classification, distribution and
analyses of soils of region covered.

1704. -----
1970e Summary. In H.A. Haantjens, Compiler
(Ref. 1069), pp. 7-12.
Overview and summaries of chapters of
Goroka-Mount Hagen Land Report.

1705. Haantjens, H.A., E. Reiner and R.G. Robbins
1970 Land Systems of the Goroka-Mount Hagen
Area. In H.A. Haantjens, Compiler (Ref.
1069), pp. 24-65.
Detailed descriptions and illustrations
of 39 "natural landscapes" of region
covered.

1706. Haantjens, H.A., J.J. Reynders, W.L.P.J. Mouthan
and F.A. van Baren
1967 Major Soil Groups of New Guinea and Their
Distribution. Amsterdam: Koninklijk

Instituut voor de Tropen.
General survey, description and mapping
of distribution of soil types for all
of New Guinea.

1707. Jennings, J.N.
1963 Floodplain Lakes in the Ka Valley,
Australian New Guinea. Geographical
Journal 129:187-190.
Description of geology and geomorphology
near Kandep, Western Highlands.

1708. Jennings, J.N. and M.J. Bik
1962 Karst Morphology in Australian New Guinea.
Nature, 16 June, 194:1036-1038.
Survey of karst formations in lower
Wahgi, Mendi, Koroba, Tari and lowlands.

1709. Löffler, E.
1974 Explanatory Notes to the Geomorphological
Map of Papua New Guinea. Land Research
Series, No. 33. Melbourne: Commonwealth
Scientific, Industrial and Research
Organization.
Booklet to accompany set of detailed
maps of distribution of major land
forms throughout Papua New Guinea;
describes landform types in detail
and illustrates with aerial photos.

1710. Löffler, E. and "J.M."
1972 Landforms. In Peter Ryan, Gen. Ed.
(Ref. 11), Vol. 2, pp. 590-604.
Descriptive survey of physiography
and landform types, illustrated with
photographs.

1711. McAlpine, J.R.
1965 Introduction. In R.A. Perry et al.
(Ref. 1088), pp. 7-9.
Brief discussion of survey procedure
and sources of data for Wabag-Tari
Land Report.

1712. McAlpine, J.R. and H.A. Haantjens
1970 Introduction. In H.A. Haantjens,
Compiler (Ref. 1069), pp. 13-18.
Description of survey area and conduct
of field survey of Goroka-Mount Hagen
area.

1713. McMillan, N.J. and E.J. Malone
1960 The Geology of the Eastern Central
Highlands of New Guinea. Bureau of

Mineral Resources, Geological and
Geophysical Report No. 48. Canberra.
Similar to Ref's. 1697 and 1698 in
format but covering are including
Chimbu and Wahgi Valleys.

1714. Ollier, C.D. and J.H.C. Bain
       1972   Geology. In Peter Ryan, Gen. Ed.
              (Ref. 11), Vol. 1, pp. 478-485.
              Discussion of geological history of
              mainland New Guinea and general survey
              of principal features; includes maps.

1715. Ollier, C.D. and D.E. Mackenzie
       1974   Subaerial Erosion of Volcanic Cones in
              the Tropics. Journal of Tropical
              Geography 39:63-71.
              Discussion illustrated by Mts. Bosavi,
              Murray, Karimui, Hagen, Sisa, Kerewa,
              Crater Mt., Doma Peaks and two lowland
              cones.

1716. Perry, R.A.
       1965a Outline of the Geology and Geomorphology
              of the Wabag-Tari Area. In R.A. Perry
              et al. (Ref. 1088), pp. 70-84.
              Description of regional drainage,
              geological and geomorphological history,
              structural and relief units, and land
              systems of region covered.

1717. -----
       1965b Summary Description of the Wabag-Tari
              Area. In R.A. Perry et al. (Ref. 1088),
              pp. 10-13.
              Brief overview of chapters in Wabag-
              Tari Land Report.

1718. Perry, R.A., M.J. Bik, H.A. Haantjens, J.R. McAlpine,
       R. Pullen, R.G. Robbins and G.K. Rutherford
       1965   Land Systems of the Wabag-Tari Area. In
              R.A. Perry et al. (Ref. 1088), pp. 14-55.
              Description of 39 land systems with
              photographs and schematic drawings.

1719. Renwick, A.
       1970a Geology. In R. Gerard Ward and David A.M.
              Lea, Eds. (Ref. 49), pp. 32-33.
              Brief discussion of geological history
              and notes regarding possible mineral
              resources with distribution map.

1720. -----
       1970b Volcanoes and Solfataric Areas. In R.

Gerard Ward and David A.M. Lea, Eds.
(Ref. 49), pp. 34-35.
Map showing locations of 38 areas,
including two in Highlands (Mt. Yelia
and Doma Peaks), currently regarded
as non-extinct.

1721. Reynders, J.J.
1964   A Pedo-Ecological Study of Soil Genesis
in the Tropics from Sea Level to Eternal
Snow, Star Mountains, Central New Guinea.
Nova Guinea (Geology) 6:159-317.
* * * * *

1722. Rickwood, F.K.
1954   The Geology of the Western Highlands of
New Guinea. Geological Society of
Australia, Journal 2:63-82.
* * * * *

1723. Rutherford, G.K. and H.A. Haantjens
1965   Soils of the Wabag-Tari Area. In R.A.
Perry et al. (Ref. 1088), pp. 85-99.
Description of soil morphology and
analyses of soils in region covered.

1724. Verstappen, H.T.
1964   Geomorphology of the Star Mountains:
Scientific Results of the Netherlands
New Guinea Expedition. 1959. Nova Guinea
(Geology) 5:101-158.
* * * * *

B.   Climate

1725. Brookfield, Harold C. and Doreen Hart
1966   Rainfall in the Tropical Southwest Pacific.
Department of Geography, Publication G/3.
Canberra: The Australian National
University.
Compendium of maps and tables showing
monthly and annual rainfall data;
includes many Highlands stations.

1726. Fitzpatrick, E.A..
1965   Climate of the Wabag-Tari Area. In R.A.
Perry et al. (Ref. 1088), pp. 56-69.
Description of climatic features,
controls, general characteristics and
relation to plant growth and land use
in region covered.

1727. Fitzpatrick, E.A., Doreen Hart and H.C. Brookfield
      1966   Rainfall Seasonality in the Tropical
             Southwest Pacific. Erdkunde 20:181-194.
             General survey of patterns in New
             Guinea, Melanesia and Fiji.

1728. Hart, Doreen
      1970   Rainfall. In R. Gerard Ward and David
             A.M. Lea, Eds. (Ref. 49), pp. 42-45.
             Discussion of maps showing annual
             rainfall, rainfall regimes and seasonal
             patterns for Papua New Guinea.

1729. McAlpine, J.R.
      1970   Climate of the Goroka-Mount Hagen Area.
             In H.A. Haantjens, Compiler (Ref. 1069),
             pp. 66-79.
             Description of principal climatic
             features, controls and characteristics;
             related to plant growth and water
             balance in region covered.

C. Flora

1730. Angus, R.J.B.
      1972   Forestry. In Peter Ryan, Gen. Ed.
             (Ref. 11), Vol. 1, pp. 447-463.
             Discussion of major forest communities
             with emphasis on silviculture and
             management.

1731. Brass, L.J.
      1941   The 1938-39 Expedition to the Snow
             Mountains, Netherlands New Guinea.
             Journal of the Arnold Arboretum 22:271-
             342.
             Detailed description of vegetation
             communities and species collected at
             camps in Baliem and Bele River areas,
             Irian Jaya; includes photographs.

1732. -----
      1964   Results of the Archbold Expeditions, No.
             86. Summary of the 6th Archbold Expedition
             to New Guinea (1959). American Museum of
             Natural History, Bulletin 127:145-216.
             Description of topography and vegetation
             of area of Eastern Highlands including
             Mts. Wilhelm, Otto, Michael and
             Elandora as well as Purosa, Lufa and
             Kassam areas; includes photographs.

733. Coode, M.J.E. (Compiler)
1969 A Dictionary of the Generic and Family
Names of Flowering Plants for the New
Guinea and Southwest Pacific Region.
Department of Forests, Division of
Botany, Lae, Botany Bulletin No. 3.
Port Moresby: Government Printer.
Not "dictionary" in usual sense but
alphabetical listing of genera,
cross-listed by families.

734. Flenley, J.
1969 The Vegetation of the Wabag Region, New
Guinea Highlands: A Numerical Study.
Journal of Ecology 57:465-490.
Detailed description and analysis.

735. Foreman, D.B.
1972 Timber, Commercial Species. In Peter
Ryan, Gen. Ed. (Ref. 11), Vol. 2,
pp. 1124-1131.
Descriptions of numerous tree species
commonly milled; many also used
traditionally as construction materials.

736. Gillison, A.N.
1969 Plant Succession in an Irregularly Fired
Grassland Area -- Doma Peaks Region,
Papua. Journal of Ecology 57:415-428.
Detailed description of plant
communities near Tari, Southern
Highlands.

737. -----
1970 Structure and Floristics of a Montane
Grassland/Forest Transition, Doma Peaks
Region, Papua. Blumea 18:71-86.
Similar to Ref. 1736.

738. Henty, E.E.
1969 A Manual of the Grasses of New Guinea.
Department of Forests, Division of Botany,
Lae, Botany Bulletin No. 1. Port Moresby:
Government Printer.
Comprehensive survey with descriptions
(including many drawings) and keys of
all known New Guinea grasses; species
descriptions include some information
on traditional uses.

1739. -----
1972 Grasses. In Peter Ryan, Gen. Ed. (Ref.
11), Vol. 1, pp. 501-505.
General discussion of anthropogenic

and natural grasslands and successions;
includes some information on traditional
uses of grasses, including bamboos.

1740. Johns, R.J.
1972 Vegetation. In Peter Ryan, Gen. Ed.
(Ref. 11), Vol. 2, pp. 1163-1170.
Brief descriptions of major vegetation
zones with outline map showing
distribution; extensive bibliography.

1741. Johns, R.J. and Peter F. Stevens
1971 Mount Wilhelm Flora: A Check List of the
Species. Department of Forests, Division
of Botany, Lae, Botany Bulletin No. 6.
Port Moresby: Government Printer.
Description of vegetation zones and
checklist of species; only includes
zones above cultivation limits.

1742. Kalkman, C.
1963 Description of Vegetation Types in the
Star Mountains Region, West New Guinea.
Nova Guinea (Botany) 15:247-261.
* * * * *

1743. Kalkman, C. and W. Vink
1970 Botanical Exploration in the Doma Peaks
Region, New Guinea. Blumea 18:87-135.
Detailed description with twenty-five
photographs of region near Tari in
Southern Highlands.

1744. McIntosh, D.H. and K.J. Granger
1970 Forest Resources. In R. Gerard Ward and
David A.M. Lea, Eds. (Ref. 49), pp. 48-49.
Forests classified in four divisions
in relation to potential economic
value; map shows distribution and
major species are briefly described.

1745. Paijmans, K.
1975 Explanatory Notes to the Vegetation Map
of Papua New Guinea. Land Research Series
No. 35. Melbourne: Commonwealth Scientific
and Industrial Research Organization.
Booklet to accompany four sheet maps
with classification and definition of
vegetation types, description and
mapping of distribution; illustrated
with thirty-two photographs.

1746.   Robbins, Ross G.
        1960   Montane Formations in the Central Highlands
                of New Guinea. In Symposium on Humid
                Tropics Vegetation, Tjiwai, Indonesia,
                1958, Proceedings. UNESCO Science Co-
                operation Office for South East Asia.
                pp. 176-195.
                    General description of major vegetation
                    communities in Highlands regions.

1747.   -----
        1961a   The Montane Vegetation of New Guinea.
                Tuatara 8:121-134.
                    Similar to Ref. 1746.

1748.   -----
        1961b   The Vegetation of New Guinea. Australian
                Territories 1(6):21-32.
                    General survey describing major
                    communities with cross-section schematic
                    diagrams.

1749.   -----
        1968   The Biogeography of Tropical Rainforest in
                Southeast Asia. In Symposium on Recent
                Advances in Tropical Ecology, Proceedings.
                R. Misra and B. Gopal, Eds. Varanasi,
                India: International Society for Tropical
                Ecology. pp. 521-535.
                    New Guinea material used in illustrating
                    vegetation communities.

1750.   -----
        1970a   Vegetation. In R. Gerard Ward and David
                A.M. Lea, Eds. (Ref. 49), pp. 46-47.
                    Very brief description of major
                    communities with map showing gross
                    distribution in Papua New Guinea.

1751.   -----
        1970b   Vegetation of the Goroka-Mount Hagen Area.
                In H.A. Haantjens, Compiler (Ref. 1069),
                pp. 104-118.
                    Classification and description of
                    vegetation communities of region
                    covered; discussion of ecological
                    controls and resulting distribution.

1752.   -----
        1971a   On the Biogeography of New Guinea.
                Australian External Territories 11(3):
                31-37.
                    General discussion of New Guinea as
                    link and dividing line between flora

and fauna of Australia and Southeast
Asia.

1753. -----
1971b   Plants, Birds and Animals. In Peter
         Hastings, Ed. (Ref. 5), pp. 23-41.
         General survey of major vegetation
         communities for entire island;
         discussion of biogeography in relation
         to Asia.

1754. Robbins, Ross G. and Roy Pullen
1965   Vegetation of the Wabag-Tari Area. In
         R.A. Perry et al. (Ref. 1088), pp. 100-
         115.
         General description of vegetation
         communities and relationship to land
         systems.

1755. Saunders, J.C.
1965   Forest Resources of the Wabag-Tari Area.
         In R.A. Perry et al. (Ref. 1088),
         pp. 116-124.
         Classification and description of
         forest types and correlation with
         vegetation communities in region
         covered.

1756. -----
1970   Forest Resources of the Goroka-Mount Hagen
         Area. In H.A. Haantjens, Compiler (Ref.
         1069), pp. 119-125.
         Similar in format to Ref. 1755 but for
         region indicated.

1757. Shaw, Dorothy E.
1972   Fungi. In Peter Ryan, Gen. Ed. (Ref. 11),
         Vol. 1, pp. 472-474.
         General description of three main
         groups and importance in human
         pathology in New Guinea.

1758. Wade, L.K. and D.N. McVean
1969   Mt. Wilhelm Studies 1. The Alpine and
         Subalpine Vegetation. Department of
         Biogeography, Publication BG/1. Canberra:
         The Australian National University.
         Detailed description of vegetation
         communities and species collected.

1759. Walker, D.
1965   Stratigraphy and Ecology of a New Guinea
         Highlands Swamp. In Symposium on
         Ecological Research in Humid Tropics

Vegetation, Kuching, 1963. Sponsored by
UNESCO Science Co-operation Office for
South East Asia. pp. 137-146.
Description of vegetation in Lake
Ipea region, Western Highlands.

1760. -----
1968   A Reconaissance of the Non-Arboreal
        Vegetation of the Pindaunde Catchment:
        Mount Wilhelm, New Guinea. Journal of
        Ecology 56:445-466.
        Detailed description of vegetation
        of region indicated.

1761. -----
1972   Vegetation of the Lake Ipea Region, New
        Guinea Highlands. II. Kayamanda Swamp.
        Journal of Ecology 60:479-504.
        Detailed description of vegetation
        in swamp in Western Highlands.

1762. Womersley, John S.
1958   New Guinea Vegetation. Australian Museum
        Magazine 12:384-388.
        Brief general survey with description
        of major vegetation communities.

1763. -----
1962   Notes on the Techniques Employed for the
        Collection of Botanical Specimens in
        Papua and New Guinea. Ninth Pacific
        Science Congress, Bangkok, 1957,
        Proceedings 4:61-63.
        Brief summary of techniques described
        fully in Ref. 1764.

1764. -----
1969   Plant Collecting for Anthropologists,
        Geographers and Ecologists in New Guinea.
        Department of Forests, Division of Botany,
        Lae, Botany Bulletin No. 2. Port Moresby:
        Government Printer.
        Handbook with description of techniques
        for collecting, labeling and preserving
        plant specimens for identification;
        indispensable if working with Papua
        New Guinea institutions.

1765. -----
1972a   Conifers. In Peter Ryan, Gen. Ed.
        (Ref. 11), Vol. 1, pp. 206-211.
        Discussion of classification and
        distribution of three families in New
        Guinea; detailed descriptions of

representative genera.

1766. -----
      1972b Exploration, Botanical. In Peter Ryan,
             Gen. Ed. (Ref. 11), Vol. 1, pp. 389-390.
             General survey of botanical research
             in New Guinea.

1767. Womersley, John S. and J.B. McAdam
      1957 The Forests and Forest Conditions in
            the Territories of Papua and New Guinea.
            Port Moresby: Government Printer.
            Comprehensive, but now somewhat dated,
            survey and description of forest
            communities in Papua New Guinea.

D. Fauna

1768. Anderson, C.
      1936 Fossil Marsupials from New Guinea.
            Australian Museum, Records 20:73-76.
            Description of finds from Upper Watut
            region, Morobe District.

1769. Brongersma, Leo D.
      1958 The Animal World of Netherlands New
            Guinea. Groningen: Wolters.
                      * * * * *

1770. Cogger, H.C.
      1971 The Venomous Snakes of Australia and
            Melanesia. In Venomous Animals and
            Their Venoms, Vol. 2. New York:
            Academic Press. pp. 35-77.
            Comprehensive survey with detailed
            classification and descriptions of
            species; includes photographs.

1771. -----
      1972a Lizards. In Peter Ryan, Gen. Ed.
             (Ref. 11), Vol. 2, pp. 651-657.
             Discussion of distribution and
             description of six families
             represented in New Guinea.

1772. -----
      1972b Reptiles. In Peter Ryan, Gen. Ed.
             (Ref. 11), Vol. 2, pp. 1012-1013.
             Very brief discussion concerned
             with place of New Guinea in reptile
             biogeography.

1773. -----
1972c Snakes. In Peter Ryan, Gen. Ed. (Ref. 11), Vol. 2, pp. 1042-1048.
General description of eight families in New Guinea, with representative species.

1774. Collins, Larry R.
1973 Monotremes and Marsupials: A Reference for Zoological Institutions. Smithsonian Institution, Publication No. 4888. Washington, D.C.
Comprehensive survey with information on classification, distribution, reproductive biology, diet, behavior traits and parasites; organized by genus; includes extensive bibliography.

1775. Deusen, Hobart M. van
1972a Bats. In Peter Ryan, Gen. Ed. (Ref. 11), Vol. 1, pp. 60-63.
General discussion of distribution relative to Asia and Indonesia; description, habits and distribution of various families.

1776. -----
1972b Echidnas. In Peter Ryan, Gen. Ed. (Ref. 11), Vol. 1, pp. 297-299.
Brief description and discussion of distribution.

1777. -----
1972c Mammals. In Peter Ryan, Gen. Ed. (Ref. 11), Vol. 2, pp. 688-694.
General discussion of distribution with list of orders, families, genera and species; New Guinea divided into vegetation zones with indicator mammal species given.

1778. -----
1972d Marsupials. In Peter Ryan, Gen. Ed. (Ref. 11), Vol. 2, pp. 711-714.
Brief description of four families and representative genera including broad distribution patterns.

1779. Diamond, Jared M.
1967 New Subspecies and Records of Birds from the Karimui Basin, New Guinea. American Museum of Natural History, Novitates, No. 2284.
Detailed descriptive species list.

217

1780. -----
       1973   Distributional Ecology of New Guinea
              Birds. Science, 23 Feb., 179:759-769.
              General survey, especially of birds
              of Highlands.

1781. Diamond, Jared M. and J.W. Terborgh
       1966   Ecological Study of the Birds of Mount
              Michael, New Guinea. American
              Philosophical Society, Yearbook for 1965,
              pp. 305-308. Philadelphia.
              General report of 1964 research in
              Okapa region of Eastern Highlands.

1782. Frith, H.J.
       1972a Megapodes. In Peter Ryan, Gen. Ed.
              (Ref. 11), Vol. 2, pp. 757-758.
              Brief description and notes on
              distribution of "fowl-like" birds
              of forest floor.

1783. -----
       1972b Pigeons and Doves. In Peter Ryan, Gen.
              Ed. (Ref. 11), Vol. 2, p. 905.
              Very brief discussion of various types
              found in New Guinea.

1784. Gilliard, E. Thomas
       1969   Birds of Paradise and Bower Birds.
              London: Weidenfield and Nicolson.
              Standard reference work with numerous
              illustrations.

1785. Gilliard, E. Thomas and Mary Lecroy
       1968   Birds of the Schrader Mountain Region,
              New Guinea. American Museum of Natural
              History, Novitates, No. 2343.
              Detailed description of birds of Aiome
              and Mt. Kominjim areas.

1786. Gould, J.
       1970   Birds of New Guinea. (Text by A. Rutgers).
              London: Methuen.
              Reprinted 19th Century lithographs;
              160 color plates with brief text.

1787. Gressitt, J. Linsley
       1972   Insects and Relatives. In Peter Ryan,
              Gen. Ed. (Ref. 11), Vol. 1, pp. 564-573.
              Very general discussion of biogeography;
              brief descriptions of major groups with
              extensive bibliography.

1788.   Gressitt, J. Linsley and A.C. Ziegler
        1973   The Effect on Fauna of the Loss of Forests
                in New Guinea. In Nature Conservation in
                the Pacific. A.B. Costin and R.H. Groves,
                Eds. Canberra: The Australian National
                University Press. pp. 117-122.
                Brief discussion of impact of forest
                clearing on animal populations.

1789.   Gyldenstolpe, Nils
        1955   Notes on a Collection of Birds Made in
                the Western Highlands, Central New Guinea,
                1951. Arkiv für Zoologi 8:1-181.
                Annotated list of 166 species collected
                in Kerowagi and Nondugl areas, Chimbu
                District.

1790.   Holthuis, L.B.
        1972   Crustacea. In Peter Ryan, Gen. Ed.
                (Ref. 11), Vol. 1, pp. 232-235.
                General description of appearance,
                habits and habitats and discussion of
                distribution of major groups.

1791.   Iredale, Tom
        1950   Birds of Paradise and Bower Birds.
                Melbourne: Georgian House.
                Illustrated in color but incomplete
                coverage; taxonomic information now
                superseded by E.T. Gilliard (Ref.
                1784).

1792.   -----
        1962   The Birds of New Guinea. 2 Vols. Sydney:
                Georgian House.
                Illustrated in color; work as whole
                superseded by A.L. Rand and E.T. Gilliard
                (Ref. 1804).

1793.   Laurie, E.M.O. and J.E. Hill
        1954   List of Land Mammals of New Guinea,
                Celebes, and Adjacent Islands. London:
                British Museum of Natural History.
                Standard check list with information
                (somewhat dated) on distribution; no
                descriptive information.

1794.   Lidicker, W.Z. and A.C. Ziegler
        1968   Report on a Collection of Mammals from
                Eastern New Guinea, Including Species Keys
                for Fourteen Genera. University of
                California, Publications in Zoology,
                No. 87. Berkeley.
                        * * * * *

1795. McMichael, Donald F.
       1958   Land of the Tree Climbing Snails.
              Australian Museum Magazine 12(9):297-299.
                 Brief discussion of snails of several
                 areas including Wissel Lakes, Irian
                 Jaya.

1796. -----
       1972   Molluscs. In Peter Ryan, Gen. Ed.
              (Ref. 11), Vol. 2, pp. 789-792.
                 General discussion with descriptions
                 of major families and some genera
                 (few above 6,000 ft. a.s.l.).

1797. Marlow, Basil J.
       1958   Mammals of New Guinea. Australian Museum
              Magazine 12:388-393.
                 Very general description of major
                 groups.

1798. Mayr, Ernst
       1945   Birds of the South West Pacific. New
              York: Macmillan.
                 General survey with colored illustrations
                 but superseded by more recent work (e.g.
                 A.L. Rand and E.T. Gilliard, Ref. 1804).

1799. Munro, Ian S.R.
       1967   The Fishes of New Guinea. Department of
              Agriculture, Stock and Fisheries. Port
              Moresby: Government Printer.
                       * * * * *

1800. -----
       1972   Fishes, Freshwater. In Peter Ryan, Gen.
              Ed. (Ref. 11), Vol. 1, pp. 422-424.
                 General description of 111 species,
                 some occurring in Highlands.

1801. Parker, F.
       1970   Collecting Reptiles and Amphibians in
              New Guinea. Australian Natural History
              16:309-314.
                 Suggestions and discussion of value
                 of assistance of villagers mentioning
                 experiences in Wahgi Valley and Chimbu
                 District.

1802. Plane, M.D.
       1972   Fossil Mammals. In Peter Ryan, Gen. Ed.
              (Ref. 11), Vol. 1, pp. 464-465.
                 Brief discussion of finds from only
                 three known sites of antiquity (Kiowa,
                 Tari and Upper Watut River).

1803.   Rand, Austin L.
        1942   Results of the Archbold Expeditions,
                No. 43. Birds of the 1938-9 New Guinea
                Expedition. American Museum of Natural
                History, Bulletin 79:425-515.
                    Detailed description of birds collected
                    in Baliem Valley and Idenburg River,
                    Irian Jaya.

1804.   Rand, Austin L. and E. Thomas Gilliard
        1967   Handbook of New Guinea Birds. Garden City:
                Natural History Press.
                    Standard reference work; complete
                    descriptions (many illustrated with
                    drawings) and taxonomy.

1805.   Ripley, Dillon
        1964   A Systematic and Ecological Study of
                Birds of New Guinea. Peabody Museum of
                Natural History, Bulletin 19:1-85. New
                Haven.
                        * * * * *

1806.   Schodde, Richard
        1972a   Birds of Paradise. In Peter Ryan, Gen.
                Ed. (Ref. 11), Vol. 1, pp. 86-89.
                    Brief descriptions of appearance and
                    habits of major forms including
                    information on calls, distribution,
                    evolution and nests.

1807.   -----
        1972b   Bower Birds. In Peter Ryan, Gen. Ed.
                (Ref. 11), Vol. 1, pp. 112-114.
                    General description, especially of
                    bowers and nests, and discussion of
                    distribution and evolution.

1808.   -----
        1972c   Cassowaries. In Peter Ryan, Gen. Ed.
                (Ref. 11), Vol. 1, p. 137.
                    Very brief description and discussion
                    of habits and human uses.

1809.   -----
        1972d   Kingfishers. In Peter Ryan, Gen. Ed.
                (Ref. 11), Vol. 1, pp. 582-583.
                    General discussion; two species
                    endemic to Highlands.

1810.   -----
        1972e   Parrots and Cockatoos. In Peter Ryan,
                Gen. Ed. (Ref. 11), Vol. 2, pp. 890-892.
                    Description and information on

behavior and distribution.

1811. -----
        1973   General Problems of Fauna Conservation in
                Relation to the Conservation of Vegetation
                in New Guinea. In Nature Conservation in
                the Pacific. A.B. Costin and R.H. Groves,
                Eds. Canberra: The Australian National
                University Press. pp. 123-144.
                    Discussion of impact on fauna
                    (especially birds) of forest clearing.

1812.   Schodde, Richard and W.B. Hitchcock
        1972   Birds. In Peter Ryan, Gen. Ed. (Ref. 11),
                Vol. 1, pp. 67-86.
                    General survey of ecology, habits,
                    distribution, evolution and relation
                    to man; includes extensive bibliography.

1813.   Sims, R.W.
        1956   Birds Collected by Mr. F. Shaw-Mayer in
                the Central Highlands of New Guinea.
                British Museum of Natural History,
                Zoology, Bulletin 3:389-438.
                    * * * * *

1814.   Slater, Kenneth R.
        1961   Reptiles in New Guinea. Australian
                Territories 1(5):27-35.
                    General survey with descriptive notes
                    and photographs.

1815.   Worrell, E.
        1963   Dangerous Snakes of Australia and New
                Guinea. Sydney: Angus and Robertson.
                    * * * * *

1816.   Ziegler, Alan C.
        1972   Rodents. In Peter Ryan, Gen. Ed.
                (Ref. 11), Vol. 2, pp. 1017-1020.
                    Discussion of conjectural evolutionary
                    history in New Guinea and description
                    of major genera and distribution.

1817.   Ziegler, Alan C. and W.Z. Lidicker
        1968   Keys to the Genera of New Guinea Recent
                Land Mammals. California Academy of
                Sciences, Proceedings 36(2):33-71.
                    * * * * *

1818.   Zweifel, Richard G.
        1972   Frogs. In Peter Ryan, Gen. Ed. (Ref. 11),
                Vol. 1, pp. 466-471.
                    General discussion of distribution
                    and habitats.

ADDENDA

The following references regrettably escaped earlier inclusion and are supplied here with appropriate section designations.

II.   SOCIAL AND CULTURAL ANTHROPOLOGY

B.   Ethnographic and Topical Studies

1819.   Bee, Darlene: USURUFA
        1974   A Brief Note on Kinship and Social
                Groupings among the Usurufa.   In R.
                Daniel Shaw, Ed. (Ref. 348), pp. 125-136.

1820.   Bulmer, Ralph N.H.:   KARAM
        1974   Folk Biology in the New Guinea Highlands.
                Social Science Information 13(4-5):9-28.

1821.   Hotz, Joyce and Mary Stringer: WAFFA
        1974   Waffa Social Structure: The Individual in
                the Group.   In R. Daniel Shaw, Ed.
                (Ref. 348), pp. 79-96.

1822.   Lloyd, Richard G.:   BARUA
        1974   Baruya Kith and Kin.   In R. Daniel Shaw,
                Ed.   (Ref. 348), pp. 97-114.

1823.   Loving, Richard: AWA
        1974   Notes on Awa Kinship Terminology.   In
                R. Daniel Shaw, Ed. (Ref. 348), pp. 115-124.

1824.   Sorenson, E. Richard: FORE
        1974   Anthropological Film: A Scientific and
                Humanistic Resource.   Science, 20 Dec.,
                186:1079-1085.

1825.   Young, Rosemary: BENABENA
        1974   The Social Hierarchy of the Bena-Bena.
                In R. Daniel Shaw, Ed. (Ref. 348), pp. 137-
                168.

III.   LINGUISTICS

A.   General Surveys and Comparative Studies

1826.   Hooley, Bruce A. and Kenneth A. McElhanon
        1970   Languages of the Morobe District -- New
                Guinea.   In Stephen A. Wurm and Donald C.
                Laycock, Eds. (Ref. 1148), pp. 1065-1094.
                Survey and taxonomic essay; includes
                MENYA, WAFFA, WAMPUR and YAGWOIA.

1827. Z'graggen, John A.
         1970   Languages of the Western Madang District.
                <u>In</u> Stephen A. Wurm and Donald C. Laycock,
                Eds. (Ref. 1148), pp. 1271-1292.
                     Survey and taxonomic essay; includes
                     GANTS and KARAM.

231

1471, 1472, 1505-1506,
1508, 1518, 1535, 1560-
1561, 1577, 1579, 1612,
1619, 1629, 1654

Daribi -- see MIKARU

DEM 459-463, 745, 1106

Dom -- see SINASINA

DUNA 110, 156, 168, 196,
198, 202, 212-217, 410-
411, 535, 651, 790,
1024-1026, 1431, 1457,
1509, 1582-1583

Ekagi -- see KAPAUKU

Elimbari -- see CHUAVE

ENGA 84, 95, 112, 115, 156,
159, 168, 192, 194, 198,
202, 212-217, 240, 263,
294, 317, 319, 323, 347,
354-355, 383, 412, 433-
434, 464, 480, 533, 563-
565, 577, 579, 581-586,
606-608, 644-645, 692,
726-728, 759, 764, 768-
786, 830, 854, 896, 903,
924, 946, 998-1001, 1002,
1023, 1092, 1101, 1169-
1170, 1177, 1217-1218,
1219, 1376, 1390-1392,
1395-1397, 1401, 1420,
1429-1430, 1439, 1442,
1444-1445, 1449, 1450,
1455, 1459, 1509, 1515,
1580-1583, 1590, 1592,
1595, 1601, 1604, 1607-
1609, 1616, 1620, 1628,
1629, 1663, 1687-1688

FAIWOL 102-103, 150-152,
155, 439-440, 549, 931,
1115, 1451, 1482

FASU 1114, 1128, 1228,
1244

FOI 95, 104-107, 110, 141-
142, 144, 170, 377, 729,
1033-1034, 1114, 1390-
1392, 1397

FORABA 702, 1006

FORE 112, 236-237, 351, 381,
432, 442-446, 448-458,
466, 559-562, 578, 609-
610, 614-619, 630, 746-
748, 934-936, 941-943,
1229, 1245, 1251-1252,
1253, 1261-1263, 1370,
1373-1374, 1375, 1390-
1392, 1394, 1397, 1402,
1420, 1425, 1434, 1437,
1443-1444, 1446-1448,
1451, 1472-1478, 1479,
1483, 1484-1490, 1500-
1503, 1504, 1516, 1517,
1519-1521, 1523-1527,
1528-1531, 1535, 1544,
1561, 1564-1565, 1572-
1573, 1585, 1602, 1604,
1619, 1629, 1632, 1634-
1635, 1655-1656, 1684,
1824

GADSUP 295, 324, 325, 370,
372, 374, 536, 568-574,
683, 742-743, 761, 829,
1016, 1104, 1121, 1197-
1199, 1242, 1390-1392,
1395, 1397, 1422, 1424,
1425, 1443, 1446-1448,
1458, 1535, 1561

GAHUKU 108-109, 112, 193-
194, 334, 354, 376, 587-
590, 650, 866-874, 1040,
1178-1183, 1280, 1416,
1425

Gaj -- see GANTS

GANATI 192, 194, 274, 278,
944, 1437, 1443, 1446-1448

Gandja -- see KANDAWO

GANTS 83, 108-109, 1827

GAWIGL 105-106, 159, 263,
468-471, 665, 744, 784,
1162-1163, 1401, 1432

Genatei -- see GANATI

GENDE 388-390, 397, 409,
413-420, 698, 710, 1150,
1172, 1433, 1449, 1571,
1664-1669, 1671-1672,
1674-1675, 1680, 1689

GIMI 351, 561, 631-635, 1375, 1390-1392, 1394-1395, 1397, 1420, 1425, 1443, 1446-1448, 1458, 1473-1478, 1483, 1485-1488, 1500-1502, 1504, 1517, 1519-1521, 1524-1527, 1529-1531, 1564-1565, 1572-1573, 1632, 1634-1635

GOLIATH FAMILY 128, 188, 724

Gumine -- see SINASINA

Gururumba -- see ASARO

HAGEN 86, 91, 94, 108-109, 115, 129-132, 156, 159, 167, 179-183, 193-194, 212-217, 228, 230, 257, 263, 335, 354-356, 359, 376, 472-479, 612-613, 646, 711, 784, 796-798, 895, 930, 945, 947-968, 971-980, 981, 982, 994-996, 1035, 1429, 1432, 1435, 1439, 1441, 1452, 1459, 1568, 1581, 1586-1587, 1592, 1606, 1611

HEWA 110, 168, 202, 212-217, 380, 937, 1112, 1174, 1457

HULI 95, 105-106, 110, 138-143, 170, 193-194, 198, 202-203, 212-217, 228, 620-627, 707, 768, 892, 1037, 1390-1392, 1397, 1401, 1420, 1430, 1451, 1452, 1455, 1509, 1536, 1568, 1581-1583, 1585, 1592, 1599, 1604, 1620, 1631, 1633

IPILI 168, 198, 202, 785, 787-788, 1401

JALÉ 171, 229, 678, 712-723, 1106

Kakoli -- see GAWIGL

Kalam -- see KARAM

Kaluli -- see BOSAVI

KAMANO 108-109, 159, 236-237, 372, 374, 376, 381, 442-447, 448-458, 593-595, 837, 1280, 1395, 1427, 1443, 1446-1448, 1452, 1473-1478, 1483, 1486, 1500-1502, 1504, 1517, 1519-1521, 1524-1527, 1564-1565, 1572-1573, 1580, 1585, 1632, 1634-1635, 1653, 1692

KANDAWO 389-391, 395, 397, 402, 423-425, 667, 1432

KANITE 236, 432, 442, 444-446, 448-458, 1237, 1280, 1390-1392, 1394, 1397, 1443, 1446-1448, 1473-1478, 1483, 1485-1488, 1500-1502, 1504, 1517, 1519-1521, 1524-1527, 1564-1565, 1572-1573, 1585, 1632, 1634-1635

KAPAUKU 101, 120-121, 146, 147, 204, 210, 219, 328-329, 465, 510-513, 567, 576, 580, 643, 709, 740, 745, 792, 838-851, 1045, 1117, 1184-1187, 1267, 1409, 1444, 1463, 1651-1652, 1683, 1692

KARAM 83, 95, 112, 113, 249, 257, 260, 359, 421-422, 515-525, 648-649, 793, 817-818, 889, 989, 1149, 1161, 1164, 1248-1250, 1385, 1410-1411, 1437, 1548, 1593-1594, 1614, 1666, 1670, 1820, 1827

Katem -- see STAR MOUNTAINS

Kaugel -- see GAWIGL

KAWOL 548-549, 1115

KEIGANA 236, 432, 442, 444-446, 448-458, 1375, 1394, 1420, 1425, 1437, 1443, 1446-1448, 1473-1478, 1483, 1485-1488, 1500-1502, 1504, 1517, 1519-1521, 1524-1527, 1529-1531, 1564-1565, 1572-